Betrayal of the Child

Betrayal of the Child

A Father's Guide to the Family Courts, Divorce, Custody and Children's Rights

Stewart Rein

Lotus Press

Tobyhanna   New York

Betrayal of the Child

A Father's Guide to Family Courts

Second Edition

First Printing

Published by
Lotus Press
For information, please contact:
Lotus
2929 Melody Lane
Tobyhanna
PA 18466
child@pnpa.net

clik.to/Betrayalofthechild

ISBN: 0-9711472-0-5

Printed in the United States of America

For
Lindsey Elena
Mildred
Aida
And Paul

"He knew that the tale he had to tell could not be one of final victory. It could only be the record of what had had to be done, and what assuredly would have to be done again in the never ending fight against terror and it's relentless onslaughts, despite their personal afflictions, by all who, while unable to be saints but refusing to bow down to pestilence, strive their utmost to be healers."

"The Plague", Albert Camus

Foreword

This book is the consequence of over twelve years involvement in the field of children's and human rights, independent examination, soul-searching and intuition. It represents no interests other than the best interests of the child. It has no support or endorsement from any special interest group. It is written in the hope that it might assist fathers to safeguard relationships to their children, serve professionals to better represent the needs of our children, spark public debate and cause a higher degree of reflection on the part of social policy makers, community and religious leaders. I want to extend my deepest gratitude to Sir James Goldiner for his patient editorial efforts. The miracle is that it exists and can be read and judged on its merits.

Stewart Rein

Contents

Notes to the Second Edition

There is no doubt that unprecedented levels of family dissolution is leading to large-scale father-absence, while loss of father is clearly imposing serious deprivation and dysfunction on tens of millions of children. This represents a human tragedy for children, fathers and all society. It is even a disaster for mothers. Therefore, this books argues for the presumption of shared parenting in the aftermath of divorce in all but the most extreme and anomalous cases

As there are multi-millions of fathers facing impending, current and ongoing custodial conflicts threatening a continued relationship to their children, I have incorporated a guide to the family courts to assist them in the conduct of cases. I have overridden well meant advice to place the Father's Guide at the front of the book. I leave it up to the reader to choose whether or not to review that chapter first.

However, the guide works together with and within the context of the development of family law, child psychology, political trends and even social pressures. Unfortunately, the complex subject matter and material are predictable artifacts of the conflictual divorce-custody conundrum. Therefore, fathers face a steep learning curve. This is true for the pro se and represented father alike. Having said that, my experience working with fathers has taught me that highly motivated dads usually prove up to the task of absorbing and using such material.

Without understanding the past and its connection to the present, fathers are doomed to repeat recent massive failures in convincing courts to maintain the integrity of adult-child, post divorce relationships. Therefore, the general advice in the guide links to historic as well as to modern psychiatric & psychological evidence. That evidence references the statistics and source material provided in the relevant chapters. *See Consequences of Parental Deprivations on the Child, Psychiatric& Psychological Literature, Re-Location Cases, Phenomena of Parental Child Abduction, Conclusions*

Chapter sub-headings provide pointers to specific problems such as parental abduction, relocation, abuse allegations and imputation of income. *See Chapter 4 Parental Abductions, Chapter 7 Modern Law*

Suitable material for legal briefs and argument is included that would take hundreds of hours to accumulate it if it could be found. That incorporated material is in textbook format (source-date-quote).

Let me set the record straight. There is no panacea. There are no quick fixes, or simple ABC 'how-to' formulas that can reverse entrenched court policies that are robbing children of their fathers. Fathers, acting as advocates for their kids, are not facing a 'level' playing field. I can only provide an intelligent, evidential, and rational approach for the beleaguered, threatened parent and child. The included material, if used properly, might just improve their chances in the hostile environment of family law courts.

Bold type, italics, parentheses and underlined words are either my contributions or case citations, not attributable to other sources. Cases and psychiatric reports reproduced are real with only the names, or parts of them, removed to protect the privacy of the individuals. Named cases are those already published in the legal literature. I have analyzed several cases and psychiatric reports for the benefit of the reader.

It is sadly evident that, in the industrialized world, there is a universal sole maternal custodial approach holding true for nearly all jurisdictions. Therefore, while anecdotal, cases included reflect general family court practice and illustrate the enormous obstacles facing children and fathers in custodial conflicts.

Limitations not withstanding, I believe that the legal, statistical and expert material included is far more comprehensive than ever before attempted in a similar work. To my knowledge, there is no other book available that advocates social and legal reform, while providing fathers with material and a strategic basis to conduct shared parenting custody cases on behalf of their children.

While the book assists fathers, it is also of interest to women. If mothers are open to the issues, arguments and proofs, they might better understand the impact on children of actions that separate those children from their fathers. Once understood, perhaps, they will reject the kind of radical and cultural feminist ideas that reinforce fatherlessness and take us towards a matriarchal society. *See Betrayal of the Child*

Additionally, one hopes that professionals involved in children's issues will not find the arguments for shared parenting, backed by the statistics and studies, lacking in reason. Further, I would remind them that much of our knowledge about children and family is *a priori*[1] and not necessarily science based. Intuition and empirical experience should inform us as much as the rather imperfect literature.

However, either out of plain ignorance or from deliberate obfuscation, many of these professionals have come to believe or represent that the family ceases to exist after a non-marital breakup or a formal divorce. Nothing is further from the truth. It may change shape, alter format and even the subtle balance of its relationships, but from the child's perspective it does not and cannot die. The child's ties to his or her parents remain a constant, while even the parents remain implicitly connected through the life of their child. One can only hope that involved professionals will see this and open their eyes to the damage done to this and future generations of children by following the principles of sole maternal custody in protection of special interests.

Finally, I write in the rather timid expectation that I will not be deliberately misinterpreted or glibly described as anti-female or anti-feminist.

---

[1] 'a priori', in the philosophical sense, prior knowledge

If mothers were to find themselves and children in the same position facing modern fathers and children, I would be taking up their cause with equal gusto. In fact, for mothers living in the very few anomalous jurisdictions where they might face unfair treatment, the same principles apply as for fathers. This is true for custody and child abduction cases. The Guide should be useful to them. My view as a child's advocate determines that the gender based special interests of adults must be set aside in order to protect the rights and best interests of our children.

As for the feminists, they are like cholesterol; there is the good and the bad varieties. When their ideals accord with principles of universal suffrage, human rights, equality and true liberation, I am a staunch supporter of their aims. I do try to distinguish amongst their various categories, separating nominal feminists from the cultural and radical elements.

However, this book is extremely critical of the cultural and radical feminists. Their private political agendas and anti-male attitudes have helped to create circumstances threatening the very core and concord of male-female relationships. Ultimately, those views and agendas, taken together with other dynamic forces, constitute a real and present danger to the human rights of children.

Part I

Chapter 1

Betrayal of the Child

Family Dissolution and Betrayal of our Children's Best Interests

"We have permitted the courts to sever the relationship between the child and his or her biological father. This is something that no court should have an opportunity to do."

Margaret Mead

Male Denial

Men are stupid. Most men have a shocking lack of awareness of the ever-increasing family issues, including divorce, custodial conflict and parental loss. Male ignorance crosses over racial, religious, social and national divides.

Unmarried men live in a world of romance and optimistic expectation. This state of mind is part of our historical socialization. Married men go about their lives also without thinking about these painful issues. Neither group even recognizes let alone accepts the uncomfortable facts about family crisis and the breakdown of modern marriages.

Men fear opening the proverbial Pandora's box that threatens their ontological safety and their inherited and reinforced systems of belief.

Men are living in denial.

When fathers are suddenly confronted by separation and divorce, by breakdown of their own family lives and the potential loss of their children, these problems are perceived as existing in a vacuum. Fathers often see nothing more than a miserable personal experience unrelated to outside influences, trends or policies. Wrong!

Men are not only ill informed on the issues, but are the most vociferous of all in denial of the facts. They are the last to acknowledge the existence of covert court custody policies set up to deny their rights to relationships with their children -until it is too late to resist. They cannot imagine the full extent of the family court's wide-ranging discretionary powers. They cannot conceive of the possible existence of radical and cultural feminist conspiracies seriously influencing legislation and maternal preference court policy. They do not imagine that their former wives or girlfriends would ever act to harm the children.

Fathers believe, rather naively, that justice will prevail in their 'personal' cases, that no court would ever take away their children from them. Friends and relatives will also deny realities, either reinforcing a misguided trust in the family law system, or distancing themselves from the 'dead or dying' fathers.[2]

Secretly, family members will ask, "What did he do to her? He must have done something to get her this angry?"

Men hiring lawyers think they can simply leave it to their representative to protect them and their children. Pro se fathers believe they are capable of self-representation in a hostile and complex legal forum. Both sets of fathers often have come to see me seeking advice, after the fact, after their cases have gone horribly wrong, when they are desperate, alone and defeated.

Male perceptions are simply out of tune with the facts!

---

[2] See Chapter 2 Dr. Bakalar on "Court Bias Against Fathers, The Hidden Mechanisms"

Lets start with a few relevant, staggering and quite conservative statistics from the "The Stepfamily Foundation" that set the scale of the problem for children and fathers.

"One out of two marriages end in divorce.

60% of second marriages fail, according to the U.S. Census Bureau

66% of marriages and living together situations end in break up, when children are actively involved, according to Stepfamily Foundation statistics.

It is predicted that 50% of children (35 million) in the US will go through a divorce before they are 18.

At present there are over 22.5 million children in the US living in single-parent homes, nearly all with a female parent."[3]

Sole maternal custody court policies have led to the undeniable statistical fact of a rapid and painful disappearance of fatherhood. *See Graphs on single-parent families-Divorces* Along with that disappearing dad has come misleading and injurious terms like 'dead-beat' dad and 'absent parent' that have sprung into the modern vocabulary. However, the truth is that the vast majority of men are not 'dead beat' dads or voluntary 'absent parents'. Very few men abandon their children. The truth is that tens of millions of women are delimiting and obliterating contact between their former spouses and the children. *See Myth of the Dead-Beat Dad*

This catastrophic scenario of divorce, separation, custodial conflict and parental loss did not erupt without warning. It was found in an early study by Hetherington (1977) that:

" Within two years some fathers could not cope with seeing their children only occasionally and gave up on visitation refusing to become "Disneyland Dads" in the face of stern and unrelenting opposition by their former wives" (Marriages and Families, Mary Anne Lamanna and Agnes Riedmann, 4th Ed., Wadsworth, 1991).

---

[3] Present guesstimates have risen to between 28 to 32.5 million children in single-parent homes, nearly all with a female parent

In the year 2000, at the time of writing, one such estranged and destabilized dad just holed up with a gun and hostages at that very same 'Disneyland', threatening suicide and murder. Nothing changes! All he wanted was access to his children. He is not alone. Figures show that tens of millions of other fathers are living out that same crisis.

Ironically, as shown by three separate studies, men, on those rare occasions when entrusted with sole custody, do not act to betray their children's trust and rights:

"Children living with fathers typically have more contact and are emotionally closer to parents, that is, their mothers" (Greif 1985, Greif and Pabst in 1988, and Lewin in 1990)[4]

One reason for that result may be that fathers, unlike huge numbers of mothers, do not act to destroy the rights and interests of their children when placed in positions of control and power. These studies on paternal custody compare favorably (and can be used in court) with studies on maternal custody showing that mothers with sole custody interfere, delimit, and act to destroy paternal relationships to children after divorce. *See Source Material on Maternal Abuse of Sole Custody Orders*

The studies are extremely important given Psychiatrist John W. Jacobs report that many of his colleagues believe **ALL** marriages will end in divorce and that we will marry at least three times in our lives. Reports indicate that the average marriage lasts only for seven years.[5]

There are also between 500,000 and 650,000 parental child abductions in the US alone each year directly related to custody conflicts, with many more going unreported. This heralds in an era of enormous crisis in family relations in America and the rest of the western world. According to The National Center for Missing and Exploited Children, "the incidence of child abduction by family members is growing at an alarming rate in the United States and will

---

[4] Marriages & Families, 4th Ed., Lamanna & Riedmann, Wadsworth, 1991 at Page 566

[5] Source, Ernie Allen, President, NCMC, 1995 Report, See Chapter 4 Parental Child Abduction

become a greater policy challenge for elected officials each year." *See the Phenomena of Parental Child Abduction*

Anecdotal evidence, supplied by a highly placed source at The US State Dept., suggests that the vast majority of parental kidnappings are by women, mothers. My own research supports that finding, as does the evidence from French Hague Convention Attorney, Dr. Alain Cornec.

The statistics and problems cited, as well as those to follow, are some of the consequences of a tragic three-step process; commencing with the facile breakdown of traditional 'intact' families, the advent of 'on demand' no fault divorce, and, finally, the imposition of universal sole maternal custody orders making children fatherless.

The knock-on effects and consequences to children of this invidious process include serious pathologies developed in childhood, adolescence and adulthood as reported by The Utopia Foundation as recently as 1997:

"Over 85% of all youths sitting in prisons grew up in fatherless homes the according to: Fulton County Georgia Jail Population and Texas Department of Corrections (1992)

70% of juveniles in state operated institutions, come from homes where the biological father is not present (US Dept. of Justice Special Report, 1988)

71% of all high school dropouts come from homes where the biological father is not present (National Principles Association Report on the State of High Schools)

85% of all children that exhibit behavioral disorders come from homes where the biological father is not present (Center for Disease Control)

63% of youth suicides are from homes where the biological father is not present (US D.H.H.S. Bureau of the Census)"

Fathers involved in custody battles in hostile forums MUST use those and other statistics in a reasoned defense of their children's best interests, arguing for joint physical and legal custody.

Even if mother, or her lawyer, attempts to undercut the statistical validity (citing other factors), there is no overcoming a 'prima facie' (on its face) case that father absence is an unmitigated disaster. These statistics, together with others and the studies in this book make a compelling case for the shared parenting of children, *See A Father's Guide to the Courts. See Parental Deprivation and Consequences on Children. See Appendix A on US Government Statistics Visitation and Child Support*[6]

How relevant is all this?

Who has not either suffered marriage or non-marital disruption personally or experienced it through a close friend, or family member? How many have experienced the pain and suffering of missed children, or grandchildren, when the children have been whisked out of loved one's lives, because of former partners desire to dispose of father? The odds are that all of you will have had one experience or the other. Further, if you have not lived through this pain, the odds are that you will within your lifetime.

"How intimate is the link between the nature of society and how its children are raised? Alternatively, as we have so often asked: Is man the father of society, or society the father of man? This question becomes no less burning with the passing of millennia". Bruno Bettelheim, "The Children of the Dream".

Perhaps a more compelling question, heralding in the dawn of a new millennium, is how to preserve, protect, or indeed, even salvage our most fundamental unit of society -the family. - Can we prevent it from disappearing into a black hole of interpersonal gender based chaos and animosity, while guarding the inalienable rights of our children to be nurtured, loved and guided into a healthy adulthood.

However, society has failed to address, let alone confront the issues of rising gender warfare, divorce, fatherlessness and an unparalleled social re-organization driving us towards female-headed single-parent families. Collectively, judges, lawyers, social workers, psychologists, law guardians and tens of millions of mothers have failed to cherish

---

[6] See Chapter 12, Conclusions, Matriarchy v Patriarchy, for further studies on adverse results for children of sole maternal custody orders

and protect our children's rights. Fathers have failed to reverse the trend, or even put a dent in it.

Despite existing evidence that 'traditional' family structure is, as the UN has declared, "the most fundamental social unit of organized society", we have allowed it to crumble to the point of devastation.

US and UK studies gave us forewarning as far back as 1988, as reported by David White and Anne Woollett, lecturers in Developmental Psychology, that this epidemic was well underway but have ignored the consequences:

"Figures from the US census returns showed 21 percent of children in single-parent homes (mother)(Laosa 1988). In the UK, sixteen percent of the families with dependent children were headed by a. (mother) single- parent (OPCS 1989). Those figures have escalated in both countries through the nineteen nineties."

Having gone on to account for extremely insignificant 'other causes' of single parenting (death, abandonment), they restated:

"Looking at these statistics in a different way, figures from the US show that 38 percent of the children born in the period 1965-69 were not living with both natural parents by age 16 years."

It is estimated that 50 percent or more of children born in the late 1970's will spend some time in a single-parent family before they reach the age of 16 years (Bumpass, 1984; Hofferth, 1985)."

As reported in 1999, in Perspectives on Father Involvement: Research and Policy, Catherine S. Tamis-LeMonda and Natasha Cabrera, Social Policy Report, Volume XIII, Number 2,1999. Society for Research in Child Development:

"Another quite different social development that has placed men in the national spotlight is the alarming rate of father-absent families."

In 1997, 24% of children lived with only their mothers (Federal Interagency Forum on Child and Family Statistics, 1998a).

Almost 70% of women on welfare were unmarried when they had their first child. It has been estimated that the proportion of children who will live with only one parent at some time during their childhood will exceed 50% (Hernandez, 1993)." *See Graphs on Lone Parenting*

Those statistics are shocking enough, but both the estimates and projections have been seriously under-reported. The trend toward female-headed single-parent families has escalated off the top of the charts. Yet, we have taken no steps, to halt the trend, implement reform legislation, alter unworkable policies or offer moral leadership.

The bells are tolling for the tens of millions of innocent children. Children have fallen tragic victims to the onslaught of divorce and estrangement from male parents, suffering the imposition of a destructive female-headed single-parent family system.

Association of Children's and Father's Rights

This book looks at the situation from the child's perspective. I wanted to speak out for the tens of millions of silent suffering children. Unfortunately, many children's rights issues remain clouded and merged into interpersonal relationships within the family nexus. Therefore, it is necessary to clarify a few things.

First, for me men's issues are only of interest if dependent on and annexed to those of the child. There cannot be any confusion here. Equally, women's issues are only of interest in respect to their connection to children's rights. The child's interests are paramount.

Nevertheless, having said that, one has great difficulty separating the interests of children and fathers in present circumstances. There is, from the child's perspective, a relative association of children's and father's rights. Both groups, forming two-thirds of the family nexus, have become in the circumstances of divorce (in a constitutional sense) cognizable minority classifications whose natural and legal rights have been seriously impaired. Both groups, in the aftermath of 'traditional' family breakdown and conflictual divorce, have become the psychological victims of millions of women.

Although White and Wollett reported that there had been recent moves in the US and UK to make joint custody arrangements to ensure the child's rights to maintain contact with both parents in the aftermath of divorce, they implicitly admitted to the hypocrisy of family courts in failing to put shared parenting into practice:

"However, the evidence suggests that changes in the legal arrangement are not reflected in the living arrangements of families post-divorce." (Families: A Context for Development (1992)

In other words, policies rooted in the outmoded doctrines of 'tender years' and 'maternal attachment' discussed in later chapters, leave sole maternal custody firmly in place despite recent lip-service paid to shared parenting and vague 'gender neutral' legislation. *See The Psychiatric & Psychological Literature on the Child, The Legal System*

Family courts worldwide with rare exception, remain driven by radical feminist politics and pressure[7]. Courts continue to exercise wide ranging discretionary powers allowing them to bypass, ignore, abuse and contravene legislative intent. Courts remain committed to personal prejudices and private political agendas supported by outdated and erroneous research in the psychiatric literature. *See Rebuttal to Freud, Solnit and Goldstein*

Universal sole maternal custody not merely rules, but is identifiable as a root cause of serious trauma imposed on our children. *See Consequence of Parental Deprivations on Children*

White and Wollett continued on to also point out that:

"Children generally live with only one parent and have few overnight stays with the other parent. Only a small percentage of children spend large amounts of time with both parents."

Confirmation for that finding comes from another study:

"In general, children do not see a great deal of their (other) parent (Maccoby et al. 1988)".

Moreover, in 2000, twelve years later, conditions have worsened as numbers have swelled. What other outcome could we expect in these circumstances? Sole maternal custody is the universal norm and granted exclusively. Control and power mostly vested in a party (mother) that seems to have, and act out of, a number of subjective and

---

[7] *See NOW Opposition to Shared Parenting Bills in New York and Michigan*

objective reasons to limit or completely deny child and father their most vital and appropriate relationship. That is what the statistics and studies in this book go to prove.

Women have brazenly admitted in surveys that, 'they see no value in fatherhood and to having interfered with visitation between their former spouses and the children'. *See Surveys of Divorced Mothers, See US Census Data Appendix A and below*

Given that bizarre and rather cruel admission it is, therefore, not surprising that only in:

"About 20 percent of cases the parents (men) see their children once a week or more (Furstenberg 1988). Contact with the parent declines with the passage of time with fathers showing a more marked decline in the frequency of their visits (Hetherington et al 1982)".

These are the kinds of emerging patterns and trends that have continued and accelerated through the 1990's and into the twenty first century, as women seek divorces, disposing of male parents using legal process to do so.

In 1994, US government sources reported that a shocking **37.8 percent of fathers were denied any access to their children** by the courts and over **54.9 percent were given little access and virtually no enforcement of that contact**. *See Appendix A* That means that in a child population in the US of some 77 million kids, roughly sixty percent of them are children of divorce. Of those, 92.7 percent of them have no fathers. Dr. John Campion in England confirms the fact that over 50% of children of divorce in his country do not see their fathers at all. These statistics tell a sad tale of injustice and deceit.

In Braver, S., & O'Connell, D. "Taking on myth 2: The no-show dad. In Divorced Dads: Shattering the myths", New York: Tarcher/Putnam. (1998):

"The authors found that the bulk of visitation problems are traceable to disputes between the non-custodial father and the custodial mother. Mothers' strategies include denying visitation, encouraging the child to feel alienated from the non-custodial father, and attaching unacceptable conditions or financial demands to visitation."

Why are 'intact' family models being torn and desecrated?

Why are millions of women obliterating the interpersonal relationships between their former spouses and the children?

How are they affecting this destructive process?

How can we as a society find more humane and rational solutions, than we have during the past twenty years, to the dilemma of family breakdown and parental loss?

What can fathers do to protect the emotional and legal rights of their children?

First fathers must come to even recognize the nature of the problem!

The Disappearance of Fatherhood

It is undeniable that two phenomena are occurring simultaneously, massive divorce rates and the disappearance of fatherhood. These bad twins are symptoms of a society split into disharmonious gender halves by myopic radical feminists and their allies. There is no discounting radical feminist influence on women or the existing causal connection between radical feminist ideology and fatherlessness.

There has been a drastic re-shaping of "societies most fundamental unit" (the family) while a popular myth has been created that it can be transmuted into and be maintained by a female single parent supported by the state. This is not merely a gross misunderstanding of human nature, but a powerful vehicle for creation of cycles of deprivation and dysfunction in our children. That is what the available studies already show is happening.

One longtime and respected critic of present court custody policies is American Psychiatrist Mel Roman. He calls for a joint custody approach, characterizing present policies as anachronistic and unjust:

"The assumptions that underlie the policy of generally granting custody to mothers are outmoded, unrealistic and damaging. They are as inappropriate to the contemporary intellectual and socio-cultural

Zeitgeist as were the rights of fathers in ancient Rome to sell their child or put it to death."

Driven by huge increases in the numbers of non-marital separations and conflictual divorces, society is drowning in a rising tide of destabilization in the lives of our children. Few among the empowered elite wish to acknowledge this fact. While numerous apologists leap forward to address only superficial aspects of the problem, acting only to reinforce the underlying policies causing these disastrous consequences for children.

While Dr. Roman rejects past gender stereotyping and the discredited psychoanalytical theories of Freud, Solnit and Goldstein (*see Chapter 2*) that support sole maternal custody, reminding us that:

"Maternal custody as a presumed preference is the shadow of a world that no longer exists except in the minds of those who unrealistically cherish the imperfect past."

In fact, I would go much further, as that world never truly existed. It was largely mythological and limited to an extremely brief historical period (Industrial Revolution).

We must reject maternal preference standards. Professor Daniel Amneus warned with justifiable impatience in his book, "The Garbage Generation":

"What needs to be done is to stop the flow of messed-up kids through the pipeline running from the divorce courts and into female-headed families, through pathological childhoods into disruptive adolescence and demoralized adulthood--the process now in full swing and programmed to continue into the next Garbage Generation in the 21st century."

Dr. Amneus calls for a return to Patriarchy of the family and for father custody where there has been family disruption. My position on custody is that we MUST make joint physical and legal custody (shared parenting) the presumption in law as a first step forward in safeguarding the rights of children. Family law should be federal and not subject to state vagaries. National 'joint custody' law can still provide for the flexibility to make sole custody orders in extreme or exceptional (anomalous) cases. Nevertheless, even in those cases, we must adduce concrete evidence meeting with all other civil and criminal law standards, unlike the allegation driven process in family law courts. *See Chapters on the Law, See Objective Evidence tests*

In principle, commonsense, intuition, logic and modern research all argue for the continuing need and rights of the child to be nurtured by his or her two psychological parents in the aftermath of separation and divorce. Only 'judicially mandated' joint custody or shared parenting best serves the needs of children . I believe that the material in this book conclusively supports this view.

We must understand that sole maternal custody in practice equates to nothing less than a serious parental loss *(See Dr. Jacobs)*. No reputable mental health professional can dispute the idea that the most significant loss to a child is the loss of one or both of its parents. Yet, we create this loss artificially when making custody decisions removing one parent (father) from the child's life. This is especially disagreeable when the basis for such removal is nothing more than sexual or gender stereotyping and abuse of power. It is not made more palatable by rationalizations like, it must be done for 'the sake of regularity and order', 'reducing hostilities' or as 'the least detrimental solution'. Nor can we use sole maternal custody as a quick, practical means to dispose of the tens of millions of cases that flow through national and foreign courts.

Even if we applied maternal preference strategies to more 'traditional' family models, there are multitudes of sound arguments against them. However, applied to the 'post-nuclear' family models in which men, at women's insistence, have taken on ever increasing roles as co-nurturers, they become indefensible. They are cruel, irrational, and visit a miserable injustice on our children. As leading psychiatrist, Dr. Jacobs, told me during a television interview:

"If the loss of a parent through natural causes presents a child with an important loss, can you imagine the traumatic affects on the child from the enforced loss of a parent due to a conflictual divorce, separation and an artificial severance of it's precious relationship." ("Wednesday's Children" 1997)

Sadly, I can imagine such trauma, and so have many responsible mental health professionals. This falls under discussion in the Chapter on Parental Rights Deprivations along with aspects of 'parental loss syndrome' represented by reunion fantasies and a quest for the missing parent.

Further, suggestions that fathers still maintain 'rights of visitation' when mothers are granted sole custody, are spurious in the extreme. Those arguments fly in the face of reality. The statistical facts and research demonstrates that paternal ties to children are lost, not maintained, through supposed visitation rights. *See US Census Figures, See Custody and Visitation, See Dr. Fay: An End to Visitation*

Despite the known affects of paternal loss on children, case law denial of the child's rights persists through continuation of sole maternal custody policies. Children's rights to treasured relationships are shattered, as the research shows, without judicial concern for the child's immediate trauma, long-term harmful effects or dysfunctionality directly linked to those policies. The legal systems of The United States, Europe, Israel as well as Canada, New Zealand, Australia and others, are alike in this betrayal of the rights and best interests of children.

The insensitivity and corruption of present family court process extends beyond married persons to the tens of millions of de facto (common law) marriages producing children. Treatment for unmarried fathers is even worse than for married ones in custody and visitation matters. One sick joke arising out of modern common law marriages (no longer recognized by most states) is that 'paternity suits' once used to force men into submission and recognition of their paternal responsibilities are now having to be used by men to force women into acceptance of male parentage and paternal rights.

While in one particular case, even the US Supreme Court has gone so far as to create a legal fiction (based on gender discrimination and an arcane California statute) that the biological and psychological father of a young child-was not (in law) its father. In this exasperating case, an unmarried father went on a twelve year Odyssey through state, federal and international courts to establish his relationship to his daughter only to be defeated. *See the extraordinary case of Michael H. v. Gerald D. in International law, UN Convention on the Rights of the Child/*

*International Covenant on Civil and Political Right, See Orders of Filiation,
See Parental Responsibility Orders*

If we all (especially fathers) fail to understand the source and nature of both internal and external forces driving family court policy, we cannot change its direction. This is true for individual parents fighting cases and for advocates of broad social and legal reform.

However, for all those outside forces, we return to the mother for one of the first questions that springs to mind. Why would millions of women, long since liberated from what all feminists call, the bonds of patriarchal, conservative, stereo-typical and 'traditional' long term relationships, (having demanded that men become co-nurturing partners) revert back to pre-liberation positions characterizing men as mere 'providers' and themselves as 'homemakers'?

Too many women, ironically, when dissolving the new style 'mutual' marital relationship, disposing of their spouses as parents to their children, are doing precisely that. The very qualities that women claimed to seek in men as husbands and fathers (partners, co-nurturers) are, suddenly, in the circumstances of divorce, completely repudiated as huge numbers have enforced maternal sole custody on their children.

Gender Warfare and Fatherlessness

One part of the answer to the question lies in the attitudinal changes of women towards men. Changes in the female view of men has been energized by social circumstances, modified behavior patterns and the fostering and interposition of an aberrant brand of cultural or radical feminism. Over time, anti-male feminism has infused itself into millions of individual male-female interpersonal relationships. *See Social Changes in Family Structure* One frightening aspect of the present trend toward dissembled families and conflictual relationships, is the collective wedge forged by women between themselves and men. We are only now seeing the first signs of this gender division as revealed by a study on adult male and female sexual dysfunction. *See Edward Laumann Study, U. of Chicago at Page 242*

As this has far reaching implications for the children of divorce, it needs discussion.

The developments of the past 30 years involving a negative shift in perception by women (anti-male feminism) has had a powerful impact on their conscious and unconscious expectations of men. It has affected their conduct in marriage and child rearing. It has forcefully affected their choices of the means and style of divorce. Over a prolonged period, we reached and crossed over an invisible threshold making men the unwitting and unwilling enemies of women. An undeclared war has begun. We have proved false the old cliché 'it takes two to make an argument' in light of family disruptions and aggrandizements by millions of mothers in divorce.

Devaluation: Man as Thing or Person?

What has all this to do with MY divorce and custody conflict?

In order to deal with the reality of custodial conflict fathers must understand the female psychological mindset operating during the divorce period. First, consider a useful general definition of man given by the Anthropologist Paul Bohannan.

"Man is, first of all, a mammal, which is to say that he reproduces sexually. Man is a sentient being. He has, in his classification of species, called himself Homo sapiens-'man the knowing' or 'man the perceiving'. Man is a social being. Man is a being who lives by culture." Bohannan differentiates between man and other mammals insofar that:

"But social man is man in touch with his own kind. Alone, without communication with other human beings, he is not wholly human."

What happens to man (and his children) when woman, in practice (during divorce), acts to deny him sociality and communication? What happens when she ex-communicates him in fact from the family? Does he, from the point of view of woman become something less than a person (subhuman) and more of a thing? Does that enable her to harm him, and of course the children?

These questions are relevant to fathers, before, during and after marriages have ended. The great gender divide, based on artificially induced negative perceptions of men, progressively widens. Evidence of this gap comes from the prodigious male scapegoating instigated by cultural and radical feminists.

As the English philosopher Wittgenstein put it, 'the thought is the language'.

The Linguistic Merry-go-Round

This is not an exercise in semantics. Social anthropologists have always characterized historical man as man the 'hunter-gatherer'. In other words, man as a person described by one of the tasks representing a part of his whole function. The term in no way implies a pejorative value or diminishes a man's worth.

However, an important early twentieth century shift in the characterization of man to 'provider' (initiated by the psychiatric literature, not by Anthropologists) carried an entirely different connotation. Perhaps, subtle and even accidental, this shift downgraded man from a person to a thing, reducing his significance in the family. The use of the language made it clear that man, in a family context, had no role other than provider. Dr. Roman referred to this world in his rejection of maternal sole custody practices.

Much later, the feminist intellectual culture reinvented man as person, at least in theory. During the sixties revolution it became extremely convenient for feminist women to describe men as 'nurturers' and 'co-parents', not merely as providers. Simultaneously, women sought freedom from homemaking-nurturing roles and expansion of their personal lifestyles. Terms such as 'provider' and 'nurturer-homemaker' (for women) dropped completely out of the vocabulary replaced by new, enhancing terms such as sharer, partner, and co-nurturer.

Moreover, from the eighties onward, co-incidental to marked increases in divorces, men suffered another reversal. Now, the perception of men highlighted male scapegoating. Commonly portrayed as oppressors, perpetrators of violence, sexual abusers, rapists, dead-beat dads, and absent parents, man had become a 'thing' and a dirty one at that. This was not just historical coincidence, but carefully orchestrated through media propaganda, social pressure, and legislative lobbying. It has had an unfortunate affect on the real lives of ordinary men, women and children. Derogation of men operates at the back of each conflictual custody case.

Feminist June Carbone even saw fit to meekly caution her female colleagues that some women might start to reject the feminist label because,

"Their focus has raised fears that feminists are anti-men and, therefore, antifamily."(Carbone, "A Feminist Perspective on Divorce" The Future of Children 1994-Notes)

I disagree. Fears that feminists have anti-male, anti-family views arise from more than mere focus. It is their rhetoric, policies and extravagant deprecation of men as a collective that should frighten us. They are anti-male.

It is also obvious that they are anti-integrated family. Their literature demonstrates the pursuit of policy objectives fostering implementation of a matriarchal system, making men peripheral, second-class citizens, if not indentured servants.

Comparing present circumstances with pre-sixties traditional family settings in which men and women had to remain committed to one another and work at relationships, one can readily understand the reasons for a similar lack of commitment in our new post-nuclear family.

Radical feminist polemic, abstract condemnation of men and the existence of alternative opportunity have taken a huge toll on women's commitment to family values. Women's new freedoms combined with their pre-emptive negative expectations and distorted imagery of men has made divorce viable. The divorce climate guaranteeing 'equal distribution' of family assets and the sole custody of the children, has actually made divorce an extremely attractive alternative to resolving even the lowest levels of family discord. *See Chapter and discussion on divorce law reform*

The generic scapegoating and deprecation of men finally caused moderate feminist Lynne Segal to bravely warn women against this kind of anti-male radical-feminism that:

"Celebrates women's superior virtue and spirituality and decries 'male' violence and technology. Such celebration of the 'female' and denunciation of the 'male,' however, arouses fear and suspicion in feminists who, like me, recall that we joined the women's movement to challenge the myths of women's special nature."(Amneus 1996)

The central ingredients to present gender warfare are, on the one hand women's natural bio-chemical predisposition to pro-create and on the other, an increasingly destructive and distorted perception of the males they require to complete their sexual function. Given these ingredients and the new unbridled freedom of women to, express themselves, earn independent livelihoods and extricate themselves from unwanted marital relationships (through recent law reform), is it surprising that we are tumbling towards rapid dissolution of marital and non-marital pro-creational relationships, at just a whisper of discord or stress.

Divorce and the De-Personalization of Fathers

From the mere abstract, one inevitably arrives at real life conflictual family dissolution and unjust custodial arrangements. Seeing female de-personalization of ex-husbands and fathers at work in the legal forum, confirms the flow -man's theoretical reduction in status translated into the real life trauma of divorce.

Fathers involved in conflictual custody cases must be aware of this factor. A woman's mindset might, in these millions of cases, be best described by psychiatrist R.D. Laing in his classic work on Schizophrenia "The Divided Self", a work partly analogous to what we call more or less 'normal' social interactions.

According to Laing:

"Depersonalization is a technique that is universally used in dealing with the other (husband) when he becomes too tiresome or disturbing. One no longer allows oneself (herself) to be responsive to his feelings and may be prepared to regard him and treat him as though he had no feelings. **A partial depersonalization of others is extensively practiced in everyday life and is regarded as normal if not highly undesirable."**

The conduct of a majority of women in millions of conflictual custody cases, framed by selfish and practical motivations, is dependent on their ability to invent a convenient rationalization that relieves them of guilt feelings.

Mothers first come to accept the radical feminist ideas that broadly dehumanize man, reducing his value and status, transitioning him from being to thing. They then might impose real life de-personalization of the former loved one in custody cases. Spouses (former loved ones), suffer summary dismissal as husbands, devalued and disposed of as fathers of the children.

This de-personalization is easily crystallized. There is separation from the spouse using negative imagery and expectations (he is dangerous). Subjective and distorted views of the individual conflictual family experience (I am threatened, victimized, vulnerable, isolated, entrapped) are developed. The role of husband (oppressor, source of entrapment) and subsequently that of father (un-necessary) suffers devaluation. Finally, mothers acquire psychological confirmation and support from outside sources (radical feminists, complaisant mental health professionals, judges, social workers, friends and family).

Confirmation of this process comes from studies showing that women are guilty of an unusual degree of distorted thinking linked to their de-personalization of the former spouse as the following one illustrates. Incidentally, the study also shows why avoidance of sole maternal custody orders is so important for the child:

"Overall, approximately 50% of mothers "see no value in the father's continued contact with his children" (pg. 125, 4, lines 1 and 2) "Surviving the Breakup" Joan Berlin Kelly and Judith S. Wallerstein"

This preposterous declaration and shocking result of interviews with divorced or divorcing mothers underscores my argument. I am certain that it also comes as a surprise to unsuspecting fathers. Do mothers say such things while content in the marriage? No. Quite the opposite, they call for, encourage and laud the male parent's co-parenting qualities and capacities. Mother's denigration of father is clearly derivative of the divorce process and the unspoken drives behind it.

Women still feel the need to rationalize stripping the child of his or her male co-caregiver and co-nurturer while fulfilling the practical need to obtain financial security (protection) from him using the complaisant legal system. The marvel in this system of false self is that it allows these mothers to remain guiltless, lacking in remorse or concern. Dr. Jacobs and others have described this process as the 'parentectomy' of father.

This behavioral style is encouraged by the Women's Movement where according to critic Warren Farrell Ph.D. a former board member of N.O.W. (National Organization of Women):

"There are two fundamental faces of the Women's Movement...the other part has honed victim power to a fine art creating a problem few people understand. With victim power goes the underlying belief you can kill the victimizer and feel no remorse."

While Amneus reports that: "Dr. Lenore Weitzman's book "The Divorce Revolution"[8], argues that ex-husbands owe ex-wives far more alimony and child support money than divorce courts now compel them to pay. The problem of the feminist movement, as Dr. Weitzman articulates it, is to use the Motherhood Card and the Mutilated Beggar argument to get that peripheral male out of the home without losing his paycheck."

The accomplishment of ridding the home of father (parentectomy) comes in two stages, first by de-personalization and second using legal intervention. Amneus continues:

"The problem of patriarchal society and, of the men's rights movement is to ensure that this separation of a man from his paycheck and his family does not occur." ("The Garbage Generation")

---

[8] See Chapter 3, Myth of the Dead-Beat Dad, Braver & O'Connell refutation of Weitzman's false economic premise

Ironically, as seen from following chapters, within the framework of our rapidly dissolving two-parent family structure transposing into a female headed single-parent family, women have come to perceive of all males as disposable lovers, partners and parents. While too many mothers have foolishly and narcissistically come to believe that our children are their own private property, thereby substituting one arcane system of injustice in which they claimed to be victims (patriarchy), with another in which they become oppressors (matriarchy).

Unfortunately, mothers, even where poorly motivated, are exclusively supported by the legal system, erroneous psychological literature, propaganda and media control, legislation, complaisant feminist males and general indifference from the public.

From the child's perspective, I would rephrase the Amneus quotation.

The problem of 'all' society and of the children's rights movement is to ensure that this separation of child and father does not occur.

Chapter 2

The Psychiatric & Psychological Literature on the Child

The Psychiatric & Psychological Literature on the Child

In principle and with rare exception, children cannot argue their own cases for continuation of precious relationships. At best, children may give evidence, if permitted, of limited or doubtful weight. *See Chapter 8, Children's Evidence*

Therefore, fathers must fight for them. Fathers cannot begin to argue the case for shared parenting without first understanding the historical impact of the literature and expert evidence on child custody cases. That literature presently underpins all open and covert court policies rooted unjustly in sole maternal custody.

Fathers also have to grasp the evolution of family models interacting with the literature. That too has played a part in present legal practice. Only then, can they make or instruct their lawyers to make intelligent and compelling arguments to refute the old literature universally supporting the sole maternal custody of children.

Those arguments refer to the resource material supplied in this, and subsequent chapters, proving shared parenting is in the best interests of children, while demonstrating the negative effects on them of sole maternal custody.

A Brief Primer on Gender Function, Child & Family

Even before reviewing the psychological literature on children one has to understand a little of the complexities of adult human relationships. This means function, purpose and development of family structure. That is the framework for any discussion on the best interests of the child. What is a family? What is its purpose?

It is obvious, at least to me, that there is a prime directive for the human race, the survival of the species. This directive operates in the presence of necessary bio-chemical and psychological conditions.

Nature, while imposing and meeting the physiological and bio-chemical criteria needed to foster pro-creation, also provided a means of rearing and nurturing offspring. Protecting children while vulnerable increases the probability for their survival. A combination of genetic imprinting, learned experience, environmental conditioning and physiology all served to evolve a system designed to continue the species. Simultaneously, this system created both family and social order.

As an extension of this thinking, family and social order rely on the divided sexual function of men and women, the physiological and biological distinctions between them.

It seems that in primitive man, copulation and impregnation alone did not serve human purpose. Women were extremely vulnerable during pregnancy, increasingly disabled from providing food and sustenance for the fetus. They were less mobile and able to protect themselves from the elements and predators. Especially after childbirth, while nursing, mother and child remained at significant risk. Therefore, over time, these fleeting 'agamous' male-female relationships changed into 'monogamous' ones. The socialization of man was the predictable outcome of natural forces.

Man was hunter-gatherer and protector.

Man fulfilled his role within the prime directive. Compelled to do more than impregnate, he had to serve as protector and provider of the means for survival. There were some pre-historic and later exceptions to the rule. However, at some point, historical man became hunter-gatherer while historical woman continued as life former-nurturer. Nature, in demanding the survival of the human species, had really dictated the eventual need for monogamous relationships between men and women and the formation of traditional family models (marriages).

Division of labor, tasks, and interests in the family model were rooted in the distinctions and differences in the bio-chemical function and physiology of men and women. Early families were close units. The young had protection, shelter, food, and were able to grow safely to adulthood provided with the necessary skills to form their own families. After breast-feeding concluded, offspring had equal exposure to the love and complementary influences of both parents. Unlike Industrial Revolution humankind, early families spent their lives as much more of an ensemble living on a simple agrarian design. These units remained undisturbed except, by sorties for food provision, or by the outbreak of disease and war.

The continuity of this simple 'traditional family unit' had a guarantee, until or unless, organized society might interpose a new set of environmental conditions necessitating revision of the structure.

That is what happened during The Industrial Revolution. Men left the home for long periods in order to provide shelter, food, clothing and protection for their wives and children. While most families remained living on the land, significant numbers of men began to work in the newly created factories or in offices. Over time, greater numbers of men owed their families' survival on work within the growing industrial complex. These numbers rose to proportions that impacted on the organization of the family and society.

Society had begun to make transitions from a purely agrarian culture into a manufacturing culture in the modest mid-nineteenth century industrial revolution. This threw up new groups of middle and working class men during the Victorian Era. As families moved from the land to the cities, so their structure changed.

Simultaneously, man began to develop a pseudo-science called psychiatry.

Our Man in Vienna: Freud and the Child

Sigmund Freud had begun to seek explanations for some ailments for which he could not find a physiological cause. One such ailment was what he described as cases of hysteria in patients. He suspected that the roots of his patient's problems stemmed from early childhood experiences. Despite the ridicule and skepticism of his conservative medical colleagues, he began to use hypnosis and psychoanalytical treatment as a methodology in defining conditions and seeking cures in his patients. His work laid the foundations of modern psychoanalysis. Freud's early work opened the door to research on the child. He stressed the importance of the 'Oedipus Complex' on child development, a theme taken up and expanded upon by others, including Melanie Klein.

The Early Literature and Melanie Klein

Having read Freud's work on dreams, influenced and encouraged by Ferenczi, Klein began to develop an interest in the psychoanalysis of children. By 1921, she had moved from Vienna to Berlin to work with children. She eventually settled in London where she continued her research and practice until her death in 1960.

Dr. Klein (troubled by a problematic relationship to her own daughter) was amongst the first to inspect family life. This review was restricted to the perspective of child development and the mother, especially in the first year of life. Father never entered into her investigations. He was at the factory or down the coalmine.

Succeeding generations of psychiatrists and psychologists considered Klein as the pre-eminent contributor to theoretical work and to clinical practice on children.

My purpose is not to demonize Klein, nor to indulge in speculations about the more eclectic aspects of psychoanalysis. However, it is important to demonstrate and explain to fathers and the general public how and why we have arrived at present misunderstandings. Misunderstandings about children and the family, manifested within psychological, social, and legal contexts.

The early psychiatric literature on child development has had an enormous impact on the present approach to deciding the legal issues inherent in divorce-custody actions. While traditional family units have transposed into nuclear, post nuclear and more recently single-parent family units, the old literature remains intact to rationalize universal sole maternal custody. This reinforces the decision making process of law courts. *See Chapters 5, 7, 8*

Melanie Klein emphasized the importance of the first year of an infant's life for its development. It is obvious that, in the typical first year of life of an infant in the traditional family structure of 1921, the focus was more on mother, mother's breast, and child. Klein's concern centered on childhood anxieties, concluding that they were rooted in the two phases of the child's first year. In the first phase, or first six months the child would recognize only parts of mother and in the second, mother as a whole.

It is important to acknowledge and understand that Klein's work was the first link in a historical psychoanalytical chain exploring child development solely from the point of view of the child's interaction and fantasies about the mother. Subsequently, absent of research on the child's relationship to father, the literature was transposed into doctrine applied **outside** of psychiatric practice. The transposition of this speculative and incomplete theory was misinterpreted and misused, finding its way into our family law courts.

Adler and Child Affection

However, it is interesting that Alfred Adler's work on children, though largely ignored, focused on an entirely different aspect of child development. As early as 1908, he had written on the child's need for affection, exploring child development from a perspective other than autoerotic behavior, depressive positions, Oedipus, and aggression.

Adler described the need for affection as having the strength of a drive and cited its existence as evidence of the child's drive life. Adler stated that, "Among the externally observable phenomena in children, the need for affection shows itself relatively early." While he concluded that, "the strength of the child's affectional tendencies, the psychological apparatus which the child can bring into play to achieve satisfaction represents an essential part of the child's character."

What does this tell us? It was clear to Adler that the child's needs and desires to be held, fondled, loved and praised by 'loved persons' were "well known and striking". He did not say mother. He said persons not person. To Adler the child's ability to form loving relationships as an adult stems from it's childhood experience and degree of success in having those earliest needs met. Quite unlike Freud and Klein, Adler had discovered and articulated a wholly distinct aspect of child development, that of social feelings. The implication of his logic is that, a father can provide this loving relationship as easily as a mother can, that these needs of the child are not gender specific, dominated or related.

Tender Years Doctrine

However, the evolution of the psychiatric literature on children, child development and it's connection to adult dysfunction, begun by Freud, carried on by Klein and later on by Freud's daughter, Anna, Bowlby, and others, continued to focus exclusively on aspects of the child's earliest experiences from inside the womb through the first year of it's life. It failed to grasp other formidable influences on the formation of the child's personality, including Adler's important observations. This limited research transposed into the formation of two erroneous and incomplete theories, **Maternal Attachment** and **Tender Years**, both of which became prime legal doctrines.[9]

---

[9] See Chapter 5, Development of Law, A Brief Historical Perspective

The Link between Early Psychiatric Theory and Modern Family Law

There is a direct link between psychiatric theory and the family law system. Over time, the notion was developed that a child of "tender years' cannot be separated from his mother, but left father completely out of the equation. This was a gross research error.

Practicing psychiatrists like Klein often saw their young child clients while in the care and control of either mothers or female nurses. Father was far less available because the Industrial Revolution had caused a social reorganization of the family leading to his prolonged periods of absence. He was at work.

The observational environment was decidedly maternal, limited and incomplete. Clinical bias had been, inadvertently skewered by the very purpose of all psychoanalytical investigations. The premise for these investigations was the need to discover causation of adult psychosis, neurosis and other associative mental disorders. That causation seemed related to early childhood problems.

I am not suggesting that gestation (life inside the mother's womb) and the first year of life are not significant, especially when large numbers of women breast-fed their offspring. Clearly, between 1900 and World War II, and to a lesser extent up to the end of the 1950's, the earliest influence on the child might flow from Klein's good and bad breasts of mother. Indeed, the life experience of mother during the gestation period has a direct bearing on the yet unborn child. In a chance meeting I once had with a Russian Psychiatrist, he said he was focusing his research into problems related to refusal of the fetus to turn in the womb. His research showed that mother's bad experience or frame of mind produced poor results with the child, while her healthy disposition supported the correct turning of the fetus.

Moreover, the psychiatric literature failed to offer a complete or balanced picture on subsequent child development, paternal relationships and the family. It ignored the data and theory on the child's necessary 'separation' from the mother and 'attachment to his or her father' in the 'second stage' of growth and development. It never considered whether a father could provide a similar or complementary influence to that of mother, especially absent from or after breast-feeding.

The influence of the psychiatric community's imperfect research eventually found its way into social and legal domains. It cemented the foundation for a generalized dictum that children of 'tender years' (primed at first by the British Act of 1839) should not be separated from their biological mothers. *See Chapter 5*

However, we could also ask whether separation from his or her biological father is healthy for a child. Perhaps, if anyone had bothered to research and analyze the relationship of father-child, one would have arrived at a similar conclusion to that of the mother-child relationship. In other words, attachment theory should apply to both father and mother. Children attach to those who nurture! This is not gender specific or dependent. Further, nurturing does not necessarily mean changing nappies or diapers!

While the psychiatric literature was in the midst of infusing itself into societal and legal thinking from 1925 onward, it still had little or no direct impact on the general population. The reason for its lack of impact was rooted in the firmly established taboos against divorce and the extremely low number of separating families.

Regardless of immediate effect, it had created an intellectual and scientific climate. Thus, setting in motion the machinery that later served to sever important links between children and their fathers. The inevitable distortions of a pseudo science (initially directed at a narrow investigation of adult dysfunction) have lead to chaos and destruction when relied on (by legal systems) without reference to social, anthropological, cultural and other influences on child development.

Later, in the aftermath of the sixties revolution that thrust radical changes on traditional family structure, the erroneous literature on child development merged with external forces to shape our present dilemma.

And as the divorce rate began to escalate through the seventies, eighties and into the year 2000, these dramatic rises produced a corresponding rise in the amount of psychiatric literature on child development, trauma, separation and custody. A veritable cottage industry was born!

Bowlby and the Theory of Attachment to Mother

Modern court reliance on sole maternal custody relies on Bowlby's theory of attachment to mother (The Maternal Attachment Theory). His ideas remain dominant to this date despite massive contemporary evidence contradicting his views and showing that the child has two psychological parents and attachment to both parents (Two Psychological Parents Attachment Theory).

Bowlby's work followed Klein and others who had pursued lines of inquiry limited to the role of mother and the mother-child interaction. Although, he would later modify his view, the central theme of his work was that early attachment did not occur through Freudian "orality", but from an innate survival strategy catalyzed by sustained and loving **maternal** touch.

A synopsis of Bowlby's biography helps to explain how the nature of his own family background, and his training with Klein, made his focus the exclusive investigation of mother-child attachments while ignoring the important father-child attachment.

"On Feb. 26, 1907, John Bowlby was born in London to rather **distant, middle-aged parents**. His father, Maj. Gen. Sir Anthony Bowlby, was surgeon to King George V. **One of six children**, the young **Bowlby was sent to boarding school at age 7**. He attended the Royal Naval College, then Cambridge for premedical studies. In 1929, after a formative year working with maternally deprived adolescents, he completed his medical studies at the University College Hospital, London. He trained in psychiatry at the Maudsley under Aubrey Lewis, but also at the Psycho-Analytic Institute with a Kleinian training analyst and Melanie Klein, herself, as a supervisor. He wrote, with his friend E.P.M. Durkin, a book that synthesized objective field studies of aggression in the behavior of great apes with Kleinian theories about aggression."

Bowlby, the professional, trained for a year working with what his biography describes as 'maternally deprived adolescents' and studied under Melanie Klein.

According to his biography:

"During the years 1950-1952 he completed a monograph for the World Health Organization that was to make "maternal deprivation" a household phrase and draw the attention of psychoanalysis and the public to early mother-child interactions."

In light of his early childhood experience so starved of affection, I am not surprised at the direction and interest his professional work took. It appears that he never found mother and, therefore, failed to reach the next stage of finding father. Did Bowlby influence the work of those who followed? Yes! Anna Freud and her co-authors would further consecrate the theme of maternal-child attachment, to the exclusion of any research on father, coming to some extraordinary conclusions on custody.

A Critical View of the Works of Goldstein, Freud and Solnit

Following the work of Klein and Bowlby, a disastrous book written in 1973 by Goldstein, Freud and Solnit took as its title, "Beyond the Best Interests of the Child". This book was later augmented by, "Before the Best Interests of the Child", and, finally by "In the Best Interests of the Child", published as an edited and revised trilogy in 1996. This trilogy spanned twenty-three years and reinforced the old 'maternal attachment' views of Bowlby.

Unfortunately, it was and still is without a doubt the most influential work on the issues of child custody viewed 'purportedly' from a purely psychoanalytical perspective. In conflictual custody cases, this book is the enemy of children and their fathers. Fathers must produce powerful arguments to offset its influence. The very title of the book is purposefully derivative of a political doctrine (The Best Interests of the Child) of the world's family law courts.

The doctrine of 'the best interests of the child' demands that family law courts follow a mandate (especially in conflictual cases) to prioritize the 'best interests of the child' and not those of parents. In fact, this doctrine relies on an even earlier concept of the 'paramountcy' of the child's interests, which meant that the child's interests overrode those of the parents. Although neither doctrine is anything more than general 'policy', they intermingle with social, psychiatric-psychological and other dynamic influences to create definitive black letter (judge made) law. That law universally defers to mother in child custody cases.

The titles of Freud's books are, therefore, quite interesting. Far from accidental, they are clear attempts to drive the legal system towards pre-conceived and pre-determined results in contradiction to the very meaning of civil legal process. Second, while purportedly addressing child custody issues from the perspective of the child, they inject a number of strict codes and legal guidelines, also usurping the administration of justice and the prerogatives of court process. Third, this was collaborative work. It combined in part, the limited and unspecified experience of Anna Freud at her Hampstead Clinic in England, with the legal perspective of Joseph Goldstein at Yale law. Children of divorcing or divorced families were not included in the research.

A careful review of the trilogy sounds an immediate warning. There is no focus on either research or case study of the particular crisis facing children thrust into the traumatic circumstances of divorce and custodial issues. However, the authors still suggest to the courts a rigid style and structure for making custody decisions, including case material and a re-writing of actual decisions using the author's own guidelines.

What cases they had followed were of children who had been 'fostered' and removed from their 'mothers'. They reached a number of conclusions chief amongst them was, that 'children should not be separated from their mothers'. I think that any one of us could have come to a similar conclusion.

However, their views on welfare cases extended well beyond that area into normal family law. They stressed the idea that children required a regularized routine to maintain their emotional balance and that it could not be disturbed even if, in normal custody cases, it meant delimiting their access to the other parent. Further, they stated, that the controlling custodial parent (mother) 'must be granted sole decision-making power over the child'.

Of course, the authors had failed to carry out any research on the interaction between child and father. They had merely worked from the suspect earlier assumptions of Klein, Bowlby and others who had researched child development during the industrial revolution strictly from the mother-child interaction.

They argued for sole custody as being the 'least detrimental alternative', and had with 'extreme prejudice' exclusively identified and associated the child's best interests with those of the mother.

The net effect of their trilogy has been to foster a strict environment perpetuating sole maternal custody decisions over joint custody ones. It has had a devastating affect on the emotional lives of children the world over.

However astonishing it might seem, Goldstein, Freud and Solnit concluded, without the slightest adduction of evidence or intuitive sense, that a child has only one primary caregiver. Further, they concluded that sole custody 'must be granted' to the mother and that mother 'must not be interfered with' by the state (court). The conditions of sole custody must be final with neither the court or the parent (father) being able to dictate special conditions-such as requirements for a special education, religious or other, to live in any one given geographical area or to grant visitation to relatives.

Not content with those authoritarian conclusions, the authors surpassed themselves in a betrayal of the child's best interests when they declared that:

"Where courts impose visitation as a condition of custody, this may itself be a source of discontinuity"

And even more astoundingly:

"The non-custodial parent (father) should have no legally enforceable right to visit the child and the custodial parent (mother) should have the right to decide whether it is desirable for the child to have such visits." [10]

In their revised edition encompassing the trilogy, "The Best Interests of the Child" 1996, the authors claim in an attempt to justify their conclusions that their views are misunderstood. I hardly think so. It is difficult to imagine how a child (facing the severance of loving contact to an important psychological parenting figure) can possibly prosper emotionally.

Further, if the parent (father) has no legally enforceable rights, then the converse of the proposition is also true that the child has no legally enforceable rights to see and enjoy a relationship with the non-custodial parent. This is the case even when he or she may be demanding contact. This is a legally, morally and intellectually unacceptable position.

The authors of this work then vainly plead that they have "reasoned" always from the child's point of view.

How could they have 'reasoned' so? Did they conduct controlled studies of divorced households, interviews with children followed up over time along the lines of Wallerstein and Kelley (much criticized by feminists) or follow the research and studies of their colleagues in the field? Were they aware of the existence of reformed family unit structures in which men had become co-nurturers of their children? Had they even considered the issues of parental loss raised by Dr. Jacobs and others?[11]

The answer is a firm and absolute no. They quite mistakenly superimposed their own value systems and flawed psychoanalytical approach projecting them onto the child. They confused their own bias with the views, feelings and psychological needs of the child on whose behalf they claimed to 'reason'. They did so in the absence of the proper adduction of evidence or support. I do not call their work reasoned. Do I too misunderstand them when they say that they are

---

[10] The Best Interests of the Child, Goldstein, Solnit, Freud, The Free Press, 1998, at P23-27
[11] See Chapter 3 Parental Alienation Syndrome, Quest for Father

not opposed to visitation, merely to the courts' enforcement of that visitation? I think not.

Clearly, the authors meaning and the consequences of their logic is the following.

In conflictual cases (and that is what we are dealing with in their millions) mother 'wins' and acts out in a hostile, irrational and determined manner to deprive her spouse and children of access to one another. Mother 'should be permitted' to continue acting in a destructive manner without court interference despite the long established psychiatric literature demonstrating the incredible harm she causes the children in doing so.

Not only do Goldstein et al support this notion, but, **they indeed are supporting authoritarian control by the parent least capable of appropriate parenting from the child's point of view**, a parent who from questionable motives and possible emotional instability acts to de-stabilize the child.

What is unstated, but obviously driving their conclusions, is that mother is nurturer/care-giver and father is nothing more than a provider. All else is derivative of and flows from that misinformed bias. It puts them sadly and desperately out of touch with the reality of family structure and research in the field.

Of course, many reputable psychiatrists have characterized the work as being intellectually disingenuous. Other critics have described the research as wholly inadequate and destructively misleading. However, it remains a painful fact that this is the cited work in hundreds of thousands of cases throughout the western world. Judges, social workers, lawyers and so-called hired experts, use it to reinforce the court's subjective predilection to grant sole custody to mothers. In a practical sense, it sets a limitation on the child's rights to access his or her father and is a denial of human rights law.

Disingenuous mothers, radical feminists, lawyers and other so-called professionals, rely on Freud, Solnit and Goldstein as one would the Bible. Their covert support of maternal preference standards, ironically, contradicts the theory of the paramountcy of the child's best interests and modern best interests doctrine.

Psychiatrists such as the misandrist Dr. Dora Black in England have full rein to impose feminist agendas over vulnerable sets of family relationships. They offer false 'neutral expert' evidence[12] ignoring the needs of children, opining for female dominated child parent relationships to the exclusion of male influence and rights. Dr. Black and others rationalize their conclusions relying on the erroneous views of Bowlby and the insipid theories of Goldstein, Freud and Solnit. Lost on the court is the fact that the Freud findings relied on impaired samplings, improper controls, personal bias and incomplete research. In order to fully understand the impact that books such as "Beyond the Best Interests of the Child" and it's later editions had on present court policy, one has to focus on the male judges who heard most of the earlier cases.

Interaction-The Literature and Male Judges

First, I should point out that family law courts did not even properly exist in their own right until the late sixties. Second, the judges had no prior training either formal or informal in the psychology and social organization of the family. Third, that the judges were drawn from a segment of the male community who had been raised in conservative traditional family structures that suffered from the sexual-gender stereotyping of earlier generations. Their value systems were firmly in place and were inflexible.

These judges were not only receptive to the idea of women's hegemony over the home and offspring but found it extremely inviting to digest the sole-custody arguments of but one segment of the psychiatric community as exemplified by Goldstein and friends. The arguments conformed to their own sexist and parochial views on women. To them, women were not equals. The Czech psychiatrist Bakalar in his paper: "Court Bias against Father: The Hidden Mechanisms", wrote:

"The judge has to decide whose arguments to believe, whom to favor, whom to support-and also whether his or her colleagues and

---

[12] See Chapter 8 False Expert Reports, Dr. Black,

society at large would approve of the decision. In such situations an inner voice appears...help the woman (especially the mother) support her, protect her, do not let her suffer, this is the right way to decide!"

He says that the inner voice has deep roots in human biological history, relating the male protective reaction to the hunter-gatherer societies of our ancestors:

"We all...are descendants of those ancestors who protected women. But there is a difference...in the past helping the woman had a function of primary importance i.e. survival of the tribe..."

He says that this "I must help the woman" behavior of judges is now anachronistic, but so ingrained through natural selection in tens of thousands of generations that it is difficult to overcome:

"...The scientists, a biologist, a socio-biologist or an evolutionary psychologist would name that as the basic reason for inequality while deciding personal and emotional conflicts between a man and a woman, a biological disposition acquired through natural selection. Now, we can better understand the behavior of judges who are not aware of the mechanisms involved."

So, while the contemporary real world lived according to the more open and flexible lifestyles predicated on the sixties social revolution, these judges were generally older men steeped in the anachronistic conservative structures of post industrial revolution life and family experience. Equally, the desire to grant women pre-eminent domain in the home and over the children may have been fueled by a desire to exclude women from traditionally male spheres of life.

In short, male judges naturally gravitated towards the settling of children into the sole and exclusive control of women. "Many judges have traditional attitudes about gender." (Robinson and Barret 1986 p.87) From a psychological point of view, it seems reasonable to conclude that these judges would have viewed the desire of the 'new' man to maintain a nurturing interest in the lives of his children as somehow rather perverse and bizarre. This has been even more glaringly obvious for English judges.

In addition, the American and British family court systems have recently incorporated a generation of radical feminist judges who, in the words of one of their number, "would never hand over custody of a child to a man".

Later Research and Studies Challenging and Rebutting the Conclusions of Goldstein, Freud & Solnit

Now we come to deal with some elements of rebuttal that are of direct interest to fathers fighting for joint custody. These opposing views are valuable taken together with statistical and further evidence provided in this book.

As I have said, Goldstein, Freud and Solnit, originally published in 1973, once more in 1979 and again broached the topic in the watershed year of 1984, re-confirming their earlier conclusions. Despite the fact that between 1975 and the present numerous research and other psychiatric material has been available to challenge the conclusions of Goldstein, Freud and Solnit, that research was not incorporated into the revised editions. Alternative views on child care and custody issues have received little or no attention in the courts or in the community-at-large. The reasons for this are both varied and complex, but begin with who controls the media.

Many reputable psychiatrists and psychologists, highly skeptical of the work and conclusions of Goldstein et al, set out through psychoanalysis, research and observational clinical studies to review the issues raised by separation, anxieties, loss and trauma consequential to family conflict and custody battles.

Between 1974-77, roughly at the same time Goldstein had first published "Before the Best Interests of the Child", Wallerstein and Kelley had embarked on a study of families with maternal custody, their attention focused on the effects to children. The conclusions they drew were that children suffered loss deprived of their treasured relationship to the other parent and intense longing to be in a continuing relationship to the departed parent (father). They also found that enhanced ease of meaningful access of the visiting parent led to a reduction in distress and trauma to the child.

Here, in a controlled study environment contrasted to Goldstein et al, we had early proof that Goldstein's conclusions were biased and erroneous. By the nineteen eighties Wallerstein and Kelley had embarked on a 10 year follow-up study of divorced couples and their children, which ultimately confirmed that children need continued, on-going and meaningful contact to both parents in the aftermath of divorce.

The study showed the children who fared best in post-divorce circumstances were those who had that contact and conversely, those who did the worst were those that had their relationships to one or the other parent either substantially reduced, delimited or completely obliterated. The work of Wallerstein and Kelley eventually had an impact on California custody law mandating joint-custody or shared parenting decisions as a presumption in law. The presumption depended on cogent judicial arguments not reliant on a generality such as the ill-defined 'best interests of the child' doctrine[13]. Wallerstein and Kelley were not the only reputable sources of information available to us in respect to the welfare of children threatened with family trauma, separation and loss.

Modern Consensus on Joint Custody as the Least Detrimental Alternative

In 1986, in the aftermath of a symposium held at the 137th Annual Meeting of the American Psychiatric Association, psychiatrist Dr. John W. Jacobs edited a book reviewing the psychiatric literature. It included monographs by Dr. Mel Roman, Dr. Frank Williams, and Dr. Dorothy Huntington, that focused not only on aspects of custody decisions but also on the role of fathers in relation to their children within a divorce context.

This insightful book, presented clear and cogent evidence that served to counter the sole-maternal custody theories of Goldstein et al. It argued that joint custody, in light of more recent research on father-child interactions, is often a far better solution to the problems of conflictual families seldom having worse effects on the child than the

---

[13]Cal Evidence Code Sec.4600.5 Presumption of Joint Custody

sole custody decisions so prevalent in the courts. (Dr. John W Jacobs, Divorce and Fatherhood: The Struggle for Parental Identity, American Psychiatric Press, 1986)

In reporting on recent clinical observations demonstrating that from early infancy onwards, children have more than one psychological parent and need both parents for different aspects of normal development[14] (Rutter (1974), Williams (1983),

Dr. Jacobs's states,

"Cultural and employment patterns have changed such that mothers as well as fathers are now frequently employed when their children are still young. Often the mother and father share bottle-feeding, diapering, play and emotional nurturing activities with each other...**This results in many infants and toddlers having two psychological caretakers**, mother and father."

He added:

"As babies move into the day-care phase (toddler and pre-school levels of development, fathers are more equally and sometimes more bonded to their youngsters..."

Jacob's findings confirmed the work of Margaret Mahler and Abelin (1976) in directly observing young children, reporting that father has a vital role in the traditional family in helping the child to "separate from her earliest attachments to mother." and stating that for many children:

"The father relationship develops side by side with the mother relationship from the earliest weeks on and shares many of its 'symbiotic' qualities."(Jacobs (1986)-Abelin (1975) p.128)

Lamb(1976) had already reviewed the literature identifying the serious methodological errors made by researchers (Bowlby, Freud, Solnit, Skynner) who had assumed a minimal role for fathers in child rearing while he had drawn attention to the mounting evidence of the developmentally critical nature of nurturant father-child interactions.

---

[14] See Dr. Rossan on Father Importance next sub-chapter

In light of modern research, studies and clinical observations, Roman and Haddad (1979) argued consideration of joint custody as being in 'the best interests of the child'. They meant by this that the parents share equally in childcare responsibilities and in the making of significant child-rearing decisions.

Remember, Goldstein et al had presented their theories about sole custody without the adduction of evidence or controlled divorce studies. While Arbanel (1979) reported that for most children little discontinuity and no evidence of developmental pathology existed in having two regular homes instead of one and strongly suggested that joint custody be considered as a viable option to the injustice and rigidity of the Goldstein approach.

Steinman's study (1981) had found that having a regular relationship with both parents enhanced the child's self-esteem. While, one third of the sample's children felt some burden in maintaining a strong presence in both homes.

Benedek and Benedek (1979) also repudiated the draconian solutions of Goldstein et al, taking the view that it was and is **the child's right to see the parent on a regular basis**. This is the first time to my knowledge that mental health professionals have addressed the position of the child from a legal point of view[15]. I will expand on this development in a later chapter that will deal with the civil and human rights of children and parents.

Dorothy Huntington, Clinical Professor of Psychiatry and Director of Research and Evaluation, Center for the Family in Transition, spoke disparagingly of the exclusionary process eliminating fathers as being an outgrowth of "tender years" doctrine based on the old and erroneous psychoanalytical assumption that children can be attached primarily to only one person that:

"...Leads to an underestimation of the viability of shared parenting as a family structure, as a positive contribution to a child's development and as a way of assuming the long-term continuation of a father's role within a child's orbit."

---

[15]A specific and defined right aligned to civil & human rights, see Chapter 7

She went on to state:

"Research, observation and intuition all indicate that multiple attachments are the rule rather than the exception for the vast majority of infants and young children and that the situational factors surrounding separation and divorce seriously influence a child's development (Waters and Noyes 1984)."("Fathers: The Forgotten Figures of Divorce, 1986")

In concurring and supporting shared parenting or joint custody decisions as a preference in law, based on revised models of gender roles, economic conditions and social expectations, Dr. Mel Roman, former Professor of Psychiatry and Director of Groups and Family Studies at The Albert Einstein College of Medicine, stated in 1986:

"Ten years ago, the influential views of Goldstein, Freud, and Solnit (1973) framed the conceptual possibilities open to legal, psychiatric and social science professionals...that children of divorce need one psychological custodial parent who should have total control over the child's access to the non-custodial parent. Entrenchment and inertia in the legal, psychiatric and social science fields have since further widened the disparity between court practice and the actual lives of divorced men and women...have not been in the forefront of change...

Most studies indicate that joint custody offers sufficient meaningful advantages to all parties to make it the preferred custodial decision. Even a cursory historical review of the logic behind custody decisions inexorably leads to the conclusion that a new operational method-joint custody- is in order."(Roman, Ph.D., "Joint Custody Fathers: An Update, 1986")

Writing in 1985, , Richard A. Gardner Clinical Professor in Psychiatry, Columbia University, stated:

"A type of custody arrangement that I believe should be tried more frequently can best be called joint-custody. In this arrangement the children at their wish, are free to go from one parent's house to the other without any kind of legal intervention or parental permission."

He notes, of course, the obvious difficulties. Gardner points to the possibility of the children having to be in close parental proximity, either manipulating or being manipulated by the parents. He points to the possible avoidance of discipline, and says it could not work in the case of extremely young children below the age of 6 or 7. However, his conclusion is that the benefits outweigh the risks. He notes that:

"It has the advantage of their having the opportunity to remove themselves easily from unhealthy parental influences." Gardner, "The Parents Book about Divorce" (1985)

Although Dr. Gardner's interesting interpretation of joint custody is not the usual one, its theme is one that is recognizable. It is really quite daring because it hints at barring the inadequate legal system from family dramas. It is innovative because it seeks to permit the children to express and realize their views on whom and for how much time, they wish to be with absent of any outside intrusions.

Other sources supporting joint custody in acrimonious divorces include moderate feminists Bartlett and Stack citing McKinnon, R., and Wallerstein, J. "Joint Custody and the Preschool Child". "Behavioral Sciences and the Law" (1986), 4:169-83; Greif, J.B. "Fathers, children and joint custody", American Journal of Orthopsychiatry (1979) 49:311,318; Roman, M., and Haddad, W. "The Disposable Parent: The Case for Joint Custody", New York: Holt, Rinehart and Winston, 1978; Wolley, P, "Shared custody", Family Advocate (Summer 1978) 1:6,7,33; and note no. 64, Wallerstein and Kelly, pp. 130-31, 218

The Importance of Father

At the time of writing, Gardner still stated his preference for mothers, up to the child's age of two years or so, but importantly adds:

"Beyond that things may equal out, especially if social attitudes regarding male and female roles in child rearing keep changing."

Another insight into nurturing and fathers from an anthropological perspective comes from Margaret Mead who said:

"Somewhere at the dawn of human history some social invention was made under which males started nurturing females and their young."

Unlike Freud and Solnit in their possibly politically motivated rush to judgment, a number of highly respected mental health professionals had taken note of Mead's comments. Also recognizing the radical changes in interpersonal family relationships that had occurred following the social revolution of the nineteen sixties. These professionals observed and reported on the remarkable impact that fathers were having on the nurturing and development of their children. Long overdue research on the role of men as fathers within intact and non-intact families was beginning to take place in earnest. The evidence grew that fathers were as important to the normal development of their children as were mothers.

Notwithstanding the fact that millions upon millions of men have become more directly involved in what researchers describe as nurturing, I take the view that we cannot judge a father's influence strictly by changing social patterns. His importance exists independent of these particular definitions of parenting.

In fact, it matters little whether or not he is home for prolonged periods of time or physically bathes an infant child or gives bottles or changes nappies or engages in those day to day activities which we normally associate with nurturing.

Father's importance, as long as he is loving, interested and concerned about his offspring, is just as prominent as a mother's importance. The evidence for this somewhat controversial point of view is really, right before our eyes. We observe in all fathers, whether 'traditional' or 'modern' a pattern of contact and interaction with their children that enables us to assume such importance measured on a qualitative and not quantitative basis.

Even more importantly, confirmation of this judgment is by direct observation of children's loving reactions to male parents. How often have we seen a young toddler child run across a room and leap into the arms of a father who has been at work all day? If mother nurturing was such a complete enterprise, then why do children crave the attention of their fathers? What is it that father provides that mother cannot? Surely, measure of time and conduct of superficial activities do not adequately express the meaning of nurturing.

Writing from a psychological rather than psychoanalytical perspective, Dr. Sheila Rossan, Lecturer in psychology at Brunel University, addressed central concerns of the effects on the child as a function of the interaction between father and his child. In addressing these concerns, she included the behavioral differences between mother's and fathers, differentiations of behavior between mother-child and father-child interactions and the differences in the quality of these interactions and their effects on the child's internalizations. ("Giving Meaning to Psychological Research on Fathering" (1991)

Rossan concluded that the role of present day fathers is crucial to the healthy development of both boys and girls. She went on to report that fathers act differently toward their children than does the mother, providing them with controlled unpredictability which allows children to develop skills required to cope with change, with disorder and with probability rather than certainty.

Observation of fathers at play with their children demonstrated that they are more likely to initiate games involving tactile sensations and movement of the limbs (Clarke-Stuart 1978). Rossan's own observations showed that mothers raising children to the air often bring them straight back down not letting go while fathers do let go. She further reported that father's hold and rock infants more than mothers do (Parke, O'Leary & West, 1972) and in interviews, husbands emphasize physical contact more than their wives (Greenberg & Morris 1974).

According to Dr. Rossan, because of father's more obvious differentiated behavior towards either male or female children, the children quickly learn to be competitive or cooperative, achieving or not, to see themselves as dangerous or vulnerable, to be concerned with the world of things or the world of people. She poses the question, "How can we think, then, that the father is of little importance?"

Where Dr. Rossan had addressed the child's position in relation to both parents (the triad) within an intact family setting, Dr. Wallerstein (1984), correspondingly in following divorced families found that:

"There was considerable evidence that the relationship between child and **both** divorced parents does not lessen in emotional importance over the years."

She further found, "Even in remarriage (mother's) the biological father's psychological and emotional significance did not disappear or diminish markedly." The research, fact-finding and intuitive analysis substantiate the importance of father, treated so dismissively by Bowlby and his colleagues. Wallerstein discovered in observing children involved in divorce, their absolute rejection of the notion that they were not still part of a two-parent family:

"And, in fact, throughout the research it has been strikingly apparent that whether the children maintained frequent or infrequent contact with a non-custodial parent, they would have considered the term "one parent family" a misnomer. The self image of children who have been reared in a two-parent family appears to be firmly tied to the continuing relationship with both parents, regardless of that parent's physical presence with the family."

Author Simone De Bouvoire, a voice that feminists and feminist literature often cited, underscored Dr. Rossan's and Dr. Waller stein's views on the importance of fathers. She claimed that all that she was and had become was as a result of her own father's love, intense interest and influence on her life, his encouragement towards freedom and self-expression that never bowed to gender stereotypes.

The self-image of the daughter is one of gratification through verbal, warm interpersonal relationships, at a point requiring the separation from the safety net of mother. It is dependent on the healthy attachment to her father who provides her with a sense of the outer world and with a sense of self-esteem, born of confidences gained in the exchange and on the growth of an ability to love, not only herself but, the opposite gender. A later chapter will review the effects of father absence on daughters and sons (*See Chapters 3, 12*), but here I include Rossan's reporting on the studies, suggesting that:

"Daughters who have grown up in father-absent homes have difficulties during adolescence in interpersonal relationships" (Hetherington 1980).

Fathers are a necessary component of the normal child development equation. It is conceivable that any custody process causing their disappearance and elimination , such as the one favored by Goldstein et al., however conflictual the nature of the circumstances, is at immediate loggerheads with the clear principles enshrining the best interests of children. Ironically, it would be antithetical to the self-proclaimed title of Goldstein, Freud and Solnit's "Best Interests of the Child: The Least Detrimental" resolution.

It is astonishing that any such theoretical view on 'the best interests of children' of divorce, could even possibly espouse a solution that emphasizes regularity, order, continuity and sole authoritarian control over protection and the fostering of powerful, natural, psychological and emotional attachments as well as bonds to a male parent.

What modern researchers have discovered was available from less publicized material and earlier work such as Radlin (1972, 1973) who found that:

" In young boys paternal nurturance is, significantly and highly correlated with increased I.Q." Jacobs commented on this (1986) and Shinn (1978) confirmed this in his review of the literature on relationships between 'father absence' and children's cognitive development.

The negative effects of father absence on the health and development of children comes under discussion in the chapter on The Consequences of Parental Rights Deprivations on Children. Included quoted material from reliable professional sources in this and other chapters, should be used by fathers in all legal actions dealing with custody. They should be included in argument, and addressed in expert evidence and during interrogation of witnesses by way of affirmation or rebuttal.

Maternal Nurturance Problems

If child development is dependent on having two available parents in more or less normal circumstances, what happens to a child who has a mother who fails to nurture and father has been disposed of as the 'previously unrecognized' second of two psychological parents? What occurs when he is no longer available to safeguard the child's needs?

In "Families and How to Survive Them"(1984), Dr. Robin Skynner engages former patient comedian John Cleese in a dialogue based on maternal attachment theory following Bowlby's ideas and relates:

"Robin: Well, remember that the child isn't fully aware of his mother as a whole person until he's reached about five or six months. This seems very startling to some mothers, but the fact is that a substitute mother can be brought in during this period without so much harm because the child isn't yet completely aware of the difference."

While he realizes that mother can be absent, Skynner forgets the possibility that the sex of the substitute parent is of no observable significance, as long as he/she meets the criteria of nurture at that stage of the child's development. Skynner, like most English males and Bowlby before him, simply had no cultural cognitive basis for identification or equation of infancy with fatherhood and therefore, made automatic assumptions based on prejudices.

Cleese then inquires:

OK. Now lets go back to what you were saying earlier. I asked what happened if the mother's emotional support isn't there for the child and you explained about Bowlby's and Robertson's work...

Skynner: ...One of the worst insults in the human vocabulary is to call a woman a bad mother...**Nevertheless there are some women who are not able to give the child as much love, in the sense of emotional contact, as he needs...**"

Cleese then remarks that Skynner had explained how mother herself may not be able to empathize with the child because of her own painful childhood experiences in which she had a mother who did not offer love and emotional support.

Skynner: And her mother did not give enough to her, all the way back generation after generation. **It is called a cycle of deprivation.**

Although Skynner erroneously makes an exclusive arrangement of the mother and child relationship ignoring present research on father's parenting, he does conceptualize the cause and effect correlating lack of proper nurturance with consequential scars that impede or block the child's growth and development. These scars are of such significance that they disable her from proper nurturance of her own young. Thus creating a cycle of deprivation that goes on over many generations with affects that we will discuss later in the book.

Of greater significance is the elucidation of a concept that is not limited to mother's (or father's) lack of emotional support and love. It expands as an abstract to encompass any deprivation of the child passed on through generations, via genetics and learned behavior. Cycles of deprivation passed from mother (or father) to child and down generations, might, for example, relate to a mother's depressive nature, transmitted to the child and the child's child through the process of learned behavior and/or genetic imprinting. The impact on the child of parental depressive behavior absent a counterbalancing parental influence is devastating and sets in motion the child's predisposition to replicate that behavior. Numerous epidemiological studies substantiate that proposition.

Professor Norman Lader of The British Institute of Psychiatry substantiated my views on depressive behavior patterns in a letter to me (1993), disclosing the danger to children exposed to depressive mothers. Every parent must make courts aware of these potential problems, by linking the above to the studies showing a high rate of child depressive behavior in fatherless homes. *See Chapter 3, Short, Medium and Long-term Damage*

The argument and case for shared parenting in conflictual divorces, gains momentum by incorporating all the resource information included in the following chapter on the affects of father absence on children.

Chapter 3

Consequences of Parental Rights Deprivations on Children

If there is a violation of father's parental rights, what are the possible effects on his child's rights and needs? Is there, as suggested earlier, an association between children's and father's rights? What is the feminist position on association of rights? What do the research studies and statistics show about children and father absence?

One interesting fallacy promoted by radical feminists claims that parental rights (father's rights) are distinct, separate and not connected to the rights of the child. On the other hand, when it suits them they contrive to subtly tie children's rights to those of the mother. *See Chapter 8 Fathers Guide to the Courts (Jacobs, Saffer, Ryder Critique of Dr. Black's Psychiatric Report)*

The reality is that the family is a fragile and complicated triad composed of separate dyads, interconnected rights and needs. Legal and psychological concepts of parental rights undertake to express the inherent balances of a child's relationship to each of its parents and do not disassociate those rights from the child's best interests.

"Jacobli is to have a garden of his own to look after, set plants in, "collecting chrysalis and beetles in an orderly, exact, and industrious manner...what a bridle for indolence and wildness." Jacobli is now three and a half.

In the passage below the young boy expresses his feelings about his father.

It would be about a year later, on the occasion of his father's name day, that Jacobli, who could not write, "half singing, half murmuring", gaily dictated to his mother: " I wish my dear Papa...that you should see a lot more and I thank you a hundred thousand times for your goodness...that you have brought me up so joyfully and lovingly. Now I shall speak from my heart... It makes me terribly happy, if you can say I have brought my son up to happiness...I am his joy and his happiness, then shall I first give thanks for what you have done in my life." (H. Ganz 1966)

Whether a four and a half year old child really can articulate as Jacobli did is of no consequence. The passage is an allegory on paternal affection. If Jacobli, were suddenly and arbitrarily removed from his father, each would suffer a loss of rights. Their rights and interests in the relationship are mutual, though the child's loss of rights might be greater. Father's personal deprivation of rights disables him from nurturing and parenting his child while the child's loss of rights deprives him FROM having nurture and parenting by the father.

Jacobli is a child nurtured by his father as well as by his mother. We have no idea how much time he actually spends with his father, if his father potty trained him, or whether father works at home. However, we do know from the child's perspective and heartfelt response that father MUST have held up that smiling mirror (Dr. Sula Wolff) to the infants face.

We know that this is what nurturing and caretaking are really about. Child nurture is not subject to measure in minutes, hours or days. It is not divisible by a prosaic balancing of physical childcare tasks. Nurturing is a state of mind and spirit that is at the heart of the family nexus, and almost ineffable.

The most striking thing about radical feminist positions on the family, children and divorce is their complete devotion to exploration and promotion of the 'exclusive' interests of women. There may be subtle divisions amongst 'liberal', 'cultural' and 'radical' feminists, but the distinctions only revolve around external strategies and tactics. Feminists, in general, are concerned not with the child, but the child as adjunct to women and women's issues.

One rare but tainted exception is the position of feminists Bartlett and Stack:

"From the point of view of ideology, rules favoring joint custody seem clearly preferable. Joint custody stakes out ground for an alternative norm of parenting. Unlike the 'neutral' best interests test or a primary caretaker presumption, these rules promote the affirmative assumption that both parents should, and will take important roles in the care and nurturing of their children. This assumption is essential to any realistic reshaping of gender roles within parenthood. Only when it is expected that men, as well as women, will take a serious role in childrearing, will traditional patterns in the division of childrearing responsibilities begin to be eliminated in practice as well as in theory. They argue that many of the criticisms of joint custody result from judicial bias and that better implementation, rather than an alternative standard, offers the best way to promote women's interests." (Carbone 1994)

The caveat is that their position does not reflect one from the child's perspective, but relies on women's rights and interests. It also makes the false assumption that men are not *'prima facie'* nurturers and caretakers. On the other hand, father's rights literature usually stresses the best interests of the child in making joint custody arguments.

The Bartlett and Stack approach, as tepid as it might be, is not even in the mainstream of feminist thinking. It is Fineman and Becker who present the 'majority' feminist case for a 'maternal deference' standard in which courts defer to a fit mother's custody preferences. It does not matter whether or not she prefers sole maternal custody, sole paternal custody, joint legal and physical custody, or something in between.

While few feminists dare openly announce the female gender-based standard, nonetheless support is implied, disguised and buried in language for a primary caretaker preference. For instance, Fineman, like Becker, "emphasizes the 'qualitative differences' between the contributions of primary caretakers (typically mother-according to Carbone) and primary earners (typically fathers-according to Carbone) to the upbringing of children."

What qualitative differences does she mean? Differences based on radical feminist reversion to the old clichés and gender stereotyping previously rejected by the women's movement? *See Chapter 2 Man as Provider*

And as June Carbone reports on extremists like Fineman, "She is particularly critical of joint custody statutes" which "formally grant fathers equal control over their children, regardless of who provides the day-to-day care and nurturing."

In other words, if the formerly rejected clichés and stereotypes do not work (father has been a co-nurturer), Fineman simply ignores the facts and the needs of the child. Even if father meets with standards that equate to day-to-day care and nurturing, he cannot have equal control or even any rights! He is a man. In seeking special advantages for women, radical feminists betray the interests of children, without love, concern or guilt.

Psychological Damage Due to Enforced Father Absence

The reduction of involvement and or elimination of male parenting figures, biological, psychological and social fathers, from the family and children has the most disastrous consequences on the lives of the children.

There are two kinds of adduced evidence to prove child trauma and to foster a change in court policy from sole maternal custody to shared parenting. One is the 'positive' evidence on joint custody discussed in the preceding chapter. Now we address the 'negative' evidence that might be of even greater interest and concern. *See Chapter 1, Chapter 2 Psychiatric Literature*

Clearly, Radical and Cultural Feminists steadfastly refuse to address the consequences of their policies promoting the absenting of male parents from the lives of children. Feminist literature is replete with references to the economic standards of mother and the 'welfare of children' (meaning their economic well-being), while deliberately ignoring the emotional and psychological needs of children faced with divorce and father absence.

Whether fathers function in the 'traditional' or in the 'modern' style family makes absolutely no difference to the child. Father's impact on children is essentially the same in either case. The importance of fathers must be understood in terms of their different (complementary) but equally significant nurturing influence on the development of children. *See Chapter 2 Importance of Fathers, Rossan*

In recent years, the term 'father absence' has come to mean or to infer and to misrepresent male parents as willful and voluntary abandoners of their children. However, father absence, but for exceptional circumstances, truly represents a legal, psychological and social invention imposed on men against their will. 'Father-exile' might be a more honest and apt term.

Furstenburg's finding illustrates the fact that mothers in possession of sole custody orders interfere, refuse, avoid and eventually destroy whatever paltry access courts have granted to fathers[16]:

"In 52 percent of a sample numbering 1,337 children of divorce, the last contact with their fathers had been one or more years prior, only one-third of the children averaged monthly contact or more with their fathers (Furstenburg 1983, Huntington 1986).

Greif had already found that:

"The separated parent becomes the 'missing parent'; the disappearing father is a common phenomenon. Paradoxically, in terms of modern changes in role assignment, the higher degree of involvement a father may have with his children during a marriage may be seen as inappropriate or impossible when the marriage is dissolved."

The neutral language of the scientist really means this; a father who fully participated in nurturing and co-parenting, is going to get ex-

---

[16] See Chapter 12, Matriarchy v Patriarchy studies on maternal interference with visitation

communicated from his children in divorce. Father's parenting (so treasured in the marriage) faces repudiation, considered rather extraordinarily as 'inappropriate' in divorce. The term inappropriate means 'inconvenient' to female strategies and goals. In light of Greif, radical feminist positions supporting a maternal preference standard in custody are absurd. It means that women want freedom, power and control in divorce. It translates into women wanting to burn the proverbial burn at both ends. What is mine was yours (as long as I wanted to let you have it and it was useful), but now that I do not need or want you, you are nothing and can have nothing of mine (my children)! It means injustice to children!

Given the well-understood importance of male parental influence, what harm is done to children through the breakdown of intact family models and subsequent legally sanctioned father-absence? Before answering, let us review and reassess the statistics and facts:

Divorce went from pre 1967 levels that were stable at 5 to 10 percent, rising dramatically concurrent to various divorce law reforms instituted in several countries between 1967 and 1984. Rates first doubled and then doubled again and more by the mid-nineteen nineties, reaching our present understated levels of from 50 to 60 percent. *See Chapter 10 Divorce Rate and Lone Parenting Graphs*

Family courts have consistently utilized discredited and outmoded expert evidence to rationalize the making of sole maternal custody decisions. Attestation derives from the wealth of available research on the benefits of shared parenting and the statistics on sole custody versus joint custody results for children. Courts have ignored enlightened and reliable evidence showing the positive affects of shared parenting on children.

One of the direct consequences of the breakdown of intact family models and implementation of sole maternal custody policies is the widespread establishment of female-headed single-parent households, as shown by the available statistics.

Simultaneously, a number of consequences have flowed subsequent to the above development demonstrating an extraordinary incidence of adult dysfunctionality, disturbance and pathologies linked to childhood deprivation of male parental figures.

Particular groups and associations have supported the radical reformation of the traditional family model and have encouraged its transposition into an arcane Neolithic form of matriarchal arrangement, despite the proofs of its extremely dangerous and socially unacceptable consequences.

Other groups, opposed to these developments have proven completely ineffective in restoring balance to the natural rights and interests of children and their fathers.

The total child population of the US is about 77 million. There are at least 22 million and perhaps as many as 35 million children in the United States missing fathers, at serious risk, living in female-headed single-parent families.

The Damage Report

Enforced father absence is often, cited, as a major cause of later anti-social behavior, depression, as well as other pathologies, in later life. This, in turn, causes further cycles of deprivation which transfer on through generations. *See Statistics in Chapter 1*

One researcher, Bloom (1975) found that, "men from broken marriages were nine times more likely to be admitted to psychiatric hospitals for the first time than were men from intact homes." As he reported, admissions for women from divorced homes ran a 300 percent higher admission rate.

Dr. Sula Wolff writing in 1981, "Children under Stress", reported that:

"It has been known for a long time that children from disrupted families have more behavior disturbances than children whose homes are intact. For other children the stresses of family disruption spring not from family rejection but from their own divided loyalties between **'an absent parent'** (father) and the parent (mother) with whom they live."

Other experts, such as psychiatrist Dr. Frank Williams, echo the theme of divided loyalty conflict in the literature. Dr. Wolff went on to acknowledge the fact that family disruption was a consequence of changing public attitudes and legislation, reinforced and **reflected in abortion and divorce law reforms and by further changes in public welfare legislation,** stating that:

"When parents split up the children more often than not remain with the mother. It should not be surprising that under such circumstances boys are at greater risk than girls of emotional and behavioral disturbance."

I do not entirely agree with Dr. Wolff's assessment. It merely seems that boys are at greater risk because it is harder to dissect and identify areas of girl's emotional and behavioral disturbances. It seems to me that boys 'act out' while girls internalize. Some argue that in the short term girls cope better than boys do, but that it is in the long term that the effects of (father loss) family breakup on girls are more apparent.

"In adolescence girls from broken homes are more rebellious, show higher rates of depression and experience more difficulty in their heterosexual relations than do children from intact, non-divorced homes." White and Wollett, 1992 (Hetherington 1988)

If, as reported by Hetherington et al., 1982 "At the time of the breakup departing (male) parents may influence the children's development" and "Regular contact with the non-custodial parent and good relationships with both parents protect children from the emotional disturbances often shown", Black (1984), then how can we permit mothers to obliterate the paternal relationship?

According to White and Wollett (1992):

"...The warmth, maturity demands and techniques of disciplining employed by 'departing' fathers all relate to measures of their children's cognitive ability and sex role development. However, a year later these fathers no longer influence children's performance. Fathers cease to have a direct influence and, lose their power to buffer or protect children from a poorer relationship with the mother. However good the relationship with fathers they cannot contribute to children's resilience unless they are available on a regular basis." (Furstenberg and Seltzer, 1986)

Why then do we continue to artificially induce the death of father when we have known for 30 years that the child, absented from his or her 'treasured' relationship either suffers serious conflicts of loyalty, regresses, displays disturbed behavior and possibly goes into a continuous state of mourning. Mothers prodded on by their advisers, lawyers and peer pressure from radical feminist anti-male groups, act to 'parentectomize' father using a complaisant judicial system. They place the child or children into an impossible psychological position. Wolff sums it up quite well when she states:

"We all have our parents inside us. In part, we are our parents. Our self-esteem and our confidence are dependent on our being able to think well of our parents in childhood. The image of a loved parent who has died is kept alive by his surviving partner and is presented to the children with pride and with the affectionate feelings that existed before his death. When a parent disappears (enforced father absence) because the marriage has failed the situation is entirely different."

Dr. Wolff also voices a conviction that "maternal deprivation" is a cliché, and confirms Dr. Jacob's comments on the consequences of arbitrary and unnatural parental deprivation or loss on the emotional life of the child. *See Chapter 1, Dr. Jacobs on Parental Loss*

The child of divorce left in the sole care, control and influence of the mother who declines to agree to **shared-parenting**, lives in a nether world of conflict, deceit, and confusion. The choices for survival of such a child run from a strategy of over-identification with the good mother, imagining a 'bad' abandoning father or sympathizing with the 'poor' father rejected by a controlling, manipulative mother.

Dangers to girl children from over-identification with mother, have been referred to by Brody and Forehand:

"Daughters in single mother homes have more negative attitudes toward men in general and their fathers in particular." (Pg. 146, 2, lines 5 - 8) Interparental Conflict, Relationship with the Non-custodial Father, and Adolescent Post-Divorced Adjustment - Brody and Forehand, University of Georgia, Journal of Applied Psychology, Vol. 11, No. 2, April - June 1990

This observation carries implications reaching far into adulthood for these children of divorce reflecting a classic female predisposition towards failure in the forming of lasting interpersonal relationships with men. More divorces, more single parent female-headed homes equates to even more divorces in future generations.

Moreover, in either case the child might develop the feeling that he or she is 'bad' and the cause of the marital dissolution. If Dr. Wolff is correct in her assumption that our self-esteem and confidence is dependent on carrying forth positive, loving images of our parents from childhood experience, then how is that possible given the present scenario where custody is granted to mothers and fathers are absented as real, meaningful and loving parents?

Contrast over thirty years literature, studies, statistics, and observations on children, with the senseless views of radical feminist authors such as Andrea Engber, Editor of Single Mother, writing in The Trenton Times, "Advantages of a Single-Parent Home" in response to a grandmother's question:

"Q: Are single-parent families bad for children? My daughter just became a single mother at the age of 30. I know she is mature and responsible, but with everything I have read about children from single-parent families, I am concerned.

H.P.,

Boston"

"The answer is no, single-parent families, ...are not bad for children."

Engber simply jettisons the studies, research and statistics related to single parent families showing the damage to children. Not satisfied with this great deceit, Ms. Engber travels further down the twisted road of radical feminist misinformation,

"Data shows that there are many beneficial effects for the majority of children living in single-parent families."

What data is that? I wonder if she is referring to the statistics on male juvenile delinquency, the Texas statistics on prison populations, the studies on female depression or school dropouts and data on hospital admissions for single-parent children. *See Chapter 1*

Using the radical feminist political line she expands, "...this growing lifestyle is bridging a gap in our culture... The family is not collapsing, but is actually re-emerging as a democracy, as more and more women gain control over their own destinies."

Democracy no doubt Greek style 'Athenian citizenship' for women, but not for children or the male slave population. Democracy built on the displacement of the rights of others and destruction of the best interests of their children. The family has been redefined, as female-headed single-parented. There is no mention of children! The basis of Ms. Engber's misandrist views is one obscure radical feminist report, "The Hite Report", that Engber refers to as, "...this carefully designed survey."

However, there is not the slightest shred of real evidence in any responsible literature on children and divorce that shows net benefits to children living in single-parent families. In a classic confusion of intellectual and psychological ideation, Engber even makes further irresponsible statements:

"Children from single-parent families in general don't experience 'torn loyalties', a crisis occurring in two parent families..."

This is a most extraordinary remark. The very opposite is true, as the literature is replete with references to torn loyalties in divorcing households! One of the most obvious observable affects of conflictual divorces and father eliminated single-parent families is the child's predisposition toward torn loyalties.

Taking Ms. Engber's remarkable insensitivity and obvious bias into account, let us review the 'benefits' of female-headed single-parent families. The truth is that there is real potential for damage in these laudable single-parent family structures.

Short, Medium and Long-Term Damage

Some of the more apparent manifestations of damage done to children due to the breakdown of an intact family model and it's subsequent replacement by a female headed single-parent unit is confirmed from reliable sources as reported by Amneus in "The Garbage Generation":

"A disproportionate amount of child abuse takes place in female-headed families. According to Neal R. Pearce, "there is a strong correlation between the single-parent family and child abuse, truancy, substandard achievement in school and high unemployment and juvenile delinquency." Most victims of child molestation come from single parent households or are the children of drug ring members. The pattern among victims parallels that among offenders. Researchers at North Florida Evaluation and Treatment Center report that "the pattern of the child molester is characterized by a singular degree of closeness and attachment to the mother." (Amneus)

According to Carl Williams, head of California's Workfare program, the unmarried teen-age motherhood resulting from the first law of matriarchy burdens the welfare system and contributes to illiteracy.

The link between fatherless homes and unmarried teenage motherhood that Williams refers to is long established, but recent research has driven home the point. Researchers led by Dr. Bruce Ellis, University of Canterbury, New Zealand, published their findings in the Journal of Personality and Social Psychology (August 1999) that:

"Girls who grew up without their father at home entered puberty earlier".

This makes unsafe and unwise sexual activity far more likely. As syndicated newspaper columnist Kathleen Parker, a longtime supporter of the family points out:

"Logically, girls don't experiment with sex-at least voluntarily-until they've reached puberty. Logically, the later the onset of puberty the better."

Sixty percent of California women under 30 who are now on public assistance began receiving welfare as teen-agers. Fifty percent of them cannot read, write, add or subtract well enough to get a job or train for one.

A survey of 108 rapists undertaken by Raymond A. Knight and Robert A. Prentky, revealed that 60 percent came from female-headed homes, that 70 percent of those describable as "violent" came from female-headed homes, that 80 percent of those motivated by "displaced anger" came from female-headed homes."

Other sources echo these findings and even if one factors in percentage errors attributed to other negative influences, there is still no denying the plain meaning of the statistics. In the absence of strong paternal influence, children are vulnerable to various afflictions and anti-social behavior.

As Hetherington, Wallerstein, and Kelley and many other mental health professionals have observed:

"Children of divorce are threatened and do poorly when confronted with the loss of a male parent", Hetherington (1977) continuing:

" When fathers withdraw from, give up, or are removed from their children, their absence has an immediate, and a delayed, devastating negative impact on their children. Children with 'absent fathers' are vulnerable to developmental dysfunction and depression."(Williams 1986).

Psychiatrist Mel Roman, in describing the effects of female headed single-parent families created out of divorce states: "The pain experienced by the children of the divorce is needlessly great, amplified by the custody decision... **Single-parent maternal custody acts to make ex-parents of fathers, deprived creatures of children...**"

These official statistics demonstrate some of the shocking effects of enforced father absence:

"A child living with his/her divorced mother, compared to a child living with both parents is 375% more likely to need professional treatment for emotional or behavioral problems and is almost twice as likely to repeat a grade of school, is more likely to suffer chronic asthma, frequent headaches, and/or bedwetting, develop a stammer or speech defect, suffer from anxiety or depression and be diagnosed as hyperactive." (National Center for Health Statistics)

In addition, as one might imagine, "Children who live in single mother households receive less adult supervision and attention." (p.

79, Col. 1, 1, Lines 13 - 15) Relationships between Fathers and Children Who Live Apart: The Father's Role after Separation - Judith A. Seltzer, University of Wisconsin-Madison, Journal of Marriage and the Family, Vol. 53, No. 1, February 1991.

"55.3% of children living with divorced mothers and 59.2% of children living with remarried mothers suffer from anxiety or depression." National Center for Health Statistics

"In 21 of 27 social adjustment measures and 8 of 9 academic measures, children of divorce show lower performance than children in two parent families. The results were far more pronounced for boys, than for girls" "Nationwide Impact on Children of Divorce Study", John Guidubaldi, Ph.D. (Former President, School Psychologists Association).

Parental Alienation Syndrome

Mothers who state that they see no value in men as fathers, when granted free rein by sole custody decisions act to isolate the father from the child allowing themselves to use the child narcissistically as a cathected object. As Dr. Miller observed:

"Someone at their disposal who can be used as an echo, who can be controlled, will never desert them and offers full attention and admiration." ("The Drama of Being a Child" 1986)

Gardner and a Typical Case of Parental Alienation Syndrome

The phenomena of the child-cathected object then extends to a condition described by American psychiatrist Richard Gardner as 'parental alienation syndrome' and is widely recognized in family courts as a valid medical problem.

It is best exemplified by a case that Gardner recounts in his book, "The Parents Book about Divorce" (1977), where an enraged mother having possession of a sole custody order, acted out her anger at the father. She infected the children with her hatred causing them to completely reject their father's love as well as all of his attempts to maintain contact with them. According to Gardner:

"The mother's obsession was so all pervasive that there was hardly an hour that the children spent with her that she did not disparage bitterly the father. Whereas previously the children had had a fairly good relationship with their father, the months of vilification of him gradually began to change their attitudes. The point was finally reached, where they too began to hate him and see him as the embodiment of evil, filth and treachery. Finally, they absolutely refused to go with him when he arrived for visits. Instead, they would spit at, curse and even throw things at him when he arrived."

In a side note to Gardner's frightening tale, he recounted that: " Actually, **the mother professed encouragement of the children's visiting with the father** and even made them available for the visits." This is a commonly recurring theme in many cases, as you will note from the following letter from a mother writing for advice to Ms. Gayle Peterson MSSW in her article "Parental rights vs. children's welfare", Parents Place.

"In our case the court has ordered that my children must spend 8 weeks every summer, and 1/2 the school vacations, and every other weekend at their father's. Their father lives 3 hours (one way) from where my children and I reside. The court has also ordered that we share driving, or mileage."

While this seems perfectly reasonable to me she goes on to complain:

"As for **my daughter, she doesn't look at her father as her dad, as she was very young when he filed for divorce.** She thinks of my husband as her dad, and **doesn't even want to be forced to have to go to see her bio-dad.** I am put in the middle, as the court order says I must make them go, or be held in contempt **I really encourage them to have a relationship with their father, but he no longer upholds the values that our family believes in. God, family, hard work and lots of love.** Rather when the children are there, **they are exposed to drinking, and second hand smoking,** and told that both are ok.

Do you have any ideas for me?"

I certainly do. Stop alienating your children from their father. However, what is the response from Ms. Peterson? Does she warn Lisa of the dangers to the children of parental alienation syndrome that are most apparent in this case accompanied by the disguised rage of mother toward father? Here is the response:

"Dear Lisa,

You have identified one of the most hypocritical situations occurring presently in our legal system. While it is very important that parental rights are protected, it is sometimes at the expense of what is truly in the best interests of the children. ...It is sometimes the case that children become "prisoners" to parental "rights" in the court's attempt to dole out justice." ...

Lost on Ms Peterson is the fact that the court is not only acting to protect parental rights but the child's rights as well, and further that this legal protection is linked to the mandate of the court that is based on the psychological needs of the child, and not on her interpretation of the meaning of the term 'law'. Peterson states:

"But somehow the courts have not found a way to understand that there is a difference between the **"ethics of justice"** which our legal system is based upon, and the **"ethics of care"**, which is at the **heart of female development**. Carol Gilligan, in her book, "In a Different Voice" marked the discovery of the very "different" nature of female development, **unrecognized and devalued in our society**. She elucidates the salient point that **our society uses the values of male development based on competition of "rights" to define "justice"**. Rather than consider the value of nurturing relationships which is at the heart of female development in the evaluation of "fairness"."

In other words, when courts follow the dictates of radical feminist values they are fair, when they attempt rather infrequently to protect the legal rights of children and fathers they fail to abide by the rules of feminist ethics of care...whatever that means.

Justice is male (presumably unfair) when it acts to balance the interests of children and parents and it is obviously blind and fair when it cuts off children from men. She has played the radical feminist card again of course and completes the cycle by reverting back to deployment of the legal system that she severely criticizes as not understanding these 'mystical' female values of nurturing, telling Lisa:

"Children are susceptible to exploitation because they have no independent legal rights."

This is a completely false and misleading statement. Many states appoint independent law guardians[17] to represent the rights of children. She also suggests that a father desperately fighting to maintain his parental identity and relationship to his children is somehow 'exploiting' them. Is this the case when mothers' thinly disguised hostility and effective alienation of the children prevents him from maintaining and continuing contact? She continues:

"However, in some states (such as California) it is possible that you can obtain help from the court at no charge through family court services. In this situation, you would be entitled to request a mediation appointment to bring up the points about your son's truncated athletic development and the negative effects on him of the current implementation of the visitation schedule."

Thus, we get to the bottom line. Ms. Peterson endorses a delimiting of father's right to maintain a relationship with his children when threatened by the mother's parental alienation strategy. This case underscores what Dr. Gardner described in his book and we can better understand his rebuke:

"Mothers such as this are obviously quite disturbed and do not realize how much they are harming their children by their campaigns of vilification. In some cases, after many months and years, the relationship with the absent parent is renewed and the children come to appreciate how falsely maligned the absent parent has been. In other cases the alienation is permanent, a sad loss for all concerned."

Moreover, as Margaret Robinson of The Family Institute of Family Therapy, London reminds us about Gardner's case and our friend Lisa:

"Sometimes, the mother protests that the child does not wish to see the father. When children under 12 years of age are forced to

---

[17] See A Father's Guide to the Courts- on Law Guardians, Guardian ad litems

choose they tend to align with the parent they are living with one parent gone, their overriding fear is that they will be abandoned by the other, so they say whatever the present parent wishes to hear." (The Independent, January 1994)

The matter goes beyond the sadness commented on by Gardner and the alienation warning from Robinson.

The Search for Father

As many mental health professionals have observed, the death of a parental figure from natural causes presents difficulties that are surmountable because the surviving parent can maintain a positive image of that parent for the child.

However, the loss (death) of a parental figure (father) based on the determined efforts of the other parent (mother) causes an impact that has short, medium and long-term effects on the child having far greater significance and effect. The child goes into a state of mourning (Freud, see also Aaron Beck on Depression[18]) for the lost loved one that cannot come to a normal conclusion, left unresolved precisely because the parent is not dead. Alienated fathers run similar risks.

The child might display numerous affects and devise many coping strategies, but ultimately it is the nature of the loss, which interferes with the child's normal development.

Quest for the Missing Parent

Lora Heims Tessman described the dilemma of the child thrust into this state as one in which there is an ongoing 'quest for the missing parent', a fact not recognized:

"The children and adults I have encountered (in her practice) have convinced me that a quest for the missing wanted person goes on at many levels and in many guises. Reunion wishes and fantasies are a

---

[18] Aaron Beck, M.D., "Depression; causes and treatment, Chapter 14, Childhood Bereavement and Adult Depression

mainstay of all separated lovers, and have also been documented in relation to the bereaved (Deutsch 1937; Parkes, 1972; Rochlin, 1965) as well as the divorced (Weiss, 1975) and their children (Wallerstein & Kelley, 1976)."

Tessman continues on to state her clinical observations related to the child's precious loss:

"Depending upon the nature of the past lost relationship, and the developmental level of libidinal wishes of the child at the time the loss was experienced, attempts at such recreation could occur through the medium of ideation, motor behavior, affective or somatic experience, or be evident in the later choice of loved persons. Although sometimes obvious, at other times the meaning of the phenomenon as linked to the quest was far from obvious or apparent. The diverse expressions of the quest included the following: searching; anticipation of reappearance, or of messages or letters; a sense of the presence of the person; daydreaming involving disguised fragments of the quest, pseudologia or 'lying' in the service of inner integrity; use of transitional objects and transitional phenomena; magical gestures meant to recreate the lost relationship; acting out to defend against painful memory; hyperactivity, motor restlessness, wandering, some types of stealing; suicidal wishes and attempts; repeating and holding onto painful affects focused on the disruption of relationships or on the choice of loved persons in later life."

The arbitrary separation of child and father, occurring consequential to the high incidence of divorce and nefarious radical feminist efforts to push for sole maternal custody (encouraging the worst possible instincts in women), lead the child into unnatural mourning and other affects.

Cycles of Deprivation

In Chapter 2, we discussed some problems of compromised mother nurturing relating that to what Dr. Skynner refers to as the creation of 'cycles of deprivation' in children.

The root of this problem lies in the disturbances of childhood experience that become ingrained in following adult generations, through learned behavior and genetic predisposition. Thus, the female child whose mother failed to properly love and nurture creates an adult who also cannot offer affection to her child and so forth.

An important English study demonstrated that while family disruption has fewer observable effects on the behavior of girls in childhood, it might profoundly influence the care they give to their babies when they themselves are mothers. "Early Life Experiences an Later Mothering Behavior: a study of mothers and their 20 week old babies", Hall, Pawlby and Wolkind 1980:

As Dr Wolff reports in "Children under Stress" 1981:

"Mothers from disrupted families looked and smiled at their babies less often, touched and talked to them less...by the age of 27 months the language development of the babies whose mothers had experienced parent death, divorce or separation, was less advanced than that of babies of mothers from united families."

The Case of Duncan Brown and his Mother

Further, Dr. Wolff is in agreement with Skynner that family patterns transmit from generation to generation and having presented an illustrative case to prove the point concludes:

"The case of Duncan Brown and his mother illustrates...how the stresses and confusions of childhood can become incorporated into adult personality structure and can lead to a recreation of the anomalous situation. The child, now a parent, holds in her hands the fate of her own offspring. Mrs. Brown, rejected by her parents as a child (absented father=rejection), felt she could do nothing right. Her misfortunes she attributed to her own shortcomings (lack of self-esteem)...She could not settle. She married a boy from a similarly disrupted home and the marriage was a failure." Instead of rejecting Duncan, she acts out an over-solicitation and at the same time cannot tolerate any expressions of discomfort from him, while he develops asthma and we have the intervention of Dr. Wolff in the case.

In another vein, unconscious repetition and imitation of childhood neglect absent of counterbalancing influence is apparent in the example given us by Dr. Alice Miller, "The Drama of Being a Child" (1986) who recalls:

"Can it be an accident that Heinrich Pestalozzi-who was fatherless from his sixth year onward and emotionally neglected despite the presence of his mother and of a nurse-had the idea of bringing up his only son according to Rousseau's methods, although he was capable, on the other hand, of giving orphan children genuine warmth and 'fatherliness'? This son finally grew up neglected, as a ten year old was considered mentally defective, caused Pestalozzi much pain and guilt feelings, and then died at the age of thirty. (M. Lavater-Sloman 1977)

Dr. Miller summed up the moral of the tale:

"It was also Pestalozzi who is reputed to have said: "You can drive the devil out of your garden but you will find him again in the garden of your son". In psychoanalytic terms, one could say that it is the split off and unintegrated parts of his parents that have been introjected by the child."

> Or as the rabbi in "Golem" asked in terror;
> "How (he asked himself)
> Could I have engendered this grievous son,
> And left off inaction, which is wisdom?
> Why did I decide to add to the infinite
> Series one more symbol? Why, to the vain
> Skein which unwinds in eternity
> Did I add another cause, effect and woe?"
> *Jorge Luis Borges (A Personal Anthology)*

A child absented, for whatever reason, from his or her father within the context of divorce is a child left vulnerable and predisposed to any number of pathologies, as reliable statistics, studies and researches show. The symptoms manifest themselves differently for girls and boys, but the bottom line is the same. Chances of girls developing clinical depressions (girls internalize) from depressed mothers are, dramatically increased, whereas boys are at risk from antisocial and aggressive symptoms (boys externalize).

The High Incidence of Anti-social behavior and crime

One way to start our discussion on the correlation between fatherless homes and the high incidences of anti-social behavior and crime is to include a positive article written by Paul Schwartz (The New York Post September 9th 1999) on New York Football Giants Safety Sam Garnes in which Schwartz reports:

"That Garnes is a success is no accident. Garnes grew up in a stable home, an honor role student at DeWitt Clinton High School, surrounded by role models, Sam and Carolyn Garnes. "Two parents that's the biggest thing, that was huge," Garnes said.

When trouble on the streets approached, Garnes had the mental toughness to go the other way. "Growing up, I used to listen to people," he said."

What makes this story both extraordinary and newsworthy is the fact that in professional sports, particularly in Pro Football and Basketball, there is an extraordinarily high degree of sociopathic incidents and histories amongst the athletes. The incidents in question range from alcohol and drug abuse to domestic violence. In the lion share of cases, we discover that the childhood backgrounds of the athletes nearly always include being brought up in female-headed single-parent homes, poverty, and ghetto like surroundings. Garnes, brought up in difficult conditions similar to those mentioned above, was according to his own account saved, by having **two** parents. Nevertheless, for millions of other children this is not the case and the statistics prove that what Sam Garnes told Paul Schwartz was the essence of the truth.

According to Ramsey Clark, "Crime in America" (New York: Pocket Books, 1970), p. 39: "In federal youth centers nearly all prisoners were convicted of crimes that occurred after the offender dropped out of high school. Three-fourths came from broken homes."

Ibid. p. 123: "Seventy-five per cent of all federal juvenile offenders come from broken homes."

While Richard M. Smith and James Walters, "Delinquent and Non-Delinquent Males' Perceptions of Their Fathers." Adolescence, 13, 1978, 21-28: "The factors which do distinguish between delinquents and non-delinquents indicate that delinquency is associated with: **(a) lack of a warm, loving, supportive relationship with the father; (b) minimal paternal involvement with children; (c) high maternal involvement in the lives of youth; and (d) broken homes.** The factors which may serve to insulate youth from delinquency are: **(a) a stable, unbroken home, characterized by loving, supportive, parent-child relationships; (b) a father who has a high degree of positive involvement with his son; and (c) a father who provides a stable model for emulation by his male offspring.** The evidence reported herein supports that of earlier investigations that fathers appear to be significant contributors to the development of offspring who are capable of adapting and adjusting to society, and that fathers who are involved with their offspring in a warm, friendly, cordial relationship are important in the child's life for the prevention of delinquent behavior."

As early as 1963 we knew that as Starke Hathaway and Elio Monachesi had reported, "Adolescent Personality and Behavior" (Minneapolis: University of Minnesota Press, 1963), p. 81: "Broken homes do relate to the frequency of delinquency. Further, if a home is broken, a child living with the mother is more likely to be delinquent than one for whom other arrangements are made. In the case of girls, even living with neither parent is less related to higher delinquency than is living with the mother."

Loss of Economic and Educational Opportunity

Another uncomfortable reality arising out of divorce and subsequent decisions establishing female-headed single-parent family models is the immediate reduction in available income. *See Chapter 11 Destruction of Intact Families*

The Myth of the Dead-Beat Dad

Although radical feminist and feminized male apologists stress that this is due to 'deadbeat dads' who refuse to pay child support, the facts lead us to a wholly different conclusion. First, one does not need to be a rocket scientist to realize that there is economic advantage in the maintenance of an intact family and deprivation in the disrupted family. The divorcing family has to divide income to provide for two separate households. As William Hess, spokesperson for CRC New York pointed out in his response to an article in the NY Times by feminists Susan Bender and Phyllis Chesler titled "Child Support System Still Lets Men off Easy":

"What reasonable person would agree that a father can support TWO households at the same level as he previously supported ONE? Yet the child support rules promulgated by biased bureaucrats state that the 'children' are entitled to be supported at 'the same level' as during the marriage...Child support guideline standards are based on the child-related costs of an 'intact family' while the basic living costs of a separated family are logically MUCH higher."

It is now also clear from a number of recent studies that The Lenore Weitzman Report in 1985, claiming a 73 percent drop-off in the post-divorce standard of living of women, based itself on flawed math and inaccurate data. Braver and O'Connell pointed out that Weitzman's findings were based on gross income and not after tax income. In fact, mothers income increases due to tax-free child support, tax credits for child-care, a lower head of household tax rate, exemptions for children and a low-earner tax exemption. Yet, the Weitzman Report was a powerful radical feminist vehicle influencing policy and practice throughout the eighties and nineties. The Braver and O'Connell study, that included 340 fathers and 271 mothers from divorcing families, found that:

"Fathers make non-support financial contributions to their children in the way of clothing and visitation expenses. Fathers other expenses include renting a larger residence that most single people due to children's visitation and transportation expenses associated with visitation...55 percent of fathers paid for their children's medical and dental insurance. Since fathers leave the home, they have the expense of finding new housing and furniture. **The study found that fathers and mothers had no significant difference in their economic well-being one year after divorce**, and that only 13 percent of mothers reported falling below the poverty line."

Second, as I have shown, there is a direct relation between the percentage of fathers who do not pay child support and whether or not they have either joint custody or at the very least significant access and contact with their children. Where men have parental rights granted, maintained and enforced, there is a high degree of compliance with child support payments as the figures demonstrate. *See Appendix A.* Now compare the real figures with the extremely unjustified claim by authors Bender, a matrimonial lawyer and Chesler, a psychologist, that:

"Studies still document that non-custodial parents (fathers of course) rarely pay child support after the first year."

Bender, Chesler and their colleagues know that there is a direct link between ongoing child support payments and viable visitation rights. Their comment is nothing short of prevarication.

Braver, S., & O'Connell, D. Taking on myth 2: The no-show dad. In Divorced Dads: Shattering the myths, New York: Tarcher/Putnam. (1998) "Found that while child support payment is enforceable, visitation is not; frequently, fathers withhold payment when they are denied visitation by their former spouse."

Scoon-Rogers, L.,(1999). Child support for custodial mothers and fathers: 1995 (Current Population Reports, Consumer Income Series P60-196). Washington, DC: Bureau of the Census, U.S. Department of Commerce, also reported that fact:

"Visitation and joint custody awards are associated with increased payment rates". Clearly where mother does not deny visitation, the payments are made. Scoon-Rogers add that, "Custodial mothers were more likely to receive child support than custodial fathers and 92% of custodial parents with child support awards have them through a legal agreement decided through litigation"

The disingenuous Bender and Chesler add an equally outrageous allegation that:

" Patriarchal judges have refused to force men to lower their own standard of spending or right to reproduce again. Judges have also refused to punish fathers for failing their children both economically and parentally." The truth is that both male and female judges are tossing men into prison on contempt charges without jury trial, stripping them of driving licenses, 'imputing' income to them without objective evidence being adduced.

The best case to illustrate this as fact comes from our authors Chesler and Bender who commend Judge Gangel Jacobs for jailing Jeffrey A. Nicholls (widely publicized case), holding "a man's feet to the fire", after imputing income to him without the adduction of evidence. In fact the absurdity of the Nicholls case, points to the political agenda of the authors and to the injustice in family court process. It appears that a vengeful mother sought child support payments amounting to over 500,000 dollars. She had independent wealth and no real economic need. Whether or not Mr. Nicholls could or could not pay the child support is a moot issue.

The real issues in his case are threefold: First, what child or children on this planet require child support payments of 500,000 dollars over a short period? Second, why should Mr. Nicholls pay any child support if the mother had independent means and Mr. Nicholls was on welfare, actively engaged in rearing two young children by his second wife (who had unfortunately died)? Third, how can it be right for a court to suspend all normal rules of evidence in 'imputing income', finding civil contempt and imprisoning a man? As an endnote to this sorry tale, the judge, so applauded by these ardent feminists, ultimately faced dismissal from the family bench.

Undoubtedly, a divorced child, with rare exception, is an economically disadvantaged child. Further, such a child often has a number of problems related to learning skills and educational attainment as demonstrated by the study produced by former President of the School Psychologists Association, Dr. John Guidubaldi's, "Nationwide Impact on Children of Divorce Study".

The modern literature on children refutes the arcane theories of Goldstein, Solnit and Freud. The information on the affects of father-absence provides fathers with solid ammunition to argue the shared parenting case. We need to look at other negative effects on children related to sole maternal custody and the conflicts caused by fathers refusing to walk away from their children. Parental child abductions tend to link directly back to custodial conflicts and injustice.

Chapter 4

The Phenomena of Parental Child Abduction

The Scandal of International & National Parental Child Abduction

The breakdown of intact families and ensuing custodial conflicts have led to one of our nastiest little secrets and one of our worst nightmares, parental child abduction. These phenomena are connected.

Moreover, experience shows that men and women (as victim parents) do not receive equal treatment and justice. *See Ray Clore Dir. Office of Children's Issues US State Dept. Admission of gender-bias*

Many parents have no idea on how to get a kidnapped child returned, the costs involved or what they face in national and international court process. The public is barely aware of an underground-railroad network set up to protect runaway wives and girlfriends. I hope the material included here will go a long way towards a better understanding and provide a starting point for legal action.

The figures on annual parental child abductions reveal the scale of the problem. There are, as even the most conservative estimates admit about 350,000 to 500,000 child kidnappings every year carried out by a family member. Dr. Huntington reported in 1986 that the numbers were possibly as high as 626,000. My research in 1997 confirms her estimates as being closer to reality. The studies of The National Center for Missing and Exploited Children and those of "The United States Department of Justice National Incidence Study of Missing, Abducted, Runaway and Thrownaway Children" explain:

"Add that these numbers are very likely to be understated, since they are based on voluntary reporting, particularly in cases involving sexual abuse, we can safely assume that the real incidence (abductions) is much higher." ("The Kid is With a Parent, How Bad Can it be? The Crisis of Family Abductions in America", 1990)

These huge numbers of attributed parental kidnappings relate to marital breakdown, fundamental gender biased injustice in judicial process and the easy opportunities for some women to remove children without fear of punishment.

Put simply:

"90% of the violence and kidnapping we have seen are in sole custody situations in which the sole custodial parent fears losing his or her custody status, or the 'parentectomized' parent kidnaps the child away from the sole custody parent who possessively blocks the visiting parent from access." (Pg. 4, Col. 1, 1, lines 3-9) Child Custody and Parental Cooperation - Frank Williams, M.D., Dir. Psychiatry - Cedar-Sinai - Presented at American Bar Association, Family Law Section, August 1987 and January 1988. - Kidnapping and Violence in Relation to Custody - Reprinted in Joint Custodian, Jan. 1988

According to Ray Clore of The Office of Children's Issues, U.S. State Department, "The office was created in 1994 because the state dept realized that there was a lot more of these international child custody type issues coming up." He added:

"It's hard to prove gender discrimination but I think it's clear that in some countries there seems to be shall we say the courts lean towards the mothers.... The point was made at the review conference that this treaty doesn't have any gender references and it should be applied in a gender neutral way." (Wednesday's Children TV Program, 1997, Rein, MNN Cable)

Unfortunately, in line with established patterns in custodial process, administration of The Hague Convention falls hostage to gender bias and nationalism in too many cases. A number of signatory nations are guilty of defeating the treaty often protecting mother's interests over those of the child and victim parent. A recent US case illustrates how this gender bias (referred to by Mr. Clore) against men resides cloaked beneath ridiculous judicial decisions making complete nonsense of The Hague Convention on the Civil Aspects of International Child Abduction.

That case is <u>Croll v. Croll</u>, 2nd Circuit US Ct. of Appeals, (2000), in which a panel of three judges reversed a federal district court decision to return children back to Hong Kong. The esteemed court decided that a father holding a visitation order (exercising his rights of access) and a ne-exeat order[19] did not qualify as a person having 'rights of custody' as meant under Article 3 of The Convention. In other words that his court ordered 'rights of access' did permit him to bring a Hague action for the return of the children. The Circuit found that only a party holding a 'custody' order could make a Hague Application. Even, if the Court was right, which it was not, it still should have returned the children (under Article 21) enforcing father's 'rights of access', threatened to the point of extinction by mother's abduction.

Is it coincidental that mother was the person who had abducted the children? No.

Does this drive a coach and horses through the meaning, spirit and intentions of the Convention? Yes.

Is it in line with 20 years of Hague decisions upholding pre or post-divorce access orders as being "custodial rights" in practical terms as far as meant in the Convention? No.

The leading case on this point is C. v. C (Abduction: Rights of Custody)[1989] 1 WLR 654 or 658 B-F and 663 G-664 A), British High

---

[19] A court order preventing the mother from leaving the jurisdiction with the children

Court Family Division. Renowned British Q.C. James Holman reported on it:

"Often a father will have "rights of custody" in the Convention sense (e.g. right to determine child's place of residence, (C v. C) without "having the care of the person or the child"

He then asked the question:

"Could a mother who had "the care of the person or the child" rely on her own "consent" under this paragraph?

Answering his rhetorical question:

"The effect would be virtually to dead-letter the Convention in a large number of cases and to limit the protected "right of custody" to persons having "the care of the person".

"As far as I know this point has never yet been taken, or, if it has, not been accepted by the Court. So far, having "care of the person" has been treated as being, or assumed to be, synonymous with having a right of custody in the Convention sense (by the courts)." (Holman, J. Q.C., First British Conference on International Child Abduction, London 1994)

Further as pointed out by the renowned Hague Convention Solicitor Sandra Davis:

"In, Re C (A Minor)(Abduction: Illegitimate Child)[1990] 2 All E.R. 449 C.A.,... the Court of Appeal held that an Order made in a Sydney Court in Australia which prevented the removal of the child from the jurisdiction without the father's consent, albeit granting custody of the child to the mother, created a right of custody under the Hague Convention, since in allowing the father the right to object to the child's removal, it thus simultaneously afforded him the right to determine its place of residence." "International Child Abduction", Davis, Rosenblatt and Galbraith, Sweet & Maxwell, 1993 Chapter 4, p.p.17-18

What this treacherous decision means is as follows:

Now, every mother who sues for divorce and obtains either interim or final sole custody of the children, is then free, whether prevented by court order or not, to flee the jurisdiction into a foreign 'refuge' Hague territory (The United States) without fear of recrimination or justice. Given that women receive custody in over 90 percent of all cases, our fears gain as abductions mount.

There are also a number of other loopholes in the Convention. These allow abducting parents to avoid the consequences of their actions. Hague Attorney Barbara Sobal has pointed out such problem areas in an article on Parental Alienation Syndrome and the Convention. "Article 13B of The Hague Convention Treaty: Does it create a Loophole for Parental Alienation Syndrome ("PAS")—An Insidious Abduction?"[20]

She pointed to the case of Blondin v Dubois, New York 2nd Circuit, District Court, Southern Division (2000) 78 F. Supp.2d 283, as an example, where jurisdictional issues converted into a best interests case for a non-return. Ms. Sobal has often stated her view that there is gender bias against men in Hague matters. She also agrees with my long held view that Article 12 is another threat to the Convention.[21]

While German courts routinely contrive the non-return of abducted children due to Germanization of children and maternal custody policies and where there is little support for male parenting and intact families according to German author Karin Jaeckel:

"…preferential treatment of women,…specifically lone mothers…,the defamation of man and father as 'absent parent'…all these and more cracks the framework of the institution of the family." "Germany Devours its Children", Jaeckel, Rowolt, 2000.

Things are no better in Britain or France. According to French Lawyer Dr. Alain Cornec, an expert on the Hague Convention:

"First abductions are by mothers. Retentions (during visits) or re-abductions are by fathers.

The Courts of the "refuge" country can try and protect the abductor, usually one of their nationals, especially the mother of young children. There may be a technical loophole, which will avoid

---

[20] See this Chapter, The Hague Convention, Article 13 defenses to return
[21] See this Chapter, The Hague Convention Article 12-one year rule defense

returning the child without refusing outright to apply the Convention. And, if a court wants to find a loophole, they will probably find one."

He continued to report:

"In the subsequent ensuing French divorce proceedings, "custody" (read residence, or care and control) was generally granted to the abducting mother in over eighty percent of cases."

The facts of general unbridled and outrageous gender bias in Britain are acknowledged even in this unusually frank and ironic official U.S. Dept. of State unclassified Memo (released under The Freedom of Information Act). The Memo passed from The U.S. Embassy in London to both Ms. Conuelo Pachon at The U.S. Department of State and to a corrupt Embassy official (found to have had an improper relationship with a local lawyer) at the U.S. Embassy in Israel:

"In dealing with minors, British Courts consider only what is best for the child. **In practice in a child custody case in the U.K.**, the parents have no rights and the **father has even fewer**." (July 1990)

How could an American father expect a fair hearing in that judicial environment? Moreover, this rather honest memo seems to be a case of the pot calling the kettle black! US State courts are not much better.

Despite international treaties and several laws dealing with this subject, numbers of such acts continue to rise. Governments, judiciaries and law enforcement agencies have been slow to act properly when tested by the brutal phenomena of parental abduction. They often abuse their powers favoring rampant gender bias and discrimination over justice. Often failing to disclose information to the public, provide accountability, or even protection against single acts or organized efforts to abduct and hide children within so called underground railway systems reaching across America and foreign territories.

We come to another question. Who abducts, why and in what circumstances.

The Three Models of Parental Abduction

In my view, there are three primary models of parental child abduction. The first two deal with parental abductions as an offense described under the provisions of the international treaty known as The Hague Convention within Article 3. The third type actually resides outside of article 3, but is a contributory factor to the second type. Though it is difficult to build a definitive model for these types of abduction, I have divided the models into the following categories:

Pro-active Abduction

Re-active Abduction

State-Authorized Abduction-State Induced Abduction

The first model; Pro-Active Abduction, is broadly, a "Precipitating Action" possibly where one parent removes a child or children from the care of the other parent **prior to the hearing of custody** matters within a jurisdiction of habitual domicile. Possibly where he or she removes the child from a joint custody order, or an order giving proper contact to both parents and where there is no breach or problem of enforcement of the orders already made.

The archetypal case is one of a removal of a child from one jurisdiction to a second jurisdiction where advantage lies by means of the 'safe harbor' offered to the offending parent. Present research and anecdotal evidence supports the contention that too many US states and foreign countries have failed to return children taken by women from their habitual residences. While, on the other hand, men taking children not only have them returned but also face extremely harsh penalties including imprisonment and fines.

The shocking fact is that anecdotal evidence exists contrary to public myth that, **most Pro-Active Abductions are carried out almost exclusively by women, not by men.** For those who doubt the strength or reliability of such evidence I can only say that whenever I have made strenuous efforts to receive hard statistics from several government sources, but am invariably told that they simply do not exist. My own research is available in the next sub chapter. Let me return to the second model:

Re-Active Abduction:

Is best described by its defensive orientation, where the relationship between the offending parent and the child or children has been severely threatened either by;

1. A Pro-Active Abduction by mother that has already taken place
2. A Constant blockage of or lack of enforcement of rights of access has occurred

The types of prejudicial court decisions made in jurisdictions that minimizes or eliminates and disposes of one parent to the empowerment of the other.

Once more, I can only offer anecdotal evidence that the overwhelming majority of Re-Active Abductions are by men. In an article in England's leading newspaper, The Independent ("I Have Paid for What I Did", David Cohen 1994), the barrister Peter Marsh explained why men might reactively abduct:

"If the mother refuses to honor the contact (visitation) arrangements (of the court) there is little the father can do. In theory, he can plump for a penal order, the flouting of which carries the threat of jail for the mother. But, in practice, the courts are understandably reluctant to imprison her because the welfare of the child is compromised."

While Cohen wrote that years of frustration might cause male child abductions:

"The options many face are dire. They can either abduct their child...or walk away to join the ranks of the 'feckless and irresponsible absent fathers" and he concludes, "Surely it is time to address the grievance (from fathers) that the system is stacked against parents who, almost inevitably, are fathers."

The third model is 'state-authorized' or 'induced abduction' that I have described and explained in the Chapter on The Legal System. *See Chapter 7, Re-location Cases*

Men do not abduct children, women do!

In a study carried out as part of my research for a television special on Parental Child Abductions, "Wednesday's Children", I conducted a random survey on the incidences of parental child abductions and used a sample of 50 cases. Out of that sample it was shown that the lion-share of the abductions were carried out by mothers, and most of the male abductions were part of a sub-cultural anomalous bias directed towards Islamic countries. The actual breakdown revealed that in 45 cases the mother abducted, in four cases, it was the father but in three of those cases, the abduction was carried out by an Islamic male and therefore atypical of the general research. While in one case a grandparent abducted ("Wednesday's Children", 1997).

Figures from The National Center for Missing & Exploited Children, offered by counsel Nancy Hammer, showed that in over 60% of cases reviewed children were abducted by their mothers.

Further, when I interviewed Ray Clore, then Director of The Office of Children's Issues at the US State Department, **he agreed that there was subjective evidence, supporting my own findings, submitted by official delegates to an international governmental conference on The Hague Convention on the Civil Aspects of International Child Abduction.** He stated that: "At the most recent Hague review conference one of the long time employees of the Permanent Bureau said that anecdotal evidence suggests that the majority of abductors are now women, primary caregivers" (Rein 1996).

When queried as to why some women abducted, Mr. Clore just shrugged his shoulders. Unfortunately, we do know why some women will abduct. They feel protected and invulnerable because of the incredible gender bias that predominates in various jurisdictions. They know there are loopholes in the law. They know that they will not face severe punishment even if caught and reprimanded and that the court will still be loathe to remove the children into the father's care (see the case <u>David B v Helen O</u>). They know that they can sometimes rely on the Underground Railroad to hide them and relocate them under different identities.

In arguing before the New York State Legislature, correlating maternal sole custody decisions with emerging patterns of parental child abductions, I pointed to the links asking the committee:

"What society can call itself civilized when it acts to deprive one or more classifications of its citizens of their human rights? When it encourages, condones, and allows its official agencies, including its judiciary, to participate in the absolute destruction of the emotional lives of its future generations? What society can call itself just when it acts to replace several centuries of gender bias against women with gender bias against men, when it practices and oversees the abolition of the rights of the child under both natural and international law?

If this State wishes to;

Reduce the disastrous numbers of abductions taking place annually,

If it desires to put an end to the "cycle of emotional and economic deprivation" that it has been instrumental in creating,

If it is anxious to redress the imbalance and injustice done to children and men,

If it wants to take any perceived advantage out of initiating divorce actions,

If it is interested in reducing the extraordinary amount of re-litigation caused by sole parenting decisions,

It will take swift action NOW, to create a shared parenting Bill." (NYS Senate Committee Evidence Rein 1995)

Citing figures dating back to 1990, Ernie Allen, President of The National Center for Missing and Exploited Children, referred to causes of parental kidnappings linked to:

"The number of divorces tripled since 1960-This year there will be over one million divorces, involving more than one million children. Today the average marriage lasts seven years-at least 150,000 divorces will involve custody battles-10 million children live with a parent who is separated or divorced-In 1989, more than 24% of all children lived in one-parent families, an increase of 166% over 1960-Single parent families have increased 252% since 1959. There have been fundamental changes in law and policy which have made divorce easier and increased the likihood of child custody disputes and contests." (Allen, 1995)

Parental Child Abduction Laws

Parental abduction problems are rooted in unethical and damaging custody process as well as in female determination to separate children from their fathers. Existing laws are prejudicial and selectively implemented, operating with poor regulation and no oversight or judicial accountability.

The origin of present day abduction law relies on Anglo-Saxon common law. Former colonies such as the United States, Canada, Australia and New Zealand transcribed and incorporated it into their common law. These acts were once called, 'child stealing', kidnapping, or false imprisonment.

By 1980, The United Nations became extremely concerned with the rising phenomena of parental child abduction and implored its member states to take steps to legislate on an international basis.

The Hague Convention on the Civil Aspects of International Child Abduction

Consequent to UN efforts, The Hague Convention on the Civil Aspects of International Child Abduction was born. This international treaty, signed by many member nations, protects children from acts of parental kidnapping when carried out across national borders into foreign countries. I cannot go into all aspects of the Convention because it is worthy of an entire book on its own merits. However, I want to layout the Convention's most salient features and its problems.

The main principles of the convention are set forth in an authoritative report by Julia A. Todd, "The Hague Convention on the Civil Aspects of International Child Abduction: Are the Convention's Goals Being Achieved?",

The 1980 Hague Convention on the Civil Aspects of International Child Abduction (the Convention) is an international attempt to hasten the return of children wrongfully abducted and to deter such abductions in the future. The Convention came into effect as law in the United Kingdom by the Child Abduction and Custody Act, 1985. The Hague Convention came into effect in the United States, implemented by passage of The International Child Abduction Remedies Act (ICARA) in July 1988.

The Convention's stated goals are relatively simple:

"To secure the prompt return of children wrongfully removed or retained in any Contracting State and to ensure that the rights of custody and access under the laws of one Contracting State are effectively respected in the other Contracting States."

The Convention seeks to obtain these goals by reestablishing the status quo and returning the child to his or her country of habitual residence, where the merits of the custody dispute can be determined.

Article 3 of the Convention defines the constitution of an act of international parental abduction:

Under article 3, the removal or retention of a child is wrongful where:

(a) It is in breach of custody rights attributed to a person, an institution or another body, either jointly or alone, under the law of the State in which the child was habitually resident immediately before the removal or retention; and

(b) At the time of the removal or retention those rights were actually exercised, either jointly or alone, or would have been so exercised but for the removal or retention.

Under the Convention, an international analysis of the "merits of any custody issue" is, specifically precluded. The court in the country to which the child has been abducted the "Requested State" under the Convention, is responsible only for deciding whether immediate return is warranted. **The underlying custody issues are properly determined only in the State of habitual residence:** "the Hague Convention is clearly designed to insure that the custody struggle must be carried out, in the first instance, under the laws of the country of habitual residence." By leaving the ultimate custody determination to the courts, in the country of habitual residence, the Convention assures that an abducting parent cannot benefit from his or her unilateral actions by obtaining a favorable custody order in the Requested State.

In recommending the Convention to the U.S. Senate for ratification, President Ronald Reagan described its goals as follows:

"The Convention is designed to promptly restore the factual situation that existed prior to a child's removal or retention. It does not seek to settle disputes about legal custody rights, nor does it depend upon the existence of court orders as a condition for returning children. The international abductor is denied legal advantage from the abduction . . . as resort to the Convention is to affect the child's swift return to his or her circumstances before the abduction . . . In most cases this will mean return to the country of the child's habitual residence where any dispute about custody rights can be heard and settled."

However, all to often there is no swift return, legal advantage is gained if the abductor is female, custody issues are brought into the Convention by virtue of local prejudice, and the use of the Conventions escape clauses, especially article 13 dealing with exceptions to the return of children. Ms Todd states:

"Despite the Convention's simple and admirable goals, it remains true that **nations often have paternalistic (matriarchal) views of family and childrearing.** To order the return of a child to a foreign nation, especially when the abductor is a fellow citizen (and woman), undoubtedly proves difficult for judges in individual cases."

As Ms. Todd notes by implication, the influence of sole maternal custody style decisions interfere with a fair and impartial administration of the Convention. The following states what constitutes an act of parental child abduction.

Article 13, governing exceptions to the return of children becomes the mechanism by which national courts can excuse the kidnapping.

The exceptions, contained in article 13, have been frequently litigated. Under article 13(a), a court may deny an application for the return of a child **if the petitioner was not actually exercising custody rights at the time of removal or retention, or if the petitioner had acquiesced in the removal or retention.** (Note 70) Article 13(b) allows a court, in its discretion, **to refuse the return of a child if there is "a grave risk of harm that return . . . would expose the child to physical or psychological harm or otherwise place the child in an intolerable situation."** A third, unlettered paragraph of Article 13 allows a court to **refuse a child's return if, the child objects to being returned and the child has attained an age and degree of maturity at which a court can appropriately consider the child's views.**

In 13 we have the basis for the meaning of the convention to be perverted by virtue of provision of a means for the abducting parent to poison the mind of the child, brainwashing him or her into stating their preference to remain in the abductors control.

Further, we have now opened the doors for the hearing of expert psychiatric testimony and experience teaches that in certain jurisdictions that evidence will be mother oriented and used to deflect away from her abduction. *See Chapter 8 on Expert Evidence, also Guardian ad litems or Law Guardians imposition into cases*

At the same time, a mother-oriented judge has acquired discretionary power to defeat the convention. Taken together with the loophole provided by judging the possibility of the 'grave risk' 13B exception, courts begin to hear custody issues by default in violation of the meaning and spirit of the convention.

Another important means to defeat justice and the interests of children is through the employment of article 12.

Under article 12, if it is demonstrated that the child is settled in his or her new environment, a court is not obligated to return the child if the return proceedings are commenced a year or more after the wrongful removal or retention. As Julia Todd reports:

"Delegates added the one-year statute of limitations to the Convention because they felt that a failure to bring a swift application may indicate acquiescence in, or mixed emotions about, the abduction.

Further, the delegates feared that ordering a return after passage of so much time might cause additional confusion and psychological damage to the child." This was a serious error as it has created a loophole in the convention.

In practice, this means that if a mother can successfully evade the father's efforts to locate her and the children for over 12 months, she can then argue that they have "settled into a new environment". The judge is no longer **legally** obligated to return the children, and all the important principles of the convention, as well as its legislative intent, fall consigned to the dustbin. President Reagan's stated purpose 'to prevent an abductor from gaining an advantage, is simply knocked on its head, because that is precisely what happens.

Of course, the difficulties unmarried fathers have in seeking a return of their abducted children under the Hague Convention are often insurmountable under the convention unless they have acquired a 'formal' document (English Parental Responsibility Order-American Orders of Filiation) recognizing their paternity and can establish psychological connection to their children. Further, they must be in possession of these orders **before** the alleged act of abduction takes place. I have come across this problem in one case that I handled where an unmarried Georgia father, without a formal document proving paternity, lost his two young children.

English Child Custody & Abduction Act of 1984

This Act is separate and distinct from The Child Custody & Abduction Act of 1985 which was the implementing national law backing The Hague Convention. In the Act of 1984, Parliament made it a criminal offense for a parent to abduct a child from the care and control of the other parent and made the deed punishable for up to seven years imprisonment. British Courts have, for the most part, been content to rely on 'contempt of court proceedings' to punish parents for the removal of children. Notably, that civil contempt in England distinguishes from American civil contempt by the difference in length of servitude. In England & Wales, civil contempt is punishable by up to 18 months in prison. In the few cases where the courts, through the

Crown Prosecution Service, have brought charges under the Act, it has been, to my knowledge, exclusively against men.

PKPA (Parental Kidnapping Prevention Act) 18 USC § 1204

The above is a federal statute dealing with international parental child abductions on the criminal level and it states in pertinent part that:

"Whoever removes a child from the United States or retains a child (who has been in the United States) outside the United States with intent to obstruct the lawful exercise of parental rights shall be fined under this title or imprisoned not more than three years, or both".

I do not know of any cases litigated under this federal statute.

The Conspiracy of Silence

When it comes to providing the public proper and authoritative information on the subject of parental child abduction, governments and treaty administrators fail to disclose vital facts.

There is a consistent failure to monitor the results of prosecutions or provide legal assistance to parents that cannot afford to locate and pay legal expenses, which in international cases mount as high as 100,000 US dollars. The fact that women are the primary abductors of children remains a public secret, unrevealed except by accident as in the case of the State Dept. disclosure on the "Wednesday's Children" program.

While The National Center for Missing & Exploited Children, The US State, Justice Department and law enforcement officials are fully aware of the fact that cases are not being treated impartially, too many children not returned and that an underground network exists run by feminists who advise and hide children, they seem reluctant to end their silence. One established female matrimonial lawyer once confided in me that there was a serious gender bias against men in custodial and abduction proceedings. She went on to cite a Georgia Hague Convention case in which a judge refused to return an abducted child to the father in Germany without even bothering to produce a learned opinion defending his decision.

State Department

American parents victimized by an international abduction, their child taken out of the United States, should contact The Office of Children's Issues, US State Dept. Washington D.C.

Foreign parents having a child removed from a Hague Convention country to the United States can contact The National Center for Missing and Exploited Children, who are handling all incoming cases on behalf of the State Dept.

One common complaint is that the State Department fails to properly monitor Hague Convention cases of its own citizens. Another is that it fails to provide legal assistance, help in locating abducted children, or to ensure compliance with treaty obligations. There are forceful arguments that the State Dept. has a responsibility to ensure that any treaty signed and ratified by the United States government involving rights and responsibilities of U.S. citizens (falling within the purview of U.S. Foreign Relations Law and The Supremacy Clause of the U.S. Constitution) is properly and fairly administered or else face constitutional challenge.

Moreover, The State Dept. acts as a referral service and contact agency for the victim parent. It will provide limited information on the procedural means to recover children from the various international jurisdictions. At best, State might intercede on behalf of women.

From a strictly technical point of view, State lacks the provision or right to interfere in the judicial process of either the U.S. or foreign signatory nations. However, it does have a variety of means to express dissatisfaction or concern to legal authorities privately and to petition extra judicial governmental agencies and parties who might affect outcomes of cases. The use of diplomatic channels can be and is at times, employed. Further there is no legal impediment to the U.S. government's ability and right to "espouse a claim" on behalf of a U.S. citizen in respect to a complaint arising from an international treaty obligation.

But when it comes to the crunch, officials at the State Department, pushed and pressured by numerous bureaucratic feminists in it's fold, will act selectively in cases involving women victims of parental abductions while ignoring cases initiated by fathers seeking a return of kidnapped children.

Two cases immediately present themselves for close examination. The first case, provided by the Director of the Office of Children's Issues demonstrates structural, pro-female gender discrimination. Mr. Clore, when stationed in Jordan, acted to petition the assistance of the Jordanian government to intercede in a child abduction case brought by an American mother seeking a return from a Jordanian father. In this case, U.S. State Dept. efforts were successful. For his involvement in the matter, Mr. Clore met his reward by gunfire sprayed at his home ostensibly by members of the father's family (Wednesday's Children interview with Ray Clore).

Contrast that case with one illustrating anti-male bias based on lack of action. A U.S. father had his child abducted from France to England by the English mother. Subsequently, having his rights in international and U.S. treaty law repudiated by gender discriminatory process in Britain he turned to the US government for assistance. However, his attempts at redress founded on human rights violations by the British government faced ridicule and rejection by legal advisers at The Office of the Legal Adviser, U.S. Dept. of State. This private State Dept. memo from Miriam Shapiro to Marina Gonatas, considered whether or not there were either human rights or discrimination issues inherent in the father's case:

"When CA (Consular Affairs) called me last week, it sounded like it was just sour grapes..." (Released under The Freedom of Information Act Doc. dated 03/28/95)

In other words, a victim father with a legitimate human rights complaint that he wanted espoused by his own government, had it characterized inappropriately as being just 'sour grapes' with him being characterized as a 'sore loser'. Was the Jordanian case in which Mr. Clore was involved treated the same?

This discriminatory attitude should be born in mind when considering another key document written in reference to the very same case. Drafted by a staff member at the U.S. Embassy in London and intended for forwarding to The British Lord Chancellor, it reads as follows:

"Proposed U.S. Embassy Petition Lord Chancellor
Re: Case of...Hague Convention
US Embassy
London Post
To
Lord Chancellor
Great Britain

We are deeply concerned over several important aspects of this case, which dates back to March 9th, 1988, when, the mother, Mrs. X abducted the child (name) from the family home and sole residence in France, and then abducted her a second time on July 7th 1988, transporting the child to Britain.

The mother was at that time in possession of a "secret" British court order, which seems to have been obtained by "Fraud" and "Deceit" and clearly is in contravention of the Provisions and Articles of the Hague Convention on Child Abduction.

We would also wish to inform your Lordship that the father is an American citizen, the mother is a British National and the child has the status of a dual national carrying her own American passport.

Moreover, according to the Hague Convention, as the family was Habitually Resident in France, it fell to the sole jurisdiction of the French Courts, under Article 310 Code Civile, governing all matters related to Divorce and Custody, to adjudicate and decide this case.

However, and most disturbingly, a succession of British judges failed to properly invoke The Hague Convention and its obligations, wrongly defining the jurisdiction as British under the same Articles of the Convention.

It would seem to us that it was the clear duty and obligation of the British High Court to correctly invoke the Convention and to immediately return the child to her father in France...

We are deeply disturbed that there have been two such cases in quick succession, and most distressed by the long-term destructive affect the X case has had on the child and father...

We beseech your Lordship to join us in discussions that might bring this case to a fair and positive conclusion.

We have barely scratched the details of this particularly disturbing case and do not wish to do so within the context of this letter, but urge your Lordship to urgently investigate the matter with a view towards a constructive and just solution, fort the sake of an innocent child." (U.S. Embassy-Freedom of Information Act Released Document No. 0-67)

Were we talking about the same case? Did this approximate nothing more than "sour grapes" on the part of the father? Unfortunately, that U.S. Embassy Post Petition never reached the desk of the Lord Chancellor.

Judging by documents in my possession from official sources, an extraordinary number of strategically placed female employees in The U.S. Department of State office of Consular Affairs, Embassies and Office of the Legal Adviser, are the ones dealing with custody and parental abduction issues. They lack all credibility in handling their duties in a fair and impartial manner. Their private memos to one another tell a tale of radical feminist driven covert policies. One little interchange between two such ladies centered on what advantages there were for British mothers shielding behind the anachronistic 'wardship' laws of the United Kingdom in custody-abduction cases. *See Chapter 5 Concepts of Wardship*

Justice Department

Fails to prosecute members of 'underground railroads' and other networks that act to aid and abet predominately female acts of parental child abduction, even though they are acutely aware of their existence. My own research shows that law enforcement officials are loathe to act despite the warnings issued by Dr. David Finkelhor, Dr. Gerald Hotaling, and Dr. Andrea Sedlak that:

"Family abductions may well be on the rise and yet could be amenable to prevention." While Ernie Allen of The National Center for Missing and Exploited Children, laments that, "Far too frequently we encounter, "parental kidnapping is not a law enforcement problem, it is a civil problem, domestic relations, something lawyers should work out, and the kid is with a parent how bad can it be? I submit that the abduction of children by family members is a large and serious public policy challenge and a threat to the health and safety of children...the numbers are staggering and deeply disturbing."

I have personally conducted interviews with 3 victim fathers, an attorney for The National Center for Missing & Exploited Children, The US State Dept., and The NY State Clearing House on this important subject. I have tried to get NOW to comment on allegations of female child abduction and the underground, but never had my phone calls returned.

Police

Police often refuse to file missing person reports on allegedly abducted children when the victim parent is male, or to act on complaints. In two cases that I researched in depth, I found the stories of the fathers to be true and shocking, that police not merely failed to act but were hostile and uncooperative.

Further, I took up the matter up with Ms. Diane Vigors, New York State Clearing House for the National Center for Missing and Exploited Children (New York State Justice Dept.), a Justice Department Quasar. She confirmed that this was an ongoing and serious problem. All U.S. states now have such clearing houses mandated to work with the national entity.

Despite the opinion of Counsel Nancy Hammer, National Center for Missing & Exploited Children, that there is federal mandate for authorities such as the police to assist in the filing of 'missing persons' reports, fathers report that the police have been non-complaisant. One father even claiming that after two days of being run around at a local station, he got into a fierce argument with one officer and was thrown down a flight of stairs. Another father refused to capitulate and eventually pestered the District Attorney in New York to take action. The sad facts of his case, taken up in the next section, made it obvious that police department inaction allowed his girlfriend to make a clean getaway with his child.

Yet, as Nancy Hammer had pointed out to me during our television interview, it is vitally important that police authorities file these missing person's reports which then allows the children to be entered into an FBI national database, the NCIC (National Crime Information Center). In the two preceding cases, neither father ever recovered their children.

Obstruction of Justice

Lack of local police cooperation with federally mandated law is only one acknowledged problem facing men. Conditions are, greatly exacerbated, by further disruptions to legal process, including the location and return of kidnapped children. Cases have come to my personal attention that disclose the fact that various state bodies refuse to cooperate in such cases often failing to reveal the whereabouts of abducted children even in the face of federal subpoenas. Authorities such as The New York City Dept. of the Homeless, The New York City Board of Education and even The British Consulate in one case have hidden behind confidentiality rules to avoid compliance with federal and international treaty law. Invariably these cases involve runaway wives and girlfriends protected by the system for the psychosocial reasons discussed in earlier chapters.

Rein: Would these authorities, whether it is a drug clinic or the Dept. of the Homeless, have a clear duty under The Hague Convention to cooperate in the location of kidnapped children?

Hammer: The implementing legislation actually says within the laws of the state, federal and state laws, so there are some gray areas.

Rein: I am interested in the principle because cases presented to us during our research by victim parents have encountered exactly this problem. If on the one hand you have The Hague Convention which is international treaty law of the United States and on the other hand an agencies privacy laws, which trumps which?

Hammer: Treaties supercede state law.

Rein: Then how can this international treaty be working, if you accept my hypothetical that these problems do exist, if state and local authorities refuse to comply and hide behind confidentiality regulations?

Hammer: If there are problems that interfere with implementation, and if these problems became something that obstructed the United States upholding it's end of the treaty, then it can be raised and they can make modifications.

Rein: Given that the New York State Clearing House has told us that law guardians, the Dept. of the Homeless here in New York and the Board of Education have definitely, in various cases, shielded behind confidentiality regulations in order to rationalize their decisions to hide children. I have evidence from one British father that this has been done in a recent case, ...why has nothing been done to this date to remedy the situation?

Hammer: I think this is something that needs to be addressed, but, by state law. It is a barrier that we face.

Rein: But if we have a felon fleeing from a crime we find ourselves in the awkward position, a contradictory position, where state agencies are protecting felons in flight.

Hammer: If there is an arrest warrant it becomes a criminal investigation and we can do much more.

Rein: OK. Let me take up a hypothetical based on a specific, fact pattern. A British Nigerian mother had permission to come to this country from England as a visitor. She definitely overstayed her visa limit, provided entry into a New York City shelter, had the children placed in a local school, and refused to return the children into the custodial care of the father in England. This is an abduction-retention case. She was even in the process of getting a green card. Now in this particular case, where I have seen all of the evidence, the father had raised serious allegations against the NY Dept. of the Homeless, who refused to reveal the whereabouts of his children after having been subpoenaed to do so. He has accused the British Consulate of refusing him knowledge of his children's address, and he's also accused both the court and The British Embassy of dealing ex-parte in the matter, ultimately making a decision for a voluntary return of the mother and children to Britain. Secretly, without father's knowledge, while he was awaiting a decision from the court. Is this not wrong?

Hammer: In that case he could have utilized a pick-up order.

Rein: He had an arrest warrant. His attorney served the warrant and pickup order at the local school where the authorities refused to cooperate. There were two police officers there. They did nothing useful.

Hammer: I think that that illustrates one of the big problems, which is, in many cases family abduction is not taken seriously. In an age of divorce and separating families, these things need to be taken a lot more seriously. ("Wednesday's Children" TV Special on Parental Child Abduction, 1997, MNN Cable)

Female Underground Railroad Networks

Compounding the difficulties faced by predominantly male parents in effecting discovery and return of their offspring from parental abductions has been the growth and development of a female Underground Railroad system that hides children. The father described earlier who had gone to the District Attorney in order to get his missing child reported, was a victim of this network. I asked counsel Nancy Hammer about this underground.

Rein: Another common complaint from victim parents but predominantly men is that children are being hidden in an underground, illegal railroad system run by women for women and that government authorities know all about it but to this date have taken no steps to prosecute it's leaders.

Hammer: We believe that there is an underground and that it does exist. I do not know about the efforts to combat it. Our position is that it is wrong.

Unfortunately, there has been only one such effort over the past several years. According to my sources, the women's underground commencement has been associated with a famous case that occurred in 1987 in Mississippi, in which two women living in Gulfport had alleged, within the context of custodial proceedings, that their husbands were guilty of the sexual abuse of their children. The court ruled against these women giving custody to the fathers. Subsequently, the women went underground hiding the children. According to one victim father (J.D.) who had done extensive research:

"The prominence of that case got wrapped up into the women's movement, it became a cause celebre of the women's movement. There are two prominent persons involved...Fay Yaeger, who lives in Atlanta and Lydia Rainer who lives in Gulfport. Both of them were alleged victim parents of child abuse. In the case of Yaeger, it was eventually shown that there were FBI warrants out on her husband for child sex abuse before their relationship.

Complicating these matters were Yaeger's fundamentalist Christian views in which she somehow came to believe that the whole family court system is Satanic and that fathers will abduct kids and use them for Satanic rituals. Stuff that on its face seems preposterous.

Within several years you have created throughout the United States a system of safe houses which are basically for women, overwhelmingly for females, are taken into the system, given new identities, new social security numbers, in some cases passports are manufactured. In some cases their sophistication is such, in response to the attentions placed on them, which reached a crescendo in 1992 when Yaeger was indicted in Georgia, they began to think internationally, saying that there were countries that they could take these children to avoid the FBI. The way they are set up, they can effectively thwart the normal procedures for finding abducted children. Because if you are using false social security numbers and fleeing from state to state with their weak laws, you are not going to have people prosecuting.

They are vigilantes who acting in such a fashion that the Rico statute should be applied to them."

As I knew this father (who was a media professional) to be an active campaigner for law reform, I asked him:

Rein: If you had a magic wand and could use it to make all things better for children, how would you use it?

JD: First I would act to make the law uniform in all states, the best model for such laws that exist in the United States are those of California and Illinois.

Second, all these problems described as child snatching, parental kidnapping and family abduction treated as serious crimes.

Rein: Would you want to see your former girlfriend (abductor of his child) in a prison cell?

JD: Frankly, I do want to see her in a prison cell.

Rein: What about the effect of that approach on your child?

JD: That is an interesting dilemma.

Chapter 5

The Development of Family Law

The Legal System

In the following chapters, I am going to deal in stages with family law. A father involved in conflictual divorce-custody litigation must have a profound appreciation of the facts and circumstances confronting him. He has to understand how present family law evolved. He must know how and why it was reformed. He must see how these reforms interact with other influences to deny his child and himself any sort of justice. These chapters relate to those on the Psychiatric Literature and Consequences of Parental Rights Deprivations. All are relevant to an understanding of The Father's Guide to the Courts.

Most fathers have no prior knowledge that the practice and administration of family law has reached a low point in quality and fairness. Fathers also are unaware of the court's inability to deal with the staggering numbers of conflictual divorces stumbling through the courtrooms of the United States, Britain, Canada, Australia, New Zealand and Western Europe each year.

According to the American Bar Association Division of Media Relations and Public Affairs "Facts about Children and the Law - How many children are involved with the legal system?", we are simply overwhelmed by the figures on child related family court cases. "Overall, the number of children involved in the legal system is staggering when taking into account children in the juvenile justice system, in dependency courts because of abuse or neglect, and in family law courts because of divorce, custody, or child support determinations. State trial courts reported 4.7 million cases involving domestic relations in 1994. They comprised divorce (39 percent); adoption, paternity, URESA and miscellaneous (27 percent); child custody and support (18 percent); domestic violence (16 percent); and 1.9 million juvenile petitions.

State courts are overwhelmed by cases involving children and families because of, among other things, rapid rises in reported cases of abuse and neglect, and federal legislation that placed burdens on state courts without additional funds.

Between 1984 and 1994, there was a 65 percent increase in domestic relations cases and a 59 percent increase in juvenile cases.[22]

In particular, one survey of 35 states found 1.29 million new divorce filings in 1992, an increase of almost 100,000 from 1988.

Another recent study noted that in New York State the caseload for child abuse increased by more than 300 percent between 1984 and 1989. In Michigan, the number of cases increased by nearly 300 percent between 1984 and 1988.

Judges in Chicago hear on average 1,700 juvenile delinquency cases per month, while in Los Angeles juvenile court judges have about ten minutes to devote to each case."

Source: ABA, "An Agenda for Justice: ABA Perspectives on Criminal and Civil Justice Issues" 111-112 (1996).

With rare exceptions, the dominating theme in the custody cases is one granting sole custody to women and little or no access to non custodial fathers, while heaping trauma, suffering and long term dysfunction on the innocent children involved in the process. That theme also involves trauma to male parents who suffer from a number

---

[22] See Lone Parent & Divorce Graphs and the Impact of Contemporary Divorce Law Reforms in Chapter 10

of pathologies related to the loss of their children (Jacobs 1986). *See Chapter 11 Consequences of the Destruction of Intact Families, Knock-on Effects*

The numbers of fatherless children are of immense statistical significance and give proof to the assumptions made by Amneus and mental health professionals that we are creating a society of 'female-headed single-parent households. Legal process and a continuous multi-marriage lifestyle have made men disposable, interchangeable, and without real impact or influence in the lives of our children.

In fact, we have literally reversed the past legal injustices visited on women and children and installed a new system imposing even more injustice and even worse legal sanctions on children and fathers.

Weaving together the disparate strands of the cloth of legal ineptitude, prejudice, mal-administration and even misfeasance of the law is no easy task. The identification of psychodynamic and motivating social factors including, the sixties social revolution, erroneous development of the psychiatric and psychological literature, radical feminist politics and economic self-interest is central to that process.

The law does not operate in a vacuum. Like language, it moves, alters course, widens and narrows. Prevailing social forces often influence how legal systems function. The law is also no better than those entrusted to administer it. Law for law's sake has no meaning. The law must serve aims of justice.

A Brief Historical Perspective

Modern family law has its roots in Roman times, inspired by Emperor Constantine's intercessions in the first century after Christ. This marked the approximate inception of a patrimonial system over the pre-existing matriarchal order. An order Amneus describes, referring to Otto Kiefer's "Sexual Life in Ancient Rome" informing us that the celebrated Swiss jurist J. J. Bachofen:

"...sought to prove that in ancient Italy the reign of strong paternal authority had been preceded by a state of exclusive matriarchy, chiefly represented by the Etruscans. He considered that the development of exclusive patriarchy, which we find to be the prevailing type of legitimate relation in historic times, was a universal reform, a vast and incomparable advance in civilization (Amneus)".

Freiherr F. von Reitzenstein, "Love and Marriage in Ancient Europe", p. 28; quoted in Otto Kiefer, "Sexual Life in Ancient Rome" (London, Abbey Library, 1934), p.8., Kiefer, (pp.8f).

American law more or less follows British Anglo-Saxon law. The first serious twentieth century national law reform in respect to marriage and conditions of divorce came from England in <u>The Guardianship of Children's Act of 1905.</u> The Act sought to create a balancing of interests between the parties regardless of their gender. Until that time, women and children (existing within the patriarchal system so despised by modern feminists) were the chattel (property) of husbands. This fact reflects clearly in common law and the statutes of many nations including those who relied on the English legal system.

Early feminist Barbara Leigh Smith Bodichon wrote a critical pamphlet in 1854 that had complained about the patriarchy, "Married Women and the Law":

"A man and wife are one person in law; the wife loses all her rights as a single woman, and her existence is entirely absorbed in that of her husband. He is civilly responsible for her acts; she lives under his protection or cover, and her condition is called coverture.

A woman's body belongs to her husband, she is in his custody, and he can enforce his right by a writ of habeas corpus.

The legal custody of children belongs to the father. During the life-time of a sane father, the mother has no rights over her children, except a limited power over infants, and the father may take them from her and dispose of them as he thinks fit."

However, as Dr. Kelley points out there already had been a shift in thinking as regards custody rights:

"A landmark change was initiated with the <u>British Act of 1839</u>, 2 which directed the courts to award custody of children under the age of seven to mothers, and to award visiting rights to mothers for children seven years and older."("The Determination of Child Custody" 1994)

Mason's book ("From Father's Property to Children's Rights: The History of Child Custody in the United States", Columbia University Press, New York, 1994"), chronicled the movement toward maternal preference accompanied by an increase in the legal status of women in the United States during the nineteenth and twentieth centuries. The book could have been more aptly, titled, "From Father's Property to Mother's Property".

By the 1920s, the maternal preference standard in custody determinations replaced the earlier paternal preference standard, both in statutes and in judicial decision making. This coincided with the psychological literature and work of Klein on maternal attachment. *See Chapter 2, Bowlby, Freud, Goldstein and Solnit*

That shift had now undergone two radical changes by the turn of the twentieth century. First, by English passage of the <u>British Act of 1839</u>, directing the courts to award custody of children under the age of seven to mothers, and to award visiting rights to mothers for children seven years and older. This first statement of "tender years" doctrine advanced by the English lawyer and author Mr. Justice Thomas Noon Talfourd, though intended to determine custody only until the children were old enough to return to the father's custody, nonetheless, provided the first major challenge to the paternal presumption.

The second change came in the balance of interests between husband and wife, especially in respect to custody issues, as <u>The Guardianship Act of 1905</u> made clear. The Act declared that the interests of the child were Paramount and that the parents were equals as litigants. Importantly, **conduct** remained a central consideration of the law upholding the moral component of marriage. It was not abridged or denied. Laws of the various American states accordingly followed the principles of The Act, just as most of them had followed previous English common and statute law.

Over the next sixty years, legal principles in domestic relations remained constant, while the law showed an ever-increasing interest in children as a special classification. This interest extended beyond the confines of state and national law into the arena of the 'Laws of Nations' and later private international law.

By 1970, in the aftermath of the social revolution of the sixties and its consequential first wave of escalating divorce rates and early retrogressive law reforms, The Uniform Marriage and Divorce Act, came into effect in the US. This provided the basis for a theoretical shift in custody doctrine from 'tender years' to straight 'best interests of the child' standard. The majority of states adopted The Act, in varying forms.

However, as historical analysis, present observations and the facts indicate, all that really happened is that the 'tender years' doctrine (favoring maternal sole custody) buried itself inside of the new and supposedly 'gender-neutral' standard. The failure of this modern 'best interests' standard meets discussion in the coming sub-chapter. However, I think it useful to include some comments of Dr. Joan Kelley on the historical development of gender-neutral language and best interests standards as a means to protect children:

"The historic shift to gender-neutral and best interests standards prepared the path for a new custody arrangement to emerge, that of *joint custody*. The concept of joint custody originated in the early 1970s from a small number of fathers, including mental health professionals, who desired continuity in their relationship with their children after divorce and strongly objected to being disenfranchised of their parental rights simply because divorce had occurred.

Newly formed fathers' rights advocacy groups provided the impetus for a joint custody movement, supported in the early 1980s by lay and scholarly publications which described various advantages of joint custody for society, parents, and children.

Several parallel developments enhanced the growing interest in shared custody as a means of preserving parental status and responsibilities. First, after focusing almost exclusively on mothers and children for decades, the child development field began, in the early 1970s, to study the father's contributions to the development of the child. The expanding literature suggested that previous literature undervalued fathers' contributions to their children's development and the importance of children's attachment to their fathers. Second, gender roles within families began to shift, particularly in dual-career families. More mothers began to work outside the home in addition to carrying out domestic responsibilities."

The question is why are fathers in the position today of having to argue and plead for equity and the shared parenting of their children? Why is there no sense and sensibility in deciding these sorts of issues given the knowledge and experience of past mistakes and injustices? Here we have to look to developments and forces that have interacted with the legal process to drive our choices into negative and narrow radical feminist channels. The first area worth reviewing is radical feminist driven implementation of divorce law reform.

The Impact of Contemporary Divorce Law Reform

Under the influences of a complex nineteen sixties social revolution, the birth of militant feminism and the institution of regressive law reform, the institution of marriage as we had understood it would be threatened. The care and nurturing of children got directed towards the unilateral control of female-headed single parent families. Those three dynamics link inexorably, one to another. Without the social revolution there would not have been a climate fostering a powerful feminist influence. Without the early feminists' push, there would not have been retrograde law reform. While the English psychologist Dr. John Campion, reviewing very similar British divorce law reform, argues from another point of view on the breakdown of the traditional intact family and suggests that:

"I do not believe that the causes of the relationship revolution are due to subtle and complex forces deep in the fabric of society. The causes of marriage breakdown are simply due to the catastrophic failure of the intellectual culture supporting social policy, especially in the area of matrimonial law, to respond to the moral pressures placed on it by material changes in post-war society."

The failure, to which Dr. Campion refers, is that reflected by post-law reform divorce rates, which had been a constant over seventy years or more, but began to increase dramatically after about 1960.

Previously only 10 percent of couples separated. In England between 1976 and 1991, they had doubled to 19 percent and are presently at conservatively estimated levels of 40 percent.

British Reforms

These statistics coincide conveniently with the implementation of the first reform of British Divorce Law, The Divorce Reform Act of 1969, which was to be followed in turn by the Act of 1984. I include this material because it is the mirror of the American experience. English Solicitor Adrian Pellman wrote a summary in 1993 of what had taken place in Divorce Law since 1970:

"Essentially what has happened is that the courts have virtually turned the Law upside down, contrary to the expressed intention of Parliament, and created a situation whereby people can break up marriages and obtain the same financial benefits as would only have been received had the other party broken up the marriage. Since actions may be taken without consequences, there is no incentive to refrain from those actions."

In specifically addressing the Law Reform Acts of 1969 and 1984 he goes on to state the new grounds on which divorces may be granted. These grounds included 'unreasonable behavior', by agreement based on two years separation, and lastly a unilateral divorce in the absence of the former conditions, based on five years of separation, provided that, there was proper financial provision for the innocent party. What had been unchanged was an existing provision from the 1857 Act, making 'conduct' relevant in regard to financial provisions so that a party that had committed adultery, or cruelty, or had deserted the family, had no right to claim maintenance.

Pellman's statement of the law was accurate and his argument that the courts had "turned the Law upside down", was proven by the court's making unauthorized and fundamental changes to the law without Parliament's consent whereas:

"The first of these was to apply a subjective and not an objective test to unreasonable behavior" which means that the party seeking a divorce only has to believe that the behavior was unreasonable in order to get on practical grounds a divorce on demand and therefore, one in which financial benefits accrued without moral cause. Pellman states:

"This opened the floodgates of petitions (for divorce) which Parliament never intended."

He points to a second fundamental development in which the courts, with the agreement of **The Law Society, brought in Legal Aid only for those seeking the divorce. While, denying it to those who sought to defend against it.** This meant in practice, women had a stake in the initiation of divorce. Men were economically disadvantaged in defending the action. The coup-de gras was delivered by the courts in a 1974 case in which it was held that conduct was no longer relevant unless it was "gross and obvious" thereby making divorce in England effectively a 'no fault' based system that delivered up financial rewards to women irrespective of conduct. Pellman concludes that:

"Since the courts take the view that wives may break up marriages without any consequence, it is not surprising there is a wave of divorce."

A Typical US State Reform

Now, for the sake of comparison, let us review the law of a typical American State.

New York State, from the time of Alexander Hamilton in 1787 until 1967 allowed for only one ground for divorce, that of adultery. In 1966, the legislature had enacted the Divorce Law Reform of 1966, which became effective the next year and extended the grounds for divorce while eliminating defenses against it.

Significantly, by 1980, New York State had adopted another law setting a new public policy, The Equitable Distribution Law 1980. The chief premise of this law was that modern marriage was an economic partnership, not merely a moral and social partnership. It had a corollary to this concept, that the assets produced during the marriage by the efforts of one or the other of the spouses, would be distributed equitably in divorce. This produced a similar statistical effect to the one observed in England.

In England and New York State (as well as the other American states), divorce had suddenly become relatively easy to obtain and effectively began to operate on a no-fault basis, although thinly veiled until only recently. Adultery had given way to mental cruelty or in England, unreasonable behavior and alternatively couples could obtain divorce by mutual consent. Marital assets now faced equitable division. That, in real terms, meant that women would receive an extremely significant proportion of family assets under the theory that they were the 'primary' caregivers and had to maintain the family home and child.

Two questions arise; first, did the changes in English and New York State legislative and common law effect the numbers of divorcing couples? Yes! Second, what or who was driving the policies that initiated the law reform? Was it a combination of feminist lobbies, social scientists, psychologists and social workers, as well as feminist infiltration of strategic professions and misplaced male liberalism?

Concepts of the Wardship of Children

The vast majority of parents have no idea of what Wardship is or how it operates. Yet, in some cases it comes into play effecting decisions taken by courts.

During the English Middle-Ages, the British Crown initiated a system permitting the State, through its courts, to intercede on behalf of children. This arcane system, known as the 'wardship' of children still exists in England and many US States in a variety of formats.

The concept was that children could be 'warded' by the Crown (court) under a doctrine known as 'parens patrie'[23] and custody vested in the State rather than either mother or father. One parent (mother) becomes a granted caregiver, while the other (father) might enjoy limited rights of visitation. It is the state acting as 'father' that holds all

---

[23] The State is father

legal rights and responsibilities over the child until his or her age of majority.

The wardship of children in the UK has often been employed as a tactic by women and their lawyers to circumvent The Children Act 1989, as well as to make the operation of international treaties such as The Hague Convention on the Civil Aspects of International Child Abduction more difficult to administer impartially.[24]

American fathers have come against this concept in parental child abduction cases. In an interesting State Department cable sent by Charisse M. Phillips, U.S. State Dept. to Elizabeth N. Blythe, U.S. Embassy Post London; the question was raised:

"By the way, can you tell me why so many British Moms have their kids made wards of the court/crown? What is the advantage?" (General Security Doc. 09/08/94, FOIA release)

The answer lies in the British Courts agency behavior supporting women to such an extent that men are considered to have rights amounting to "fewer than none" as another State Department memo clearly states. The mother can hide behind the shield of the court, acting to deprive a former spouse of his rights to a meaningful relationship with the child. This is true for custody and child abduction cases.

In simple terms, father has one representative in court and mother has three, including her own counsel, the official solicitor and the judge. In some US cases, law guardians interpose themselves into the proceedings, with similar consequences.[25]

In America, the term 'ward' or 'wardship' ordinarily carries a different meaning. Unlike British law, US wardship normally operates in 'public law' cases, not private law. Such cases affect children either orphaned or removed from parents and into the placement of various welfare agencies in extreme cases of abuse, abandonment, or inability of the family to care for it's young.

---

[24] Delegates to The Permanent Bureau have in the past expressed concern to the British government over wardship as a means to thwart the Convention
[25] See Cases David B v Helen O, Stephen S

Concepts of wardship have and continue to play a part in the legal process of England, America and other nations, sometimes as alternative law, and often as a subtle influence on the manner in which the courts conduct their more traditional business.

Some Distinctions in American and British Law

Of course, there are other distinctions between English and American family law. Chief amongst them that all English legislative acts flow solely from Parliament and have the force of national law, while in America we have a dual system of law, federal and state. In our system, state courts hear domestic relations cases, in the UK, a national court is usually (although County Courts also hear cases) hearing cases.

England does not have a written Constitution. We do. Perhaps, in light of our Constitution, it is arguable that we actually have three systems of law (State, Federal and Constitutional) with the Constitution acting as tiebreaker when disputes, controversies and conflicts in law arise over protected rights. This has at least an important theoretical bearing on the legal issues of custody. Many learned jurists have argued that rights related to the family and children are liberty interests. Interests that are in theory, constitutionally protected producing cases heard by federal courts, not state courts. An alternative argument is that while State Courts can continue to hear domestic relations cases, federal courts have a concurrent jurisdiction and can review them.

Remember, no state or federal law is valid if it violates the Federal Constitution. So if Congress or State legislatures pass laws that violate the Constitution, and those statutes are judicially reviewed and found wanting, they are overturned. Equally, private and state actions, as well as particular lower court judicial decisions are open to scrutiny, review and remedial action by our Supreme Court based on constitutional considerations.

In fact, up to the mid-eighteen hundreds in America all domestic relations cases were heard by federal courts and were considered to be Article III controversies of vested 'liberty interests'. [26]

Unfortunately, a major change developed in the mid-eighteen hundreds that had an enormous impact on domestic relations law. The federal courts simply opted out of and abdicated their responsibilities to protect these liberty interests, turning all domestic relations matters over to the state courts.

A recent and important Supreme Court case <u>Ankenbrandt v Richards (1995)</u> produced a useful opinion that discusses the history of domestic relations and the domestic relations exception doctrine commencing with <u>Barber v Barber (1859)</u> .

Ankenbrandt provides an example of the Court's selective reasoning in deciding whether or not to accept particular cases and/or aspects of domestic relations matters into the federal purview. In order for a court to hear any particular case, it must have two kinds of jurisdiction. It must have jurisdiction over the 'subject matter' and it must have 'personal jurisdiction' over the principle actors. This case fell under diversity jurisdiction.

Ankenbrandt clearly establishes the right of federal courts to hear child related matters so long as they are not being required to make a custody determination. However, the Court has to some extent, collapsed under various political pressures. It has been pressured into rampant gender bias and discrimination by allowing women access to the federal courts (in financial matters) while denying men and even more importantly, children, the same degree of access on far more substantial (family and rights of association) matters. (Sahid: Second Circuit Taskforce-Fairness in the Courts(1996). The issues of association are quite different from those seeking a custody determination.

One of the most obvious and immediate consequences of self-imposed federal judicial restraint is that domestic relations matters previously heard under constitutional protection and in uniformity (due process), now face hearing in diverse state courts. These crucial

---

[26] See Appendix B Ankenbrandt v Richards for an explanation and Opinion

matters face distinctly different common and statute law, operating under local prejudices and practices.

The transfer of domestic relations cases from federal to state courts immediately removed all of us one huge step from the uniform interpretation and administration of the law and from constitutional protections. Revisionist judicial views of the 'domestic relations' exception to federal courts jurisdiction over aspects of domestic relations cases has caused and promulgated serious gender bias in gaining access to the federal courts in favor of women and against both children and men.

The English Children Act of 1989

Getting back to the idea of national legislation (that I endorse for the US), we have the interesting example of the British Children Act of 1989. This Act effectively regulates the conduct of child custody proceedings in the United Kingdom. At its threshold, the issues of legislative gender bias and equal access to the law arising in the American context are absent. In practice, it has not worked, but that is another issue. This is precisely the kind of national act that the US should put into place. Thus, doing away with the vagaries of state courts who fail to provide a uniform approach to the law or guarantee equal rights to children and parents. It would also bring us into line with our treaty obligations under The UN Convention on the Rights of the Child. *See Chapter 6 UN Convention on the Rights of the Child*

The Children Act, at least in theory, makes the conduct of child custody proceedings uniform and fair, however biased it turns out to be in practice. The principles, scope and administration of the Act were intended to reform the system in such a way as to make an association of the best interests of the child with the principle that children have and need not one but two parents.

However, just as solicitor Adrian Pellman pointed out how family law courts perverted the wishes of Parliament on divorce law reform, this is precisely what they have done to The Children Act 1989. They have consistently refused to incorporate shared residence orders into practice, failing to implement Parliament's expressed wishes and intentions.

And the evidence of Parliament's intentions is adduced from their working documents and in particular from The Children Bill (Bill 104 of 1988-89), Major Amendments to the Children Bill in Standing Committee added 26 June 1989 (Reference Sheet No. 89/5)(Kim Greener & Mary Barber) reproduced in pertinent part:

Part I: General Principles, (a) Residence Orders

"In some cases, the order will provide that the child shall live with both parents, even though they do not share the same household. If such an arrangement is practicable, there is no reason to discourage it.

More commonly, however, the order will provide for the child to live with both parents, but to spend more time with one than the other (e.g. school term time with one and holidays with the other; or two out of three holidays from boarding school with one and the third with the other). It is a more realistic description of the responsibilities involved in arrangements of this sort to make a residence order covering both parents rather than a residence order for one and a contact order for the other"

Judge for yourselves! The law clearly contemplated shared parenting and equal rights, while the courts in practice ignored the parliamentary mandate and imposed universal sole maternal custody on children. His Lordship Mr. Justice Ewbank once declared in a case that:

"This is not the sort of order (Joint Custody) that is in favor here"

This is a useful general lesson for parents. *See Chapter 8 Father's Guide on adduction of evidence*

Returning to US law; from the turn of the last century we saw the gradual equalization of rights between men and women, husbands and wives, coming before the courts in respect to the issues of child custody. There was a growing interest in the idea that children required special protection. At the same time, a number of charitable organizations, some with state charters, began to express a direct interest in the welfare of children.

Judicial practice in general, in England and America, accepted the notion of the 'paramountcy' of the child's interests over those of the parents within the context of divorce and custody. *English Guardianship Act of 1905*

By the nineteen twenties, with the social organization of the family altered by the events of the industrial revolution, general perceptions of the male role pigeon-holed him as sole provider and not much else. Courts began to reflect these changes incorporating them into case law.

A doctrine was born called 'tender years'[27] (from the English Act of 1839). It meant that young children of 'tender years' should not be separated from their biological mothers. Courts considering child custody issues were extremely hesitant to hand over custody of young children (especially girl-children) to fathers. They operated in light of prevailing, however inadequate and mistaken, psychiatric literature and universal notions of women as nurturers and men as mere providers.

Despite legal perceptions formed out of the new literature, the population at large felt little impact. Social, religious and psychological taboos in place served to seriously impede efforts of men and women to obtain divorces. Therefore, divorce affected relatively sparse numbers of children.

Dr. Campion confirms that divorce numbers in England, before 1960, never exceeded one in twenty marriages ending in divorce, roughly the same as in America. Various courts from Admiralty to the Chancery, and their divisions, heard most cases. No special family law court system was established until the nineteen sixties either in England or America, coincidental to the steep rise in divorce rate.

Interestingly, fault was a consideration in the granting of divorce and custody decrees. Juries heard cases not the bench. Relevant to the grounds and defense, evidence was taken, examination and cross-examination permitted. Moral judgment formed an important part of the legal process, linked to marriage vows and in recognition of its esteemed estate within society.   Although many amongst us now

---

[27] Also See Chapter 2 The Psychiatric & Psychological Literature

might view prevailing conditions as restrictive and even marginally oppressive, they served a utilitarian purpose. They not only preserved matrimony in which the state has an overwhelming interest, but maintained social order against the invasion of anarchy and chaos. As the eminent psychologist B.F. Skinner pointed out:

"The function of cultural norms, although appearing arbitrary and oppressive to the individual, is to bring individuals under the control of the long-term social consequences of their behavior."

While family law issues came before these courts (prior to the formation of special domestic relations courts such as the Family Law Division in England and various US State Family Courts), it is significant that they followed all of the normal rules, procedures and practices of civil process. This included: due process, innocence before guilt, proper adjudication of evidence, application of 'objective' evidence tests and of real importance, a jury acting as finder of fact. Present family law is accusation driven. It has: subjective evidence tests, no fault, no jury, and as statistics reveal, makes predetermined decisions on the custody of children that runs counter to constitutional protections and statute law on discrimination.

However overbearing and burdensome a process divorce may have been in the past at least it complied with notions of a fair administration of justice. Contemporary family law practice diverts us away from due process, equal protection and all other universal norms of the proper administration of justice. It has drifted and been driven into decision by accusation style without the proper adjudication of evidence.

Family law operates on pre-conceived notions dictating the conclusions reached by judges while depriving children and men of their rights in law and their natural rights. It opens the doors to abuse, manipulation and deceit because it incorporates nothing more than contrived and ill-defined theories that fail to utilize rational criteria. It relies on covert political doctrines supported by out of date, disingenuous and inappropriate psychiatric and psychological assumptions.

The modern court places us at the mercy of and interdependent on current behavioral trends, social and political pressures that represent only one particular special interest group within the larger community, that of women.

Radical Changes and Corruption of Process from 1982 to the present

On the one hand, the nineteen sixties unleashed an optimistic social revolution that led to the radical re-structuring of our traditional intact family units, on the other hand it led to an unparalleled acceleration in rates of divorce amongst the populations of America, Britain, Western Europe and other advanced nations. General naivety accompanied a torrent of social enigmas, ills and unworkable contradictions with extremely onerous consequences for children, adults, families, and society. *See Chapter 10 Graphs on Divorce Rates and Single-Parent Families*

In many ways, the changing pattern of post-sixties family life, driven in part by sexual politics, has dulled our senses to the repercussions of these changes. We seem to have either ignored or not understood the greater meaning of their impact on this and future generations.

Our family courts have become one-stop clearing-houses for women to dispose of their former spouses, claim the children as their chattel and receive life long economic scholarships. Thus, enabling them to indulge in further, transitory, relationships with males without regard to the health well being and safety of our children. None of this would have been possible but for the political pressures brought to bear on the 'despised' patriarchal system (which had ceased to exist in fact) resulting in the creation of advantageous matriarchal divorce laws.

Numerous professionals, knowing better but lacking the will for forthright condemnation of radical feminist ideals, have aided and abetted the process. Professionals have failed to plead conclusively for commonsense and justice. One psychiatrist admitted to me that he had vacillated for years before coming out for the principles of shared parenting and recognition of the two psychological parent thesis.

A classic example of mental health professional writing on the subject of custody comes from Dr. Joan Kelley who seems to fear some feminist backlash against her for taking a truly disinterested position favoring a joint custody approaches over maternal custody:

"While clearly there is growing convergence on a number of divorce-related findings, they currently remain inconclusive or contradictory with respect to a number of important issues, and continued well-designed research is needed. The current practice of feminist writers and fathers' rights groups to use a particular research finding to bolster a political or gender-linked point of view while ignoring other data makes it difficult for legislators, judges, attorneys, or parents to obtain a balanced, informed view."

She vacillates, equating the two divergent points of view as being 'equally distorted or biased', while stating that on the one hand there is "growing convergence of divorce related findings" and on the other hand "the findings are inconclusive or contradictory".

Considering that Dr. Kelley has spent 30 years conducting research, observing children of divorce, and is extremely sensitive and knowledgeable, it is extraordinary that she cannot come to a definitive conclusion on the issues. Interestingly, she is a leading advocate for legal and psychological recognition of father's equal influence on the lives of children.

It is really quite a simple matter. Are the feminists right or wrong? Are her findings about fathers and children right or wrong? She goes on to report (not endorse):

"Some feminist critics argue that the best interests standard disadvantages women by discounting the importance of primary care-taking usually undertaken by women, reduces women's bargaining power."

She fails to come out and state the bottom line. Radical Feminists are driving female opposition to implementation of fair decision-making in custody cases because they might lose control, power and money.

Rather than condemning radical feminist thinking, she tries to reassure them:

"The best interests standard does not inherently discount the importance of primary care-taking. Indeed, in many states, the primary care-taking role is one of the criteria to be considered in determining custody."

She explains to them that:

"In this sense, the best interests standard dilutes the presumption that the primary caretaker shall continue exclusively in that role after divorce, and thus it receives the support of fathers' rights groups and many professionals who believe there should be continuity in the relationship between both parents and child after divorce, unless found to be inappropriate."

But again she attempts to assuage radical feminist doubts, "**Recent research indicates that women do not appear to be disadvantaged in the bargaining process** by the best interests standard, that is, the uncertainty of custody outcomes does not cause women to trade off child support to avoid risk. **The existence of mandatory child support guidelines reduces further such potential bargaining inequities.**"

Dr. Kelley knows full well that radical feminists violently reject **any** notion of gender neutral best interests standards as well as any notion of shared parenting because it absolutely does affect their bargaining power. They are also aware that having won important legal concessions in the recent past, only conceptual contradictions forced them to accept a notion rejecting 'tender years' doctrine. So compromised, they pay lip service to the principles of gender-neutral language as part of that legal reform package. June Carbone admitted this in her article on Feminist Perspectives on Divorce:

"The express maternal presumption common earlier in the century has disappeared and is widely believed to be unconstitutional. Virtually all states decide custody in accordance with a "best interests of the child standard." Thirty-seven states authorize joint legal and physical custody awards, with a few states requiring the agreement of both parents and a few states recognizing a rebuttable presumption that joint custody is in the child's best interests. One state, West Virginia, has adopted a primary caretaker standard in which sole legal and physical custody is awarded to the parent who assumed the greater responsibility for the child's care during the marriage. See Bruch, C.S. "And how are the children?" Internal Journal of Law and the Family (1988) 2:106-26."

It is enlightening to note that Ms. Carbone was quick to recognize what father's rights and humanist organizations have been complaining about for years, that, "The express maternal presumption...**is widely believed to be unconstitutional**". She fails, of course to comment on why it is that her feminist colleagues push for its return as a standard, or to recognize that maternal presumptions still predominate in fact and practice as shown by the available statistics. In New York State, an area of high population density, huge numbers of divorces are granted each year, few of which are of the joint custody variety unless there is no opposition from mother and the court merely rubberstamps a prior private agreement between the parties.

Virtually all divorces end up with sole maternal custody decisions and fathers are often left with little or visitation. Carbone cites figures from California showing 73 percent of decisions in favor of 'legal' joint custody although the majority of them grant full control of 'physical custody' to mother. This misleads us as to the meaning of the statistics. These are still sole custody decisions in practice. She also claims that men did not oppose these circumstances.

The truth is that fathers have little choice in the matter as Dr. Thompson (1994), Mnookin (California Study) and other experts have explained. *See California Study.* The fact is that the principle of joint custody in California has been manipulated away from its intended purpose of presumed shared parenting (*See California evidence Code 4600 Presumed Joint Custody*) into a legal fiction that in reality grants sole custody to mothers. Father's rights are merely theoretical.

The bottom line is that radical feminists are promoting matriarchy, with men wholly relegated to the status of indentured servants, providers of sperm and paychecks. The system's integrity depends on women gaining full and absolute control over the children of divorce. If we were to assume that the new standards really implemented shared parenting, then the implications that follow are:

Each parent is going to have equal rights

Each parent is going to have equal responsibilities

Each parent, in practical terms is liable for the support and maintenance of the children.

Therefore, there will be no huge endowment upon mother in terms of, maintenance, alimony or child support monies

Therefore, she will be unable to 'parentectomize' father from the lives of the children, or to re-locate with boyfriend to distant parts taking the children with her. In short, she is likely to lose unwarranted power and control over him and them.

Let us now turn to a careful examination of these brave new 'best interest' guidelines.

The Manifest Failure of 'Best Interests of the Child' Doctrine

In addressing this purportedly guiding principle as doctrine one must absolutely bear in mind that the relatively recent family court systems in America and abroad have an almost limitless set of inherent powers. These powers, unlike any other civil and criminal law, are wide-ranging and discretionary. The courts do not have to concern themselves with accountability, as none exists. How does one determine the best interests of children? How do we make courts accountable?

If anything illustrates the difficulties and dangers of doctrines such as 'the best interests of the child' standard, it is the manner of operation. It has become a cliché phrase, lacking in any objective criteria, disabling reasonable assessment of whether or not and how the child's best interests can be met either from a psychological or legal perspective.

This doctrine can mean nothing without a clear definition of terms. Nonetheless, it has been instrumental in determining the fate of our children's lives, the make-up and character of the post-divorce family structure and even produced larger social effects that we are just now beginning to experience.

It is not hard to see how the clever use of a title such as Goldstein et als work, <u>"Beyond the Best Interests of the Child"</u> could have impacted on the court systems own similarly stated doctrine, as peculiar as that might seem.

Judges hearing cases over the past thirty-five years have happily given credence to this book that appears to substantiate the court's doctrinal theory. This book underpinned the old court's own conservative male prejudices and value system. It underpinned more recently appointed feminist judges personal prejudices. It allowed the court to automatically associate the best interests of the child exclusively with those of its mother. While on the other hand, mental health authors opposing what they have known to be erroneous positions espoused by Freud et al, have been reluctant to state those views with equal conviction, possibly fearing feminist backlashes from their 'politically incorrect' views.

No doctrine has ever done greater disservice to our children. In the recent past a number of interested professionals have attempted to define the terms and lay down the foundations of social, psychological and legal guidelines that would lend some sense to 'best interests' doctrine, but efforts have met with steely opposition and rejection.

In a letter from the British Lord Chancellor, Lord MacKay to The Minister for Health, Right Honorable Virginia Bottomley (who had written with an endorsement of my briefing paper), His Lordship firmly rejected a proposal I had offered to redefine the best interests standard arguing that, "it would take discretionary powers away from my judges". The reasons for such obstinate refusal to concede the necessity for clarification and ultimately the willingness to cooperate meet discussion in the chapter dealing with the literature on child development. Dr. Kelley has commented on broad attempts to construct some sort of objective criteria. However, they simply do not exist except as vague references lacking the clarity to force the hands of prejudiced judges.

Given the wealth of psychiatric and psychological literature on child development as well as the rather conclusive evidence on the consequences of father absence (see chapter on Parental Deprivations), no amount of posturing by radical feminists and their allies can deflect from the truths on nurturing that command our attention, respect and compliance.

The association of the 'best interests' of the child with a two-parent system (either in marriage or after divorce) needs promotion, enforcement and monitoring by the courts. The former thesis of maternal superiority must face definitive rejection. This is true in principle and for the most part in fact. For those few anomalous cases demanding draconian decisions, court powers are still reserved. In those cases, decisions must remain based on standards of evidence applied in all other legal process, not controlled by unsubstantiated allegations or subjective tests.

Clever legislators, radical feminists, social scientists and others have paid lip service to gender-neutral language revisions in family law, but the fact remains that a seductive charade is taking place. There is promotion of a false impression that there is a level playing field, due process and equal rights. The exact opposite is the case. Psychologist Ross Thompson, professor of psychology and associate director of the Center on Children, Families, and the Law at the University of Nebraska—Lincoln writing in <u>The Future of Children</u>, had to admit:

"Today, the most common standard is the gender-neutral "best interests of the child" standard which reflects (among other things) the view that parents should be preferred as custodians, not on the basis of gender, but rather because of their relationships with children, and gives social recognition to the diverse care-giving roles and responsibilities that mothers and fathers can assume in modern families. **But striving to avoid sexism in divorce standards can be a difficult task because men and women are treated differently.**"

How do we know that sex discrimination is at work? We know from the divorce statistics that show mothers as receiving over 90 to 92 percent of all custody decisions. We know from the figures on female-headed single-parent homes. We know from the statistics on crime, depression and mental breakdowns pointing toward the installation of male absent matriarchal families.

While we are all too aware of continuous feminist pressures to defeat and reject the association of a child's best interests with its two psychological parents as elaborated by Michigan President of NOW,

Gloria Woods, reported in this book. Ms. Woods comments that 90 percent of men accepted sole maternal custody, reflects only a disingenuous and spurious argument. She argues that fair standards are not necessary and the public is deceived as to the real pressures on fathers not to fight for joint custody. While Professor Ross Thompson describes the reasons for father's reluctant acceptance of sole maternal custody:

"Fathers may agree to maternal custody awards because they believe that they could achieve no better than a visiting relationship with offspring if they were to dispute such a claim."

While the research supports his view, as he goes on to report:

"In an important longitudinal study of 1,100 divorcing California couples with children conducted recently by Eleanor Maccoby and Robert Mnookin of Stanford University. In the mid-1980s, these scholars and their colleagues interviewed parents periodically throughout the divorcing process, beginning with the initial separation and continuing for several years after the divorce. They compared each parent's preference for the custody award shortly after the petition for divorce was filed with what that parent got."

Why was this so? **Maccoby and Mnookin suggested that many fathers may have decided that their efforts to achieve a more generous physical custody arrangement were likely to fail in the face of the mother's determination to have sole physical custody of offspring.** There was, in fact, considerable reason for their fear. **The Stanford study reported that, when parents made conflicting physical custody requests, mothers' requests were granted about twice as often as fathers' requests.**

Indeed, even when both parents agreed that fathers should have sole custody of offspring, judges contravened this agreement about one quarter of the time. The authors concluded that:

"Although gender stereotypes are no longer embedded in the statute books themselves, and California law is certainly viewed as sympathetic to more androgynous forms of physical custody, **the actual custodial out-comes still reflect profound gender**

differentiation between parents: the decree typically provides that the children will live with the mother."

The authors simply reiterate what we already know. The judicial system runs amok and disregards the meaning and intention of legislative bodies in their enactment of law, and does so with immunity from real accountability. The most casual reading of the relevant California statute makes it patently obvious that the judges cannot rely merely on production of a covertly interpreted 'best interests of the child' standard as a reason for making maternal sole custody decisions.

Yet, fifteen or more years after passage of the statute, results remain the same as before incorporation into law. As I show throughout this book, gender discrimination is so endemic that children and fathers can have no expectations of receiving justice in a family court environment.

Chapter 6

Children's Rights and International Law

Deprivation of Human and Civil Rights of Children and Fathers

Fathers conducting cases might also want to consider the position of the child under important international treaty law. Although US courts might very well disregard arguments and references to these treaties, some have made concessions in this area and have allowed consideration on the record. *See UN Convention on the Rights of the Child*

As important as it is to adhere to established intuitive and scientific values in relation to the needs of children, we cannot ignore other aspects of their dilemma and that of their fathers.

We cannot ignore the issue of the human and civil rights of children. They are enshrined in various instruments of international law. Unfortunately, while the western industrialized countries pay lip service to such instruments, their real focus seems directed towards the business of the impoverished and underdeveloped countries. Our attention is, cleverly, diverted from gross 'miscarriages' of justice and inequities within our own precious sovereign territories. A young child working in a sweatshop in Indonesia is thus a cause for concern.

At the same time, an American or British child deprived of his or her father is none at all! *See Appendix C of President Clinton letter*

If it is clear that individual states have consistently failed to apply humane and sound legal standards to protect our children, then we have to look in other directions. In the absence of an acceptable federal standard, we require a 'universal standard' promoting the legal rights of children. Therefore, we look to international law.

International Law: The UN Convention on the Rights of the Child

International Law had broached the issues of child related issues as early as the turn of the twentieth century as expressed through The Guardianship of Infants: Hague Convention of 1902. A number of further declarations and other instruments of international law have culminated in

The UN Convention on the Rights of The Child, which has declared in its Preamble that it is:

"Convinced that **the family, as the fundamental group of society and the natural environment for the growth and well-being of all its members and particularly children, should be afforded the necessary protection and assistance** so that it can fully assume its responsibilities within the community."

"Recognizing that the child, for the full and harmonious development of his or her personality, should grow up in a family environment, in an atmosphere of happiness, love and understanding...."

The family that the United Nations refers to is the intact family unit which has a mother and father who provide the psychological parenting making it possible for the child to have it's legal rights, as defined by international law, maintained in accordance with their solemn declaration. In Article 18 the Convention is definitive in setting forth the rights of the child in respect to having both of it's parents linking the concept of best interests to shared parenting:

"**Article 18**

1. States Parties shall use their best efforts to ensure recognition of the principle that **both** parents have common responsibilities for the upbringing and development of the child. Parents or, as the case may be, legal guardians, have the primary responsibility for the upbringing and development of the child. The best interests of the child will be their basic concern."

If there were any doubt as to the meaning and legislative intention of The United Nations, I put that to rest on the authority of no less than the second most responsible figure in <u>The UN Human Rights Commission.</u> Dr. Purificacione Quisumbing, Personal Representative of the High Commissioner, Head of The New York Headquarters, historian and lawyer. Dr. Quisumbing stated during a TV interview, that the United Nations intended that article to mean that <u>joint custody</u> should be the <u>principle</u> right of the child, not of the parents. "The Human Rights Enigma", Director S. Rein, MNN Network (1997)

However, although, state parties to international treaties, are bound by that law there are a number of loopholes through which they creep in order to evade their responsibilities. Such is the case of the United States refusal to properly implement the Convention. President, Bill Clinton has, while magnanimously authorizing his Ambassador to sign the Convention, contrived to make it impossible for parents or others with legal status to prosecute cases involving children based on the Convention in any US court. He stated in his personal letter to me that:

"These reservations and understandings will ensure that the Convention does not infringe upon the central role of parents and the family and that it is consistent with our federal system of government. **I also want to make clear that this Convention will not serve as a basis for litigation in America's courts.**" *See Clinton Letter Appendix C*

Did the former President, or his Advisers, take us for absolute fools? The ratification of an instrument of international law makes it a law of the United States to which we are bound. To sign and ratify the Convention subject to reservations and understandings that prevent the implementation of the law is a legal contradiction (conflict of law) and moral turpitude of the worst kind.

"Before sending the Convention to the Senate for advice and consent to ratification, we will undertake a final analysis of how it would be implemented domestically and propose **appropriate reservations** and understandings"

Apparently the President is concerned, on the one hand, to analyze how the Convention can be "implemented" while, on the other hand, he informs me:

"...that the Convention will not be used as a basis for litigation in America's courts."

Logic dictates that if one cannot litigate based on the Convention, it is unimplemented and is not law of the United States. Further, lack of implementation places us in the invidious position of having violated our international treaty obligations, while depriving US citizens of their rights to protection as subjects of international law. No doubt, that Article 18, declaring the UN's determined view that children are entitled to both of their parents, is being rejected because radical feminists (backed by Hillary Clinton and NOW) are determined to identify and associate families as being units composed of women (victims) and children. This strategy contradicts the meaning and intentions of the UN Convention on the Rights of the Child.

It is worth noting that principles of international jurisprudence indicate that the intended reservations of the president are in violation of treaty law as seen from Judge Lauterpacht's statement obiter dicta[28] in The Boll Case, Netherlands v. Sweden, Guardianship of Infants, Hague Convention of 1902, International Court of Justice 1958, Rep 55:

"A state is not entitled to cut down on it's treaty obligations in relation to one institution by enacting in the sphere of another institution provisions whose effect is such as to frustrate the operation of a crucial aspect of the treaty."

It follows from what the esteemed Justice opined that a state cannot sign a treaty implementing it restrictively and in such a manner as to

---

[28] "Obiter Dicta" is not definitive law but is a powerful policy statement on the law

"frustrate the operation of a crucial aspect of the treaty". Nevertheless, that is precisely what our former president proposed to do. If there are still any doubts, then we need look no further than **Article 51** of the Convention itself:

"**2. A reservation incompatible with the object and purpose of the present Convention shall not be permitted**"

The above is concrete evidence that President Clinton's letter expresses an intention to violate the meaning and spirit of the Convention. Lodging the reservations referred to in his letter undercuts the very instrument that he purports to uphold and ratify. *See Appendix C*

The rights of children as determined by The United Nations have little to do with the operative facts in various jurisdictions dealing with domestic relations issues. They are in fact, human rights. Human rights are nothing more than the legal extension and expression of those rights described by Thomas Paine as 'natural rights'. Natural rights never surrender to national states. Such rights pre-dated the American Constitution. Modern International Law is all about making all persons subjects of human rights laws with a defined set of rights.

These human rights in respect to the child, if properly implemented by the US government, would mean that fathers acting on behalf of their children might sue in federal courts. Recalling the earlier discussion on federal court abdication (the domestic relations exception) of their responsibility to hear family cases, one can better understand the previous President's reticence to properly incorporate The UN Convention into US law.

Additionally, powerful agencies and forces are at the root of his decision not to permit litigation based on the Convention, because left to their own devices state courts can continue to support female-headed single-parent families as an institution. This is a defiance of international law. State courts, left unfettered, are unaccountable to the children that The United Nations has sought to shield and protect from the affects of family breakdown and loss of their biological-psychological parents.

One enterprising and determined 14 year-old boy from Canada, Clayton Giles, has engaged in a single-handed campaign to get nation states to abide by the provisions of the Convention. Without any organized support he has been marching from Winnipeg, Canada to Washington and finally to The United Nations in New York as a protest. Along the way, he is telling his own story of paternal loss.

The International Covenant on Civil and Political Rights

One absolutely shocking case that illustrates the need for international adjudication of United States violations of it's own constitution and international treaty on human rights refers not to The UN Convention on the Rights of the Child, but to The International Covenant on Civil and Political Rights, ratified in 1992 (ICCPR).

The ICCPR, signed before our limited endorsement of the UN Convention, provided the sole means for the following case to express concerns in international law after exhausting local remedies in the US legal system. The key elements of the Covenant follow. I have included footnotes defining the terms, arbitrary and unlawful.

International Covenant on Civil and Political Rights, (G.A. res. 2200A(XXI). 21 U.N. GAOR Supp (No 16) at 52, U.N. Doc. No. A/6316 (1966), 999 U.N.T.S. 171 (1976)

Part II Article 2

Each State Party to the present Covenant undertakes to respect and to ensure to all individuals within its territory and subject to its jurisdiction the rights recognized in the present Covenant without distinction of any kind, such as race, color, sex, language, religion, political or other opinion, national or social origin, property, birth or status.

Where not already provided for by existing legislative or other measures, each State Party to the present Covenant undertakes to take the necessary steps, in accordance with its constitutional processes and with the provisions of the present Covenant, to adopt such other measures as may be necessary to give effect to the rights recognized in the present Covenant.

Each State Party to the present Covenant undertakes:

to ensure that any person whose rights or freedoms as herein recognized are violated shall have an effective remedy, notwithstanding that the violation has been committed by persons acting in an official capacity;

(b) to ensure that any person claiming such a remedy shall have his right thereto determined by competent judicial, administrative or legislative authorities, or by any other competent authority provided for by the legal system of the State, and to develop the possibilities of judicial remedy;

(c) to ensure that the competent authorities shall enforce such remedies when granted.

Article 17

No one shall be subjected to arbitrary[29], or unlawful[30] interference with his privacy, family, home or correspondence, nor to unlawful attacks on his Honour and reputation.

Everyone has the right to the protection of the law against such interference or attacks.

Article 23

The family is the natural and fundamental group unit of society and is entitled to protection by society and the State.

---

[29] ARBITRARY: unreasonable, arbitrary=with no purpose or objective; unreasonable= with a purpose which is excessively imposed, Modern legal usage, Garner, Oxford U. Press, 1987: 1. Not fixed by rules but left to one's judgment or choice; discretionary [arbitrary decision, arbitrary judgment 2. based on one's preference, notion, whim, etc; capricious 3. absolute, despotic SYN: dictatorial, Webster's New World Dictionary, Simon & Schuster 1987.

[30] UNLAWFUL: illegal; unwarranted or unauthorized by the law; lacking the qualifications prescribed by law, contrary to and forbidden by the law, Black's Law Dictionary, West Publications 1979

The right of men and women of marriageable age to marry and to found a family shall be recognized.

No marriage shall be entered into without the free and full consent of the intending spouses.

States Parties to the present Covenant shall take appropriate steps to ensure equality of rights and responsibilities of spouses as to marriage, during marriage and at its dissolution. In the case of dissolution, provision shall be made, for the necessary protection of any children.

Article 24

Every child shall have, without any discrimination as to race, color, sex, language, religion, national or social origin, property or birth, the right to such measures of protection as are required by his status as a minor, on the part of his family, society and the State.

Every child, shall be registered immediately after birth and shall have a name.

Every child has the right to acquire a nationality.

Article 26

All persons are equal before the law and are entitled without any discrimination to the equal protection of the law. In this respect, **the law shall prohibit any discrimination and guarantee to all persons equal and effective protection against discrimination on any ground such as race, color, sex,** language, religion, political or other opinion, national or social origin, property, birth or other status.

Case of Michael H. v Gerald D (1989) S.Ct. 491 U.S. 110

The case of Michael H involved an unmarried father who had been living with a woman who had not obtained a formal divorce from her husband and with whom he had fostered and raised a child. I am enclosing it's chronology because it says much more about the dedication and love this father felt for his child than anything I might write. It shows the absolute madness and blatant sexual-gender discrimination that generally controls the hearing of custody and visitation matters in violation of human rights and other principles of international law:[31]

1982- Complaint to establish paternity and get visitation rights in Los Angeles Superior Court.

03-83 Court assigns a child's attorney

08-84 (Husband of mother enters the case although mother has lived with the putative father for a number of years)

09-84 All parties undergo family evaluation

10-18-84 Based on evaluation report the judge orders a three year visitation schedule

01-21-85 There is a summary judgment in favor of defendants (mother and husband) against the biological and psychological father Michael H. in which his parental rights are terminated forever as of that date.

03-87 Michael H. seeks temporary visitation order pending his appeal of the prior decision

05-87 California Appellate Court upholds the lower court decision. Ruling appealed by Michael H.

08-87 California Supreme Court denies this appeal

09-87 Complaint for paternity and rights filed in New York State Family Court

10-28-87 Jurisdictional Statement filed from California. United States Supreme Court asked to hear the case.

12-87 Judge Marks, NY Family Ct. refuses to hear the case and fines the Plaintiff Michael H. $4,025.00. Appealed but withdrawn appeal

02-27-88 The US Supreme Ct. agrees to hear the case and the A.C.L.U., files an "Amicus" Brief on father's behalf to the Supreme

---

[31] The Children's Rights Council submitted an Amicus Brief on behalf of Michael H.

Court. The National Council Children's Rights files an "Amicus" Brief on behalf of the father

10-11-88 The Supreme Court hears oral argument

06-15-89 A deeply divided court rules 5-4 against the appellant father Michael H.. Case becomes known as Michael H. and Victoria D. v. Gerald D.

07-10-89 US Supreme Court receives Petition for a rehearing

08-30-89 Supreme Court denies further consideration of the appeal

10-90 Suit filed in New York Supreme Court for visitation, Westchester County

12-13-90 New York Supreme Court refuses to hear the case. Michael H. fined again $6,500.00 and appealed

03-91 US Supreme Court receives a second petition for hearing

04-91 U.S. Supreme Court denies the appeal without comment. Justice Scalia recuses himself.

05-91 Suit filed in Los Angeles Superior Court for visitation

10-91 LA Superior Court rules against Michael H. and fines him again $8,250.00, and says he should file in New York. Action appealed, appeal withdrawn

04-92 Motion filed to clarify, recall and/or amend U.S. Supreme Court decision

05-92 U.S. Supreme Court denies motion without comment

10-92 Defendants ordered to pay a fine of $4,500.00. The only hearing ever won in 12 years by the father Michael H. against them

11-92 Appeal filed in New York State Supreme Court, Appellate Division

10-28-93 Oral arguments heard in the Appellate Division. Court denies father the right to tape record oral arguments, marking the first time in twenty years anyone had been refused

11-19-93 Court upholds trial court, whereas no court had ever provided an evidentiary hearing

01-94 Appeal filed to NY State Court of Appeals

03-94 Appeal denied

Having exhausted all legal options in the United States over a twelve-year period, father's attorney then wrote in 1994 to The UN High Commissioner for Human Rights, Jose Ayala Lassos, seeking to initiate a human rights complaint against The United States, representing that:

"A single father in America who has a child with a married woman may have no parental rights to his own child. This human rights violation is gender based. It is only a man that can have his children taken from him like this---not a woman."

Michael H., Victoria's father, made a doomed attempt to get the United Nations to hear the case based on his and his child's denial of human rights. That case, previously heard by the US federal courts, failed at each level from district court to appellate level and finally in The Supreme Court (case of Michael H.) It opened up the issue of child and father's rights to have access to one another where the parents were not married, and the mother (separated from her husband for a number of years) denied her consort his rights of visitation to his biological child. The issues revolved around the rights of an unmarried biological and psychological father to take part in the nurturing of the child. The father had to overcome a California statute (California Evidence Code Section 621) left over from the early part of the century, stating that the children born to a married mother but derivative of an extra-marital relationship were "presumed to be the children of the husband". As preposterous as this might sound, the Supreme Court, in a retrograde divided 5-4 decision stated that the unmarried biological father had no legal rights or standing to have visitation to the child and "terminated all previous parental rights".

David Levy, J.D. CRC President reports:

"The Court ruled 5 to 4 that a court had to provide a hearing to a never married father (where mother returns to her husband) to determine his rights, 4 saying that there should be no such hearing. Justice Stephens was one of the five. He believed that Michael H. had

had a hearing. He did not. Hirschensohn twice asked Stephens to look at the California record and reverse himself. Stephens refused."

What does this tell us about the manner in which our most esteemed court functions? Does it have the capacity to make clear-headed and morally upright decisions? Is it able to rise above petty politics to make judicial judgments in accordance with important human and civil rights related principles? How strange it is that the U.S. Supreme Court becomes an active participant in the betrayal of the rights of the child. In the words of Michael H's attorney addressed to the UN Commission:

"Michael is a loving father who only wants to parent his child."

I guess that is too much to ask for if the applicant is a father and mother does not permit it!

According to David Levy J.D., President of the Children's Rights Council:

"CRC filed an Amicus Brief because children need two parents and Michael Hirschensohn was indisputably (by DNA tests) the father of the child. He was also the psychological father of the child, because he helped to raise her in the first few years of her life."

Inevitably, the father's application to the UN under the auspices of, The International Covenant on Civil and Political Rights, failed. Sadly, he has had no further contact to his child. Applications such as this one, without the United States agreement to submit to the jurisdiction of international legal forums, must fall on stony ground.

For the most part, I have been concerned about the state of marriage and the type of custody decisions depriving children from having bonded relationships with fathers. However, one cannot ignore the case of Michael H and the millions upon millions of cases involving non-marital long-term procreational relationships in which similar problems arise. What does a marriage certificate mean to an innocent child suffering from the imposition of lost loving relationships?

Chapter 7

Modern Family Law and Injustice

The Civil Rights Act: 42 USC 1983

It was Thomas Paine who in the 18th century, said:

"Every civil right grows out of a natural right, or, in other words, a right exchanged...the power produced from the aggregate of that class of natural rights cannot be applied to invade the natural rights which are retained in the individual, and in which the power to execute is as perfect as the right itself."

Just as the president's approach to the UN Convention on the Rights of the Child denies children's access to international law, the corollary is in the US government's refusal of access to the federal courts. Access rests on the principles and statute law of 42 USC 1983, The Civil Rights Act. This Act serves to protect our 'civil' rights, giving right of actions against persons who, under color of state law, custom or usage, subjects another to deprivation of any rights, privileges or immunities secured by the federal constitution. There is a long line of

143

cases establishing the Rights of the Family, parents and children as Constitutional liberty interests.

Case of a Federal Civil Rights Complaint on behalf of a child

A federal complaint arose on behalf of a child who had been the object of sexual abuse within a family. The mother was involved with a boyfriend. Divorce and custody proceedings commenced. Welfare workers had disclosed that there were signs that the child suffered sexual abuse and the court acted summarily to immediately cut off all contact between the father and the child. Subsequently, the court discovered that the boyfriend of the mother had committed this horrendous offense and the father had done absolutely nothing to threaten the health and well being of his child.

However, despite the demand for re-instatement of his access, social services arbitrarily and shamefully refused to recommend the commencement of visitation between father and child. The lawyer for the child decided to file suit against the judges, welfare agency and others who had deprived the child of his civil rights under The Civil Rights Act. The case went to the Federal District Court (2nd Circuit) in New York, dismissed as part of their ongoing efforts to refuse access to the federal courts using the pretext of the 'domestic relations exception' doctrine. The lawyer, a determined fellow, appealed and the case came before the Chief Judge of the circuit Chief-Justice Newman. Newman dismissed the appeal and threatened the lawyer with heavy monetary and other sanctions for having brought the action in the first place. Father and child have had no contact for several years.

Is it coincidence that each time I have encountered a children's case (not seeking custody) coming before the US 2nd Circuit Court of Appeals (several in all), the Chief Justice of the Circuit, former Chief Justice Newman, sat at the head of the judges panel on the case. He and the Panel dismissed all the cases. Additionally, in at least two of them, Newman threatened sanctions against the plaintiff for having brought the action. Later I discovered that Judge Newman is a relation of Judge Jackie Silberman of New York State Court dealing with divorce and custody matters. That court has a history of consistent denial of children's and father's rights, and is one of the more reactionary family courts in America.

Double standards are present when important federal judges like Newman deny fathers access to the courts on civil rights issues while allowing cases brought by women on child support issues (given flimsy Congressional legislation). On the one hand, Congress rushed to enact a federal child support statute, overcoming 'domestic relations' exception, while on the other hand no similar federal statute is contemplated enforcing paternal access, contact, visitation and the constitutional rights of children and fathers association.

Further, it is clear as crystal that cases brought by fathers in the federal courts have been based on issues also falling outside the 'domestic relations' exception. Under the analysis of the seminal case of <u>Ankenbrandt v. Richards</u>[32], those cases deserve hearing. However, from the Supreme Court down the judicial food chain, courts manipulate legal process in accordance with political considerations, covert goals and private agendas. They are under the influence of powerful extremist self-interest groups and lobbies driven by radical feminist objectives.

Men have no such effective lobbies, remain disorganized, lack group funding, personal wealth and are dysfunctional. Men, battered by the psychological defeats suffered in the wake of divorces removing them from nurturing and other parenting roles, remain passive victims. Children have, therefore, no voices to represent their interests and rights.

Feminist Driven Anti-Child-Father Alliances

Determined collusion on the parts of millions of mothers, lawyers, judges, social workers, guardian ad litems, psychiatrists and radical feminist groups leads to the fracture of two-parent post divorce families. It is a sad but incontrovertible fact that children's rights have faced sacrifice on an altar of shallow political intrigue, narrow female

---

[32] See Appendix B Ankenbrandt v Richards, a tort action under diversity jurisdiction

self-interests and anti-male ideological warfare. The evidence is clear from statistical analysis on the incidence of childhood, adolescent and adult dysfunction rooted in female single-parent parenting.

If anything argued more for the return to patriarchy that Amneus calls for, it is the consequences we now face for passive and ineffectual resistance to the subversive installation of a new matriarchy. This matriarchy threatens to disenfranchise children and male parents of their human and civil liberties. It would deprive them of human dignity. It would rob them of their natural rights to filiation. It will create a classification of male indentured servants, while granting rights and freedoms (absent responsibility) or merit to women.

One can understand the position of the male intellectual culture that refuses to accept these conditions. It is arguable that however oppressive the patriarchy might have seemed, it at least served to regulate female sexuality. It created contractual bonds that brought women into a controlled environment. This fostered social order, progress and stability in the nurturing of children, while offering women life-long protections and economic provision.

In the face of anti-male coalitions and alliances driven by radical feminist political agendas, men have little recourse but to defend patriarchy and bemoan the death of traditional family structures. Thus the disposition of matters concerning the health and welfare of our children have become subject to the machinations and intellectual chaos of a raging war defined by a Patriarchy versus Matriarchy debate. Feminists, with fixed ideas, initiated this debate and have the means to pursue their policy objectives in practice.

Moreover, no discussion of these alliances to set up an anti-male matriarchal system can be complete without including the second tier assailants. This list includes the politicians who exploit the situation for their own short-term self-interest. They court the vote of what is in practice an activist female majority, trading off promises of empowering legislation as well as state and federal grant funding in return getting comfortable offices, limos, and power. Shadowing them are the army of plebeian social scientists and mental health professionals acting as apologists. State employees (cautiously described as civil servants) add to the injustice acting without any accountability whatsoever, making secret policies and decisions endorsing the politics of matriarchy.

Custody and Visitation

I want to make clear that it is the vast majority of ordinary conflictual cases that are of concern and not anomalous ones in which extraordinary conditions exist. Those might require more individual examination, adjudication and careful consideration. Despite external appearances and personal interpretation the lion-share of all contested custody cases involve nothing more than commonplace struggles for power and control over children and family economic assets. Sexual politics, avarice, prejudice and personal vendettas drive these struggles.

Men do not start custody power struggles

As statistics and researches prove, men do not initiate these power struggles. Indeed, the Stanford study showed: "mothers received sole custody of offspring more than two-thirds of the time when their request for sole custody conflicted with fathers' request for joint custody." The majority of fathers have opted for shared parenting, and most often initiate the consideration of joint custody. (Roman 1986)"

In dealing with custody issues we are confronted with the problem of defining the needs and best interests of children and then, in what is essentially a damage control operation, finding **solutions that offer either the best possible resolution or at least the one perceived to be the least detrimental to the children.** Taken from the point of view of the child, I have not the slightest doubt that all the contemporary evidence supports my conclusion that shared parenting or joint custody must be the preference and presumption in law. Is it a perfect solution? No. The psychological displacement suffered by children due to separation and divorce will effect them whatever our approach may be. However, the only humane and sound resolution to their emotional dilemma is the re-enforcement and protection of their ties to both psychological parents. This is especially true in cases where both parents have established powerful bonds with the child.

Nonetheless, the sad fact is that courts are not acting in the best interests of children in opting for sole maternal custody. By the time father goes to court or even reads this book for that matter, it is too late. The court has pre-judged the issues and decided against him in favor of mother. Ironically, it was a feminist-anthropologist, Margaret Mead, who warned:

"We have permitted the courts to sever the relationship between the child and his or her biological father. This is something that no court should have an opportunity to do."

In rebutting the radical feminists who would seek return to Neolithic period matriarchy, implicitly criticizing the followers of Bowlby and Goldstein et al. and in observing the consequences, she added:

"We have given the kind of preference to the mother-child tie that belonged about a half million years ago, and as a result, we are eroding paternal responsibility at an appalling rate in this country..."

Finally commenting from the humanist position on the rights of children and fathers:

"...The courts, by refusing to recognize the rights of fathers and children, were practicing reverse sexism that was insulting to real women."

Each man, in my experience, walks naively into the courtroom somehow believing that despite the fact his spouse wishes to get divorced, he will get justice. He believes that no court would strip him of his children. He has never harmed them. His relatives and friends will testify to his parenting ability, love and affection for his kids, his capacity to provide a livelihood for them. He does not associate his case with all other cases. So that even where he has some passing knowledge of the courts acting to delimit male rights, he does not imagine that that will happen to him and his children. He is quite alone. He is without any emotional, financial or professional support other than his lawyer, a man who already knows the probable outcome given the limitations of the system.

The statistics state the obvious. Women have sole custody of the children in over 92% of all cases, receiving generous financial benefits in maintenance and child support from middle-class men. Fathers might have some limited access to their offspring and within 18 months after divorce, fewer than 50% of fathers will have any contact with the children. Courts will not act to enforce visitation rights Children will show signs of short, medium and long term dysfunction. Welfare rolls and social services will reflect increased burdens from among divorced female poor[33]. Fathers will exhibit pathologies related to their emotional loss. Productivity at work will decrease among men. Women will take up new male consort relationships that end in further disruption to the children.

Men that I have interviewed, in line with most research findings, have almost universally requested either joint custody or very generous visitation to their children. The lion share of them believe that shared parenting is the solution best meeting the needs of their children and reflects their own sense of love and commitment. Women almost universally project a desire to have sole custody, care and control over their children and as the statistics suggest get what they want.

Although legislators have recently come to employ **gender-neutral language** in statutory language seeking to create the impression that men and women are equal in custody disputes, in practice (as a long line of case law in several jurisdictions demonstrate) this merely camouflages radical feminist driven court policies. These policies prejudice the rights and interests of fathers and children. In short, the concept of shared-residence or joint physical and legal custody faces denial and rejection through covert court policies. The court will not act to impose these decisions over mother's determined opposition.

Contrary to the oft-heard arguments of sole custody proponents that sole maternal custody decisions eliminate stress, disruption and strife, the opposite is the case and conflict is more often continuous. While the Ilfeld study (1982): "Does Joint Custody Work? A First Look at Outcome Data on Re-litigation" on the incidence of re-litigation in

---

[33] See Chapter 11, Rein Briefing Paper to Chief Sec. of The British Treasury, M. Portillo

cases where joint custody was judicially mandated, often in the face of opposition by the mother, showed litigation significantly reduced by that process.

Even feminists like Bartlett and Stack, favor imposition of joint custody when "both parents do not at the outset agree to such an arrangement" and support additional research and experimentation to promote increased use of joint custody in relatively difficult cases.

As evidence of the successful use of joint custody in acrimonious divorces, the authors cite McKinnon, R., and Wallerstein, J. "Joint custody and the preschool child". "Behavioral Sciences and the Law" (1986), 4:169-83; Greif, J.B. "Fathers, Children and Joint custody", American Journal of Orthopsychiatry (1979) 49:311,318; Roman, M., and Haddad, W. "The Disposable Parent: The Case for Joint Custody", New York: Holt, Rinehart and Winston, 1978; Wolley, P, "Shared custody", Family Advocate (Summer 1978) 1:6,7,33; and note no. 64, Wallerstein and Kelly, pp. 130-31, 218.

However, the observable and quantifiable reality of family law both here and abroad is that there is not nor will there be justice for children and their male parents. Dr. Robert Fay M.D., F.A.A.P., a practicing Pediatrician and Forensic Consultant on Child Abuse Issues has gone so far as to call for an end to visitation if courts cannot meet the needs of children by making joint custody a preference:

"I urge that the term visitation be tossed into the dustbin of American (and European) sociological history like " a woman's place is in the home" and "spare the rod and spoil the child".

Our children (and their parents) deserve no less than co-equal parental rights and responsibilities which means JOINT CUSTODY in the vast majority of cases." He continues:

"...because "visitation" when "awarded", IS THE END OF PARENTING. Visitation in an old and dusty edition of Webster's Dictionary, which, I have at home, is defined as, "an exchange of civilities and salutations". Can anything be more repugnant and non-parental than that? This cruelly but accurately defines the brief and superficial encounters experienced by so many divorced parents and children today."

Taking up Dr, Fay's theme of "an end to visitation", viewed from the legal rather than humanitarian perspective, one could easily argue that there should be an end to the process described as visitation or access. Perhaps, men would then finally get galvanized into action, having to acknowledge the fact that they have become a minority classification worthy of society's protections. A kind of sub-species used for their semen and checkbooks to subsidize rampaging females hell bent on the destruction of their human and civil rights and those of their children.

If the process is not just, then why should men continue to participate in it?

Imagine a circumstance in which a thief invades your home, steals your valuables and then turns to shoot you in the head, pausing only to ask that you write him a check. Do you think it likely? Would you comply? This is precisely the situation that fathers are in when they enter family court, acquiescing to a kangaroo legal process that has pre-determined the issues and will reduce them to childless servitude for life. Richard Gardner, Clinical Professor of Child Psychiatry, Columbia, wrote in 1985 (The Parents Book About Divorce) that:

"The only way a father could gain custody in contested cases was to prove that the mother was significantly unfit to care for the children. So partial have courts been to mothers, and so committed have they been to the notion that mothers make better parents than fathers that **only the grossest negligence on the mother's part would result in her being deprived of the children.** Only when the mother could be proven to be a chronic alcoholic, severe drug addict, prostitute, or extremely abusive or neglectful of the children could father even hope to gain custody."

Nothing has changed in the past fifteen years.

While Dr. Fay is correct in stating that visitation itself is an expression of non-parenting, my objections to it go beyond his assessment. The very moment when a court acts to vest either interim or permanent custody in one parent (mother), it divests the other parent from important legal and natural rights. Let us examine but one case I handled to see the impact of an interim decision of a New York State Court on the eventual outcome of the dispute.

Custody Case of JI and abuse of the court's discretion

JI was an Israeli research scientist married to a German woman doctor with whom he had two young children. After the marriage ran into difficulties the couple engaged lawyers and went to court in New York over the children. Mother sought sole custody. Father sought joint custody. The father feared that mother would remove the children to Florida or Germany. The court made an interim order that neither party could remove the children from the jurisdiction of the court pending a final disposition of the custody dispute. Mother immediately acted unilaterally to remove the children to the state of Florida in defiance of the court order. Father's attorney sought an order holding in her in contempt of court and a further order to have the children returned into the jurisdiction.

In part, the case had become a parental abduction case, although, this aspect was missed by the father's attorney. The judge, in line with numerous other gross violations of paternal rights perpetrated by family courts, failed to make an order for the immediate return of the children. I can assure the reader that if the positions reversed, the court would have acted swiftly to restore the rights of mother and children. The judge merely ordered that mother produce the children in time for the next scheduled hearing in the matter and gave father a visitation with the children in Florida. Not surprisingly, mother made that access impossible and father returned to New York without seeing his children. Aside from the monstrous travel costs imposed on the man, he lost time from work and suffered serious trauma from the experience. He felt that his children were becoming dysfunctional due to their perception that father was abandoning them. There were also other problems related to the usual blocked phone calls to the children.

In the meantime, another division of the court had no difficulty at all in assigning a hefty interim child support bill to the father, although his income certainly (on it's face) did not justify the amount and while he had his children removed from the jurisdiction in defiance of an order of the court. Naturally, the judge hearing the child support matter simply "imputed" the income and refused to consider the abduction matter. One might very well inquire as to where the justice in this matter resided or if it existed at all.

When the father contacted me, I made a number of suggestions some of which he initially followed. I appeared for him and provided him with a legal brief on more significant aspects of the case as it stood. Fearing to act pro se, he ultimately returned to the care of his attorney and I lost track of the case. The reason I cite this particular case is that it illustrates the nature of several problems encountered by fathers in family courts. First, the court allowed an upset of the "status quo" taking no action against mother's abduction of the children. Second, it took no appropriate action to redress the balance. Third, it gave mother a rather powerful tactical advantage in obtaining the sole custody award she sought. Her untoward actions so hostile to the children's interests severed ongoing contact between father and children. The court permitted her to establish a new domicile over 1,300 miles away from the family home, while acquiring child support. Fourth, it set the stage for the inevitable sole maternal custody decision followed by the "relocation" of the children to Florida or Germany.

Guided by peer pressure from radical feminists, lawyers and the courts, women who might be motivated by feelings of hatred, greed and vengeance, often act to destroy the theoretical legal and natural rights of their former spouses and their offspring. It is rather sad and frightening for the children.

Unprincipled Reliance on Discredited Theories in the Psychiatric Literature

Disingenuous expert testimony often underpins what Dr. Gardner accurately reported as being the norm in custody proceedings. Expert Evidence from psychiatrists, psychologists, social workers and guardian ad litems often relies entirely on the disproved theories of Bowlby, Freud, Solnit and Goldstein. Their approach calls for sole maternal custody and by inference, the elimination of father as a significant parenting figure to the children. Dr. Jacobs calls this quasi-legal quasi-psychological process as being the "parentectomy"[34] of father, or the cutting away of his close and meaningful ties to his

---

[34] The phrase first coined by psychiatrist Dr. Frank Williams

children (Jacobs 1986). Although the professionals are well aware of the research studies and clinical observations endorsing joint custody as being the **least detrimental alternative**, (having access to the overwhelming evidence that female single-parenting often leads to a number of pathologies and dysfunction in children) they continue to drive present sole custody decision policies.

Here we must question the use of these mother-preference ideological concepts. We can measure them against what we know to be the truth about children, how they develop, what they require in nurturance, what the effects are on them of arbitrary deprivation of parental interactions. Then, we can ask, **why** have experts deliberately ignored or distorted important literature on the child? Is it deliberate? What evidence supports the argument that there has often been abuse of the literature? How important is the psychiatric literature within the context of divorce and custody?

The literature represents a powerful underpinning factor in the process enabling the court to rationalize its decision making while giving the appearance of due process and judicial disinterest. Bearing in mind that all the court must do is to state its intention to follow an un-objectified 'Best Interests of the Child' standard. It then takes subjectively tested evidence from the parties to the conflict and hears the opinions of so-called experts. If the expert evidence is slanted or skewered in favor of mothers, the court now has the ammunition to grant sole custody to her. Even if critics accuse the court of gender bias in the matter of parental testimony, the charge lacks substantiality because the court emphasizes its reliance on the broad psychiatric or psychological evidence to survive such criticism.

The answer to the question of ignoring or misrepresenting the literature is in the affirmative.

Once, in England, I sought out (on behalf of father) an independent psychiatrist to give forensic evidence in a case. The one pre-requisite that I had was to find an expert who at least in principle supported joint custody, known in England as 'shared residence'. To my dismay, I discovered only three psychiatrists who fit that description. And after numerous discussions with them I also discovered that they were unprepared to come to court giving evidence that in any way sounded of shared parenting in principle or in the particular case. When I questioned them, they admitted that the courts had covert policies rejecting these ideas however sound they may be. They believed that a psychiatrist giving this kind of evidence would have his or her practice seriously affected while the court imputed his professional worth.

I had a working familiarity with the British Family Court System and knew virtually all of the psychiatrists who most often gave expert evidence. I learned that they uniformly gave evidence based on the outdated maternal attachment theories of Bowlby. I knew they also relied on Goldstein, Freud and Solnit whose similar views laid particular emphasis on regularity, routine and order to the detriment of the child's psychological need for the male parent. I knew that fathers were completely unaware that these experts had a covert preference for sole maternal custody. I carefully observed their slanted parent-child interview process and reporting in order to arrive at obviously pre-judged conclusions.

When the feminist Dr. Dora Black entered the courtroom, she met with reverential respect by judges such as the ultra conservative Mr. Justice Ewbank. While his attitude would shift to disdain when confronted with a rather weak supporter of joint custody such as Dr. Bentovim (making an infrequent appearance before the court against his better judgment). The scenario is similar in the United States. Fathers are faced by these hostile psychiatrists, social workers and guardian ad litems all giving similar evidence. Most will be operating covertly to support the maternal preference standard carrying the latest edition of "Best Interests of the Child" in their attaché cases. While the literature that supports joint custody, is either denied elucidation or thrust aside by the court.

One of the common tricks often played on fathers is the court's insistence that the 'best interests' of the child face examination by a 'mutually agreeable' or court appointed psychiatrist.[35] The court posture is that this ensures 'independent' assessment. In reality, once father accepts this proposition he leaves the door open for abuse of his child's rights. The court appointed 'mutually' assigned expert is wholly dependent on the court and the father for rather generous

---

[35] See Chapter 8, Expert Evidence and Analysis of False Expert Reports

economic remuneration. Equally, that expert is wholly dependent on court and mother for obtaining future assignments and a great deal more money. There is a paper mache appearance of neutrality making attack on the court even more difficult.

Moreover, various courts in numerous jurisdictions have now required the child either to have his or her own attorney and/or a guardian-ad litem to theoretically protect their rights and best interests. These professionals, while purportedly representing only the best interests of the child, often advocate covertly for mother. They distort the literature, misreport and become a lightning rod reinforcing unjust judicial decisions. I illustrated the all too often illusory notion of impartiality when guardian ad litems appear. *See David B v. Helen O., See the Case of Stephen S*

As to the evidence on the impact of self-serving and distorted use of the literature, omitting key research and studies, one might find it in the expert reports and in written court opinions. Further, we see it in the factual results in custody cases in which women gain sole custody in over 92% of all cases, joint custody is granted in only 4% of them and father gets custody in the remainder. Normally father gets custody only if mother is either hospitalized or dead.

American Orders of Protection & British Ouster Orders Based on False Allegations of Sexual Abuse or Domestic Violence

One of the most notorious techniques for placing male parents in untenable and inferior legal positions is the unprincipled use of 'orders of protection' in America or 'ouster orders' in England. Courts make these orders on allegations of either sexual abuse of the child or domestic violence of the wife, sometimes both. Due to the serious nature of these allegations, they frighten even a moderately disinterested judge into taking immediate remedial action. That action often undertaken on the inherent powers of the court occurs without even the most rudimentary hearing. Such a draconian order serves to cut off the father (a) from his home and (b) from his children. Feminist propaganda and misinformation has entire populations believing that male sexual child abuse and domestic violence is a commonplace occurrence, but numerous studies have shown this not to be the case. Professor Amneus reports:

"In September, 1989 a social service officer in Milwaukee County, by name Terrence Cooley, wrote an inter-office communication titled "AFDC/Child Abuse Information," a copy of which found its way into the editorial office of "The Family in America", pointing out that of the 1,050 cases of child abuse and neglect in that county an astonishing 83 percent occurred in households receiving Aid to Families with Dependent Children (read: female-headed households)."

For every reported case of alleged abuse or domestic violence within the context of divorce/custody, there are nine shown to be nothing more than false on their face, as a key study at Peterborough Hospital in England (1993) had shown. An article by Daniel Goldman, "Studies Reveal Suggestibility of Very Young Children as Witnesses" concluded:

"Over the past decade such testimony has led to convictions in many child abuse cases and the younger the child, the less likely psychologists have thought it was that information could have been fabricated. But, now a series of recent studies has turned this conventional wisdom on its head. Researchers have found new evidence that persistent questioning can lead young children to describe elaborate accounts of events that never occurred, even when at first they denied them."

Sex and other child-abuse allegations made primarily by women within the framework of custody cases are exacerbated by both improper scientific bias of experts acting for mother and the persistent pressurizing influence of mother on the child to convince him or her that they have been abused. Dr. Maggie Bruck, a Psychologist at McGill University reports: "Many people who specialize in these cases have a pre-conceived notion of what happened (read: going solely by mother's accounts, claims and allegations), and in the course of questioning suggest it to the child, who then report it as though it was true."

Attacking the use of Dolls as a technique, Dr. Stephen Ceci, a psychologist at Cornell University stated, "The experts are correct about whether or not the child's account is accurate about one-third of the time. That's worse than chance."

Author and forensic consultant Dean Tong exposed the nature of false allegations best in "Don't Blame Me, Daddy, False Allegations of Child Sexual Abuse: A Hidden National Tragedy", commenting:

"A false allegation of child sexual abuse places a child in an intolerable situation: They don't want to hurt Daddy; they don't want to lie; they don't want to disappoint Mommy or make her angry. Placing a child in this position is itself a serious form of child abuse.

Children are easily coached and easily manipulated, especially when they are emotionally and physically dependent upon the accusing parent for all their needs. During the course of an investigation of child sexual abuse, the child is expected to go through the same questions and exercises, time after time, to satisfy everyone's requirements for testimony. By the time the child has been exposed to the same round of questions and the same round of coaching over a period of weeks, it is not difficult to convince the child that the incident actually occurred."

While, ardent radical feminists spread misinformation about male incidence of child sex abuse, the truth is that the vast majority of abuse is by mothers and or other female figures. Numerous studies support this fact. So that not only are the lion-share of allegations made during the course of custody proceedings patently false, outside of these actions the figures argue that it is women who are far more abusive than men. As is shown by Female Abusers: What Children and Young People Have Told ChildLine. Harrison, H. Chapter in Book pp. 89-92 Copyright 1994 Elliott, M. (Editor): "Female Sexual Abuse of Children":

"This chapter reviews the statistics and provides examples of situations reported by callers to the ChildLine helpline. Nine percent (780) of calls to the helpline from April 1, 1990-March 1991 reported sexual abuse by females. In 34 percent of the cases, the perpetrator was the child's mother. Twenty-two percent of the abusers were another female relative or acquaintance. Abuse by sisters, aunts, stepmothers, and both parents together were also reported."

Another report; "Child Abuse and Neglect in a Developing Country." Farinatti, F. A. S.; Fonseca, N. M.; Dondonis, M.; Brugger, E.(1990) from Santo Antonio Hospital in Brazil on 63 abused and neglected children, ages 23 days to 11 years, who were treated by the hospital's Committee of Children's Rights, a multidisciplinary team dedicated to child protection while maintaining family unity. Approximately 60 percent of these children were female. Almost 70 percent of them suffered physical abused, 21.5 percent suffered neglect and 8.9 percent victimized by sexual abuse. Most of the children's caregivers were in their 20s(female single parents), illiterate or with little education, unemployed or with minimum-wage jobs, had previous marriages or partners, and had a history of drug and alcohol abuse. **Mothers were most often the abusers.**

The sad fact in custody situations is that a number of unscrupulous women and their lawyers have employed this type of complaint as a tactical means to get father out of the house and away from his children **prior** to a custody case even being heard. There are a number of consequences related to 'allegation' based strategies. First, the psychological warfare wears down the father convincing him to cease further efforts to maintain his filiation. This removes him from the family home creating a 'de facto' legal status in which mother establishes the family home as the residence of her and the children. Cut off from the home, father is no longer a parent to the children and his 'absence' used against him in expert testimony. It becomes a more or less self-fulfilling prophesy of his emotional detachment from the children. Suddenly, various pathologies and disturbances observed (by mother of course) in the children relate to mother's allegations about his limited visitation rights. Further, he might face allegations of sexual abuse. According to psychiatrist John W. Jacobs ("Wednesday's Children" TV Program, Rein MNN Cable (1997):

"The use of false allegations of child abuse made by mothers in conflictual custody proceedings do such enormous psychological damage to the children that there ought to be a penalty imposed on them for having made them."

Now what exactly are these orders of protection or ouster orders? Simply stated they are injunctions, orders of the court forbidding a person of a particular type of behavior and having the net effect of depriving them of normal family rights. An 'ouster order' is exactly what the title suggests, an order ousting or removing the father from the family home, to which the court might add further directions that he cannot have contact with his wife or children **pending** a further order of the court. While 'orders of protection' have precisely the same effect as their British counterparts assuming the wife and or the children need protection from the father. The court will normally order the father from the family home, enjoin him from coming closer than X distance to it and his wife pending a further order of the court in the central custody and divorce proceedings.

I have investigated numerous cases of allegation driven orders of these types. I interviewed, observed and followed the cases in which the allegations were without foundation. These allegations turned out to be nothing more than a shameful and repugnant tactic employed by wives. Courts, in the cases that I had followed, did not penalize or criticize the mother or even consider her false allegations in making their custody determinations.

Use of Sexual Harassment Laws as a Means to End Contact

There are cases in which however hard mother has tried to dispose of father as a parent, the male parent refuses to concede and accept the loss of his relationship to his children. In one recent case in England, mother accessed the courts outside of family law in order to cut off the child from her father. She used a law, created by radical feminist pressure, focused on "stalking" by men against females. This Act is an extension of similar style legislation addressing so-called "sexual harassment" within The American Civil Rights Act. This law, "The British Sexual Harassment Act of 1995", was used by a mother in the following case:

Case of sexual harassment law use to sever contact

An American father had his child abducted by the mother and taken to England. He fought through the courts to obtain the child's return. He lost the case based on prejudice and circumvention of international law.

Subsequently, he had recovered his child by an extra-legal action but once again had the child taken back to England, where she remained a ward of the British Family Court in the care and control of the mother. The child had for some time demanded contact with her father, and so, she had written to him initiating the contact on her own and eventually the father tried establishing a means to deliver presents to his child through the intercession of a neutral third party.

The mother kept objecting to this most minimal and desperate conduct, finally obtaining legal aid to bring a civil suit against the third party intervenor for "harassment" under the provisions of the Act, which was intended by Parliament to deal with 'stalkers' and not issues generally heard in the family court. The man acting as an agent for the child and father was submitted to the embarrassment of legal proceedings and when he demanded that the child be heard as a witness, the court declined to allow it unless sanctioned by the family court. Naturally, removed of his witness he lacked the means to a defense. The court should have dismissed the case. Instead it made interim orders forcing the man into the position of agreeing to cease delivery of further presents to the child having him give 'an undertaking'[36] not to do so until such time as the case was resolved. The case could not resolve because the defense could not call its witness.

The court denied legal aid to the man just as quickly as it had granted legal aid to the mother and therefore being of limited means he could not properly conduct his defense. The mother, her lawyers and the court knew that he was disabled and simply got the court to suspend the matter indefinitely, while it made a 'finding of costs'[37] against him in advance of a final trial and decision of the case. This preposterous misfeasance of law resulted in the loss of what was the last line of contact between the child and her father.

---

[36] A guarantee or promise to the Court (British law)

[37] Costs are normally assigned or taxed at the end of the case, on the losing party to an action. It is unheard of to assign costs prior to a case being heard.

This use of a civil statute outside of the family court marked a significant departure and further debasement of the rights of children and parents to maintain contact. It even attacked those well-intended persons who would dare to bring humanitarian assistance to them, while setting new scales of criminal penalties including jail sentences and fines.

There are, believe it or not, feminists who disagree with these tactics and who have challenged the militant matriarchal radical feminists use of unconfirmed, untruthful, and seriously misleading presentation of statistics to support their thesis of the predominance of male perpetration of sex crimes, child abuse, domestic violence. In an article for The Women's Quarterly, IWF wrote an expose of the facts:

"Factoids and Facts 07-Aug-96 DOMESTIC VIOLENCE COVER-UP?"

There are factoids, and there are facts, about domestic violence in America.

FACTOID: According to the FBI, a woman is beaten every [fill in the blank] seconds.
FACTS: First, the FBI does not calculate, tabulate, or track data on domestic violence.

FACTOID: There are four million women beaten and abused each year.
FACTS: Same problems as above.

The Straus, Gelles, and Steinmetz survey estimated that: "2 million women were abused each year by their husbands". Straus and his colleagues speculated that if all the respondents told the truth and if ex-husbands and boyfriends were included, the number could be as high as 4 million. However, no study to date using a representative sample and measuring severe violence has found more than 2 million abused women each year.

FACTOID: Domestic violence is the leading cause of injury to women between the ages of 15 and 44 in the United States,-more than car accidents, muggings, and rapes combined.
FACTS: This factoid has been attributed to both Surgeon General Antonia Novello and the Centers for Disease Control. The actual

primary source of this "fact" is research by Evan Stark and Ann Flitcraft. It was probably Stark and Flitcraft who supplied the fact to CDC, which then included it in material supplied to the Surgeon General. Unfortunately, as good a sound bite as this is, it is simply not true. The original source of this statement goes back to two papers by Stark and Flitcraft. First, the actual research the "fact" is based on is a rather small survey of one emergency room. Second, in the original articles, they said that domestic violence *may* (emphasis added) be a more common cause of emergency room visits than car accidents, muggings, and rapes combined. Linda Saltzman from the Centers for Disease Control tells all journalists who call to check this fact that the CDC does not recognize this as either their fact or a reputable fact.

FACTOID: The March of Dimes reports that battering during pregnancy is the leading cause of birth defects and infant mortality. FACTS: The March of Dimes actually reports that they know of no such study.

FACTOID: Sixty-three percent of young men between the ages of 11 and 20 who are serving time for homicide have killed their mother's abuser.
FACTS: Sarah Buel often uses this factoid in her speeches. It appears to be yet another fact from nowhere. The FBI has published no data that support this claim. The FBI's Uniform Crime Reports has no tables that report on prison populations, let alone a table or figure that breaks down prison populations by age of offender and relationship to victim. There are no Department of Justice reports that report on what number or percentage of young men kill their mother's batterer.

FACTOID: Family violence has killed more women in the last five years than the total number of Americans who were killed in the Vietnam War
FACTS: This factoid was often used by Dr. Robert McAfee, past president of the American Medical Association. There were about 55,000 American casualties in the Vietnam War. According to the FBI, Uniform Crime Statistics, about 1,500 women are killed by their husbands or boyfriends each year. The total number of women homicide victims each year is about 5,000. Thus, in 5 years, even if every woman who was killed was killed by a family member, the total

would still be one-half the number of American casualties in Vietnam.

FACTOID: Women who leave their batterers are at a 75% greater risk of being killed by the batterer than those who stay. FACTS: Women are more likely to be victims of homicide when they are estranged from their husbands than when they live with their husbands-but not a 75% greater risk. The risk of homicide is higher in the first two months after separation. SOURCE: Wilson, Margo and Martin Daly (1993). "Spousal homicide risk and estrangement." Violence and Victims, 8, 3-16."

FACTOID: Women who kill their batterers receive longer prison sentences than men who kill their partners.
FACTS: This factoid is often attributed to someone from Pace University. There is no actual published source for this. According to the Bureau of Justice Statistics, "Violence between Intimates" (November 1994), **the average prison sentence for men who killed their wives is 17.5 years; the average sentence for women convicted of killing their husbands was 6.2 years.**

OTHER FACTOIDS FROM NOWHERE

"4,000 women each year are killed by their husbands, ex-husbands, or boyfriends."
FACTS: "The FBI reports that approximately 1,500 women are killed each year by husbands or boyfriends". Even if one factors in the number of women killed by unidentified or undetermined assailants, the number could not be 4,000.

Women of all cultures, races, occupations, income levels, and ages are battered-by husbands, boyfriends, lovers and partners. FACTS: While this fact is technically true, it is also true that domestic violence is more likely to occur in homes below the poverty line, in minority households (even controlling for income), and among men and women 18 to 30 years of age. Nationally, 50 percent of all homeless women and children are on the streets because of violence in the home.

FACTS: An interesting factoid stated by Senator Biden, but one without any actual published scientific research to support it.

There are nearly three times as many animal shelters in the United States as there are shelters for battered women and their children. FACTS: Another great sound bite, but not one actually based on a verified count of either type of shelter.

Attribution: Richard J. Gelles, PhD., Director Family Violence Research Program; University of Rhode Island.

As we see from the examples given above, radical feminist organizations such as NOW seek to insidiously invade the collective consciousness producing fear in the minds of legislators, judges and mothers. This promotes secret agendas for the revision of social order in favor of the installation of a matriarchal system derisive of children and dismissive of men. Amneus provided ample demonstration of their intent in "The Garbage Generation" citing feminist sources, rhetoric and policy statements. I have attempted to show what means and in what manner those tactics are used to effect change in social policy and the style of divorce that causes so much distress and trauma on our children.

It is also significant, that radical feminists never refer to the huge amount of domestic violence perpetrated against men by women. An example of which is revealed by an article in "The New York Times" on November 23, 1999 by it's Boston Bureau Chief Ms. Carey Goldberg, "Spouse Abuse Crackdown, Surprisingly, Nets Many Women" that:

"The National Violence Against Women survey found the gender gap was less pronounced then previously thought: it estimated last year that 1.5 million women and 835,000 men annually were raped or assaulted by an intimate partner, a ratio of just under two to one." She also reported that:

"The issue of women's arrests sometimes takes on a gender-wars edge. Some women's advocates see a backlash among predominantly male police officers. Some men's advocates see a silent epidemic of domestic abuse of men by women, and call the arrest numbers further proof. But, virtually no one claims to fully understand the phenomenon, which mystifies because it so diverges from the widely accepted estimate that 95 percent of batterers are men. Officials say efforts are under way both to study the phenomenon."

Alas, this comes as no surprise to those of us following these trends over a number of years. Does, a "Violence against Men Act" exist? No! Is 1.6 billion dollars allocated to dealing with abuse by women of men? No! Are women, scapegoated by men? No! When it comes to divorce and custody issues, how do public perceptions of males as sole batterers effect decisions taken in family courts?

Re-location Cases as Legalized Abductions

Now let us turn to cases that arise in the aftermath of custody decisions granting mother sole custody and father only a limited form of access with reduced rights. Mother at some point in time, unilaterally decides to re-locate to a geographical area no longer in the proximity of the original family environment. These are re-location cases and, before 1995, most courts in America frowned on mothers disappearing with their children. They seemed to understand that re-location would have made a legal fiction of the father's theoretical rights to visitation which the court had been in the habit of stating as being in 'the best interests of the child'.

In England, the re-location position had been similar to that of most US states. However, that position was reversed as early as 1993 in a case involving a mother allowed to re-locate from London to Australia, with her new boyfriend and two children, while the psychiatric report (which I reviewed) indicated that the two young children loved and needed their natural father. As I had reviewed this psychiatric report, I was astonished, having read through all the paragraphs of evidence arguing for a denial of mother's right to disappear, to read the conclusion in which the psychiatrist (against his own evidence) then recommended that mother be permitted to leave the jurisdiction with the children. The father in this case too had no legal aid while the mother did. I remember sitting in an austere court corridor of the English High Courts of Justice with him, his eyes reddened with tears, his body slumped in a position of utter defeat. He forlornly asked for my advice while he awaited the summary execution coming within minutes. Even as I recommended he appeal, I could see he had given up. He had already said goodbye to his children.

The American case which overturned the previous, steadfast court policy to at least maintain the fiction of visitation rights to men, was a case called Tropea v. Tropea (NYS Ct. Appeals 1996) in which a mother was allowed to re-locate, making father's ability and the child's rights to have ongoing contact, a practical impossibility. Since Tropea, other courts in America have followed this shocking policy reversal. Further, Tropea reduces the already tainted concept of visitation for parents (men) to a complete and utter nonsense, signaling the lack of concern for the best interests of the child that only the most hypocritical of us could deny.

The case of Irene Ireland v. James F. Ireland, (SC 15769) S.Ct. Conn (1998), relying in part on Tropea illustrates the false reasoning of courts under the influence of radical feminist pressurization. Not only do they deny the natural and civil rights of children and fathers, they actually impudently re-formulate social policy on what constitutes a family. Decisions such as Tropea and Ireland are aiding in the creation of de facto post divorce female headed single-parent units, reinforcing the goals of matriarchy in it's worst and most terrifying aspect. The Court in Ireland stated rather astonishingly:

"Historically, most states have discouraged the relocation of a custodial parent with minor children, in part, to protect and preserve the children's relationship with the non-custodial parent, under the assumption that it is in a child's best interests to live near both biological parents. **A growing number of states now presume, however, that the custodial parent's good faith decision[38] to relocate is in the best interests of the child[39].**"

How can that be possible given all the psychiatric, psychological, social and anthropological research over the past 20 years that argues so conclusively that the best interests of the child can only be maintained by continued, meaningful and ongoing contact between

---

[38] This is a prejudicial 'subjective evidence' test based on maternal preference.

[39] This signals the overturning of the understanding of the best interest standard.

children and both parents after divorce. The court completely contradicts that research, its own guidelines and public policy by maintaining that a child's best interests as upheld by a removal from one of its two psychological parents. It is complete illogical nonsense!

The thinking and language in the seminal case, <u>Tropea v. Tropea, 87 N.Y.2d 727, 736-41, 665 N.E.2d 145, 642 N.Y.S.2d 575 (1996)</u> (overruling previous three-tiered analysis requiring custodial parent to show "exceptional circumstances" to overcome presumption against removal of children) is far worse and more damaging to children as the next paragraph of the opinion declares:

"It may not be realistic to try to preserve completely the quality and nature of the relationship that the non-custodial parent enjoyed with the child, especially if such preservation is maintained at the cost of the custodial parent's ability to start a new, potentially improved life for herself or himself and the child. Consequently, **many states now recognize that marriage dissolution results in the creation of a new family unit, consisting of the custodial parent and the child**, and that what is beneficial to that unit as a whole benefits its individual members.[40]"

The Judge Green Australian Relocation Cases Paper

Having given examples of cases drawn from American and British experience, I'll give one last one taken from a paper delivered at the <u>New Zealand Law Society Family Law Conference</u> by (Ms.) Judge D.F. Green, "Custody and Access Disputes-Parents at a distance: Intractable Access 1995", in which as reported by Stuart Miller, she argues that:

"The priority in the rulings quoted is the well-being of the mother (the custodial parent in all the cases). In some, but not all, of the cases, it is argued that this coincides with the well-being of the child (children), even though contact and relationships with the father are adversely affected."

---

[40] The Court Opines in favor of recognition and sanction of the matriarchal ideal.

(Judge Green quoting His Honour Judge Boshier, also p.137 of his opinion) " ... where there is genuine reason to wish to move ... the mother's enhancement as a primary care-giver is more important than the father's wish to have ready contact".

She concludes the section with:

"A relatively liberal approach emerges from the cases examined in this paper. A parent wishing to prevent departure is likely to have to prove a significant and positive relationship with both the child and perhaps a custodial parent in order to prevent departure." (p.138)

Case 1

Judge Green goes on to describe a 1993 case of clear parental alienation by the mother where the mother wished to take the children out of the country and the father wanted custody. The court granted custody to the mother because, among other things, the children would feel punished if made to see their father and the girls were approaching puberty and therefore needed their mother. The judge in that case said:

"The girls, ... are approaching puberty, one of the most dramatic and important changes in their growth and development. I believe in the guiding through period of life the mother, to whom the girls are close, is essential. I do not make the slightest criticism of the father's wife and I am in no doubt, that she could handle the situation adequately but she is not and never will be, the mother. Just as the mother's husband, the step-father, is not, and never will be, the father." "Empirical Studies Related to Access/Visitation with Regard to the Family Dynamics of Divorce, Separation and Illegitimacy", Miller & Price, Esq. (1994)

Here, carefully consider two things. First the courts own prejudice in favor of maternal preference and second the following report made by the court appointed psychologist. Bear in mind the warnings I have given about the deliberate use of outmoded theory or refusal to recognize recent research in order to underpin pre-determined sole maternal custody decisions and how this now comes into play when the court considers the relocation of the children from New Zealand to Holland[41]:

"The father's case, supported by a witness, was that "if the children do not have an opportunity for a good relationship with both parents this can give rise to psychological problems" was rejected. The sort of problems mentioned were, depression, lack of trust, ability to form and hold a relationship, dependency and divorce. The case was rejected due to the Court appointed psychologist's assertion that:

"While [he] agrees ... in principle he said that over the last nine to twelve months he has come across evidence which questions the theory and suggests the basis and research is not accurate enough to make general statements". The child's mother wished to relocate to Holland (language and other difficulties for the children at that age?), and the judge found that the **father's attempts to enforce his guardianship and access rights "had contributed to the alienation [of the children],** because he was seen by the children as thereby controlling the 'new' family".

One can only describe this psychologist's work as highly disingenuous. His work represents unprincipled and negligent reporting and his presentation of expert evidence was falsification of theory and fact. It is nothing more than a sophisticated fraud. The mere suggestion that a natural and psychological parent "alienates his children" by attempting to continue to have a relationship with them goes beyond Kafkaesque bounds of absurdity. It would be difficult to imagine that the expert was unaware of long established theory based on numerous studies and observations of children leading to Gardner's "Parental Alienation Syndrome". Wives fighting against the granting of access to fathers and children fit Gardner's description as the culprits and agent provocateurs of this particular syndrome. The psychologist should face disbarment for even suggesting that father was alienating his children by trying to see them!

He even played fast and loose with the expert evidence submitted on behalf of father pointing out the serious consequences befalling

---

[41] See Chapter 8, Expert Witnesses, Analysis of the False Expert Report of Dr. Black by Dr. Jacobs, Dr. Saffer-Cohen and Dr. Ryder

children when deprived of meaningful ongoing contact to the non-custodial parent, claiming that:

"Over the last nine to twelve months he has come across evidence which questions the theory and suggests the basis and research is not accurate enough to make general statements"

While he produced no such evidence nor adduced any that would support his negative conclusory allegation that the theory (attachment to both parents-damage to children of absence) was not accurate or generally accepted.

Is it any wonder that as Amneus reports: Feminist Hazel Henderson writes a piece titled "Thinking Globally, Acting Locally," in which she complains of "fathers who refuse to pay their child support payments ordered by courts."

Is that so surprising when courts act arbitrarily to implement unauthorized social policies, benefiting not children but self-interested parties, in effect legislating? When courts turn their own avowed best interest guideline for child custody on its head acting to deprive men and children of constitutional rights under 'color of law'. The consequences of parental rights deprivations are that many men refuse to pay child support. As the statistics prove, men who have either joint custody or proper rights of visitation almost universally pay their child support. Compare that to the statistics that deal with the correlation between absence of access and or rights and delinquency on payments! *See Appendix A.*

Why would anyone expect a father to be financially "responsible" if he has his children stolen by his former wife, is left alone without his children, betrayed and no longer parent, father or even a whole person.

I have come to term these re-location cases as nothing more than **Legalized Abductions** (Rein, New York State Senate Hearing (1996. They are only distinguished from cases where mothers have simply absconded with the children, either during the marriage or, post-custody decision, by the court's endorsement of the abduction giving it the appearance of a lawful act.

What we learn from the newly developing line of re-location cases is that they accord with social, political and economic pressures as well as destructive social trends. We know that they rely on undisclosed court policies and false psychiatric evidence. We know that the evidence is mounting that Amneus' claims that these developments are a direct artifact of the persistent and effective espousal of matriarchal, anti-male radical feminist demands is a factual and compelling reality. We also learn that clichéd rhetoric about focusing on the best interests of our children is deceitful contradiction and nothing more.

Rights of Unmarried Fathers

If married men in practice have few rights **then un-married men have virtually none**. Their legal position falls on far shakier grounds, open to the vagaries of state-by-state statutes and common law and the national law of foreign territories. Most of the extant state statutes that deal with un-married fathers are leftovers from formation of the United States, nineteenth century practice and modest mid-twentieth century revision. There has been little or no revision of those statutes. Despite the fact that ever since the late nineteen sixties we have observed and quantified the incredible escalation in the numbers of un-married parents, the law has not developed in recognition of this rather important social phenomena, with rare and pointed exception. Of course, the exception is that women can bring paternity suits against men in order to obtain child support payments, while men often have to sue women in order to be recognized as parents to the child and obtain a measure of legal rights in regard to them.

As a general rule, un-married fathers who have not managed to acquire a legal document[42] stating in effect that they are the 'natural' biological father of the child, and who cannot establish their psychological role in it's nurturing and support, find that courts have no inclination or indeed, obligation to grant them either custody or visitation. Further, as a general proposition, children born out of wedlock are legally the children of the mother and not the father. She

---

[42] See Orders of Filiation, Parental Responsibility Orders next sub-header

is in principle the sole custodian of them. Recent Supreme Court pronouncements underscore the gender bias that drives legal conclusions. Here is the Lead opinion of Mr. Justice Stevens in Miller v. Albright No. 1997-056 (1998):

"Our conclusion that Congress may require an affirmative act by unmarried fathers and their children, but not mothers and their children, is directly supported by our decision in Lehr v. Robertson, 463 U.S. 248 (1983). That case involved a New York law that automatically provided mothers of "illegitimate" children with prior notice of an adoption proceeding and the right to veto an adoption, but **only extended those rights to unmarried fathers whose claim of paternity was supported by some formal public act, such as a court adjudication, the filing of a notice of intent to claim paternity, or written acknowledgment by the mother.** Id. at 251-252, n. 5, 266. The petitioner in Lehr, an unmarried putative father, need only have mailed a postcard to the State's "putative father registry" to enjoy the same rights as the child's undisputed mother, id., at 264, yet he argued that this gender-based requirement violated the Equal Protection Clause. We rejected that argument, and we find the comparable claim in this case, if anything, even less persuasive. **Whereas the putative father in Lehr was deprived of certain rights because he failed to take some affirmative step within about two years of the child's birth** (when the adoption proceeding took place), here, the unfavorable gender-based treatment was attributable to Mr. Miller's failure to take appropriate action within 21 years of petitioner's birth and petitioner's own failure to obtain a paternity adjudication by a "competent court" before she turned 18."

One bizarre development we have seen over the past five years has been the huge numbers of fathers having to demand recognition of their paternity and rights of access over the objections of the mother.

I discussed the position of unmarried fathers in respect to rights of custody and access in the case of Michael H, showing the courts lack of respect for the child's rights to have contact with both parents. As far as abduction cases go, the rights of an unmarried father remain threatened under international treaty law loopholes.

American Orders of Filiation and English Parental Responsibility Orders

This brings us to the means that un-married male parents must use in order to get recognition as natural fathers, possibly leading them to acquire some theoretical custodial rights, while accepting immediate and absolute financial responsibility for child support payments. In America, most states have provisions that allow for proceedings proving paternity and for acquisition of 'Orders of Filiation' to the child. In England, the same orders have a different name, 'Parental Responsibility Orders', but are for all practical purposes, the same thing.

Of course, the civil state is gratified to entertain these proceedings because they stand to profit from those men coming forward to declare parentage. This translates into state subsidies and payments to female headed single-parent families being significantly reduced, the burden on the state being replaced by the one placed on the fathers.

Child Support

Despite the fact that the issue of child support is one effecting tens of millions of men, women and children, it is one that I am normally loathe to get involved. It is anathema to me. In the past, I have turned away cases centered more on financial issues than issues of custody. I have decided to include child support issues because they have become interconnected to female custodial strategies and follow on from universal sole maternal custody orders.

We cannot deny that child support is part of the injustice suffered by millions of men who have seen their homes demolished and their children removed from their care. Child support issues serve as a means of male scapegoating. That child support is a red-herring issue used to deflect our attention away from primary concerns is another undeniable fact. Radical feminists consistently misrepresent facts about child support and the material that counters feminist propaganda seldom receives publication.

The sad truth is that financial resources are seriously impacted when families split apart and as Sociologists Jay D. Teachman and Kathleen M. Paasch writing in "The Future of Children (1994)" "Financial Impact of Divorce on Children and Their Families", state:

"The preponderance of evidence suggests that, following divorce, custodial parents—almost always mothers—suffer considerable decline in economic well-being. Why is this so? To some degree, the **economic distress suffered by mothers and children is structural. That is, given the nature of fixed costs (for example, housing and transportation), it is cheaper to live in one household than in two. Because two households are formed when a couple divorces, the same resources must now cover greater fixed costs. Moreover, costs attendant to marital disruption, such as legal fees and relocation costs, can drain either partner's financial reserves.**"

Compare those findings with a letter to The New York Times titled, "Child Support System Still Lets Men off Easily", written by matrimonial attorney Susan Bender and psychologist Phyllis Chesler. This is a first rate sampling of radical feminist perversion and debasement of child issues.

While I am not surprised to find a female attorney authoring such an article, I am nothing short of infuriated (sadly not shocked) that a psychologist whose concerns ought to be the emotional well-being of children contrives to make a partisan argument over the financial arrangements of divorcing parents. Ms. Chesler, in referring to father's efforts to share in their children's lives as being a 'backlash', lends her professional credentials to malicious radical feminist propaganda:

"There is an increasing trend of fathers both fighting for and winning custody. This is primarily a backlash phenomenon. Contrary to popular myths, and despite an increasing number of exceptions, the majority of fathers, unwed, married and divorced, are still rarely responsible for even 1/20th of the primary child-care tasks. Fathers who do anything more than the minimum are viewed as exceptional. Increasingly, non-caretaking and even violent fathers who contest custody tend to win either sole or joint custody." (NY Times September 15 1995)[43]

One hardly knows where to begin when one encounters such monstrous lies, hidden implications and unmitigated nonsense. This comes from a scientist who one can only call disreputable. Lie number one. We know that fathers do not merely fail to get sole and joint custody orders, but in 37.9 percent of cases get NO visitation and in 54.9 percent of cases get LITTLE visitation and no enforcement of that visitation. Lie number two. **There are no popular myths that fathers participate in caretaking tasks.** One reason for this book is to dispel the popular mythology that women are sole caretakers and men have NO role in the lives of their children despite scientific evidence to the contrary.

Hidden in Chesler's disagreeable statement about male backlash (lacking supporting evidence of course) is the implication in the word 'backlash'. What this psychologist and her lawyer friend are saying is that men only seek custody (joint custody) as a means to avoid becoming primary supporters of their children. It is truly depressing that a psychologist would lend her support to such arguments, deflecting the public's interest away from fundamental issues that concern children. The reader should consider this psychologist's motives in concert with those of the reporting psychologist in the New Zealand relocation case, and others I present elsewhere in this book.

While I cannot agree with some fathers advocates and scholars who suggest that if a woman 'withdraws her wifely services', agreed as part of the marriage contract, there is no reason for a former husband to go on subsidizing her life style, I consider that aspects of present child support policies and laws are inherently injust, unrealistic and unproductive. It is my position that if men and women join together in marriage or not and have children, that they are jointly responsible for the care, protection and well being of them until they reach an age of majority and become independent adults.

---

[43] New York virtually never grants sole custody to fathers, also see The Mnookin Study on who gets custody and why.

As I have pointed out, prodded on by extremist radical feminist leaders, women have used custody issues to impose conditions of economic servitude on men. Many mental health professionals have commented critically on the implied meaning of a mother gaining a sole custody order over the children insofar as it effects the division of family assets in such a way as to install her with a perceived scholarship for life, while her former husband is left in penury.

There is little debate amongst informed sources that radical feminists lambaste men over their intense desire to co-parent after divorce centered on their fear that women will lose their present enjoyment of control, power and money. It does not seem to bother them that children suffer exploitation in this process or that their interests are not recognized and respected or that men are injured.

The real reason for NOW (National Organization for Women) and a host of radical feminist groups opposing joint custody initiatives in state legislatures is their conviction that it will impact on the concept of parental responsibility and have a practical effect on division of family assets and income division. Equity in parenting will force women to contribute equal amounts of real money to the care of their children. If one hypothesizes the elimination of economic advantage in divorce, logic dictates that this would lead to far fewer unwarranted divorces, stabilizing conceptual and physical long-term relationships.

Having said all this, let us go on to deal with the more superficial and specific issues of child support.

US Interstate Child Support Act & English CSA

Married and un-married fathers have an obligation to support their children. This legal fact has force through The Child Support Agency in England, and through US state laws, underpinned by the federal Interstate Child Support Act.

Despite the fact that there is a general dictum in England and in America that issues of child custody 'cannot be mixed' with issues of financial support, courts in both countries consistently abuse the doctrine when and if it is convenient to do so. Case law and experience show that if the father does not or cannot pay child support he will not see his children. While on the other hand, if he is fully compliant and denied access, the court employs no sanctions to guarantee his custodial or visitation rights. The following case is illustrative of the problems facing fathers.

Case illustrating court's mixing financial orders with contact

An American father resided in the family home in France from which mother kidnapped his child to England in a unilateral action. He demanded the return of his child and refused to pay child support and maintenance to the mother as ordered by an English judge. The father had previously received an interim order granting him some limited rights of access to his child in France and in England. When the father insisted on taking up those rights to have the child on visitation in his home the English court, in defiance of it's own rules and doctrine, made payment of child support a pre-requisite of that visitation and subsequently denied it altogether.

The anecdotal evidence supports the contention that the case is all too typical in England and America. It was reported, in The Washington Times that in the Bobbitt case, a judge linked child visitation with support payment. Legislative analyst, Stuart Miller wrote to the paper in response:

"Although most men cringe at the thought of John Bobbitt being dismembered, we also cringe when he speaks. John Bobbitt is not an icon of the men's/father's movement and is most certainly not a spokesman for the supermajority of disenfranchised fathers, who desperately want to be involved in the physical, financial and emotional support of their children.

In spite of this, a point worth noting in your "Bobbitt Update" [People - 8/13/95, pg. A-2] is that you reported that Mr. Bobbitt "would be **allowed** to visit [his] toddler **after**...[emphasis added] " he pays $50,000 in child support to the mother.

If this is reported accurately, the Judge who issued that Order is violating the United States Constitution's guarantee to a right of association [with family] and a plethora of State and U.S. Supreme

Court rulings indicating that such right is an inherent Constitutional right, which may not be abridged, absent a showing of imminent danger to the child. Why didn't the headline read "U.S. Constitution - Void Where Prohibited by Law?"

This raises the same issues that were raised in our sample case, where neither US constitutional protections nor The English Children Act serve to protect children's inherent rights to have relationships with both parents. Just one more reminder to fathers that the law lacks proper administration, often seizing legislative authority not vested in it. There is a pattern of judicial misconduct consistent with the manner and conduct of aspects of child related matters.

On the one hand, courts act punitively in denying rights of association (constitutional) and children's human rights (international law) where money issues are involved. On the other hand, in stark contrast, courts have consistently failed to enforce their own visitation orders.

Courts have relied on the doctrine not to mix visitation issues with financial ones while demanding payment from fathers even when denied ANY access to their children by their former wives. Are sanctions are ever enforced against mothers for refusing access? The answer is rarely, if ever.

Courts act immediately to fine and imprison men for failure to pay child support using contempt proceedings to toss them into jail without the blink of an eye or any concern for the impact on the children. While these same courts almost never fine, sanction or imprison women for failure to provide court ordered access to take place between the children and their father. Courts will often state that they cannot imprison mother because that will harm the children. *See Pellman on law reforms* Yet, without real sanctions mothers who obstruct contact will continue indefinitely until father gives up and disappears.

Mealy-mouthed radical feminists like Hazel Henderson complain of:

"Fathers who refuse to pay their child support payments ordered by courts."

She ought to look at the published data that shows men pay up as long as they have proper access to their children. *See Appendix A See also Chapter 3 Myth of the Dead Beat Dad, Loss of Economic and Educational Opportunity*

Courts have buckled under radical feminist pressure to have men pay for and underpin their new world order of female-headed single parent families. The courts have placed all real emphasis in custody conflicts on collecting money from fathers. While they have shown scant regard for the children's rights or their best interests.

This cooperation between special interest parties and the judiciary is hardly surprising given present trends. Damage to children aside, it fails to consider the consequences on the public indebtedness caused by subsequent female single parenting. In 1994, I presented then Chief Secretary to the British Treasury, The Right Honorable Michael Portillo, with a Briefing Paper on the real costs to the public and the Exchequer of radical reformation of divorce law and its creation of female-headed single parent homes. *See Chapter 11 Destruction of Intact Families*

Chapter 8

A Father's Guide to the Courts

A Father's Guide to the Courts

As one astounded male non-matrimonial attorney confided in me, "I went to family court with a home, children, family and a thriving legal practice, driving a nice car...I left in a state of shock... childless, homeless, my law practice under threat of extinction. The new rules on division of assets included not only the value of my law degree but the value of my firm...I took the bus back."

The binding of our guide to family court systems, whether, local, state, national or foreign, consists of a common fabric: injustice, brutality, gender bias, and criminal lack of regard to the important needs of our children. While there may be local variances, the principles remain the same for all jurisdictions. I have broken down the elements of the general process to provide a means for a more intelligent approach to cases.

Having read the material on law and psychology, you are prepared for what follows in the guide. Understand that you are not fighting on a level playing field. You and your children have a number of enemies surrounding you, a collective 'Goliath'. You are 'David' without his proverbial slingshot. It is you, and maybe your lawyer, standing up to the judge, your former spouse, her lawyer, her social worker, her law guardian and her expert witness, not to mention precedent, practice and outside radical feminist influences.

And, remember that, if you choose representation, most family lawyers are either unaware of or often fail to incorporate the kind of data provided in this book in their briefs, oral argument or interrogations. An intelligent, knowledgeable client is a nuisance to a lawyer used to running the show without query, instruction or complaint.

A General Appraisal

The hard evidence shows that state and foreign family courts exclusively favor sole maternal custody over a shared parenting approach with no reversal in sight.

For thirty years, courts have ignored the theoretical concepts of joint custody or shared parenting, while giving the appearance of acceptance of gender-neutral language and standards. The ignorance and prejudice of family courts flows into custody matters, relocation and child abduction cases. The lower the court's level, the worse are the conditions.

The first advice for fathers with or without counsel

Fight where you chances of success are increased. For example, an American father, living in New York, should avoid Family Court and litigate in State Supreme Court. A British Father should avoid County Court and take the matter to The High Court, Family Division. This saves both time and money and gets the matter heard by more sophisticated judges who tend to write more erudite opinions that might, ironically, be more reversible on appeal. Parents having to fight international child abduction cases in US courts must avoid state court and use the federal district courts.

Seek joint legal and physical custody, or shared parenting orders. Do not attempt to gain sole custody unless there is present, clear, cogent and virtually irrefutable evidence that mother is a danger to the children or an impediment to post divorce continuation of nurturing by both parents. Do not argue that your spouse is an unfit mother, or let personal feelings of anger toward her interfere with good sense.

Do not accept Joint **Legal** Custody, while having **Physical** Custody vested in mother. This will leave her in de-facto control and the courts in practice, at subsequent hearings, will treat her as though she has actual legal custody.

Do not accept any 'negotiated' agreement between the parties that calls for your wife to have sole custody while you get 'generous' visitation, especially without clearly defined access. Beware! This kind of agreement is probably worthless if mother wishes to be difficult. Statistics, studies and other research show that courts will not act to enforce your access to the kids. *See Appendix A US Census Data.* Also, as the recent line of re-location cases in America, Britain and New Zealand show (*Relocation Cases*), once a sole custody order is in place, the courts are prone to permit mothers to re-locate out of the local area and even out of the country.

Although, judges face prohibition from confusing the issues of custody/visitation/access with financial issues, they can and will do that, when and if it suits them. Plain and simple, even if your wife consistently acts to deny visitation to the children, the court will insist you continue to pay child support. On the other hand, if you cannot or will not pay child support, the court will use that against you suspending all access to the children in breech of their own best interests standards. [44]

Unfortunately, the chances of success for gaining a shared parenting order in the face of mother's opposition and present court policies are less than 1 in 20. *See Divorce/Custody Graphs* Realize that

---

[44]   Braver, S., & O'Connell, D. Taking on myth 2: The no-show dad. In Divorced Dads: Shattering the myths, New York: Tarcher/Putnam. (1998). The study found that while child support payment is enforceable, visitation is not; frequently, fathers withhold payment when they are denied visitation by their former spouse.

your case might continue for months and in many instances over several years and involve numerous court appearances.

Accept the reality of the odds, but do not give up. You have a long hard fight ahead and must learn to cope with the stress, and trauma of a prolonged and possibly de-stabilizing custody case. Do not allow dispiriting circumstances to influence your commitment to fight on for your children's sakes. Even if you should lose, the message sent to your children is of monumental importance to their long-term health and self-esteem. This is true even if the children do not in the short-term either understand or are alienated by mother against you, as often happens in conflictual cases. *See Chapter 3 Parental Alienation Syndrome*

You may face the possibilities of a number of rather unfair and prejudicial interim orders being made, including disproportionate maintenance and child support, custody to your wife, limited access, and even an order of protection (ouster order). Courts will attempt to convince you that these orders do not prejudice your defense, and case, but, of course, they do.

Do not blindly accept and agree to reports prepared by so-called court appointed 'neutral' experts that deal with the psychological needs of the children and what might or might not be in their 'best interests'. Where the law allows, get your own expert to testify. *See Expert Witnesses See False Expert Reports*

In states or foreign territories using an 'independent' lawyer, law guardian or guardian-ad-litem for the children, I warn you that the majority of these professionals are seriously biased and will generally support mother no matter what the circumstances might be. They will pose a threat to any father's case for joint custody. That means you! *See the case of David B v. Helen O. See the case of Stephen S. See Expert Testimony. See Judge Green New Zealand Relocations Cases*

In the following sub chapters, I will deal more explicitly with advice on how to conduct a case, either by an appointed attorney-solicitor or as a pro se litigant.

Argument in the 'Star Chambers' of Family Courts

From coast to coast, Alaska to Texas, and in many foreign territories, family courts have excluded all objective evidence tests. *See Counsel Adrian Pellman, Chapter on Law Reforms.* Family Court process is allegation driven, gender discriminatory, and nothing more than a sophisticated 'star chamber'. The courts are set up to process cases based on a pre-determination to hand custody of children exclusively to mothers, delimiting or obliterating the rights of children and male parents alike.

So how does one argue in such an atmosphere? By being extremely aggressive, but never manifesting signs of anger or resentment, using a raised voice, or anticipating proceedings with interjections, objections and cynical responses even when provoked. You must vigorously prosecute your case as allowed by the law. You cannot cave in to pressures that brought to bear on you by the judge, opposing counsel and even your own lawyer if represented. Devise a pro-active strategy that implies that your case is the right and normal one, assuming the court's agreement and force it to rebut your presumptions.

The Core Arguments

What are you going to argue? Given the 'star chamber' environment, the statistical reality, and social pressures militating against the protection of your children's rights, what case can you present?

1 You are going to argue that nothing less than shared parenting or full joint custody can possibly satisfy the rights and needs of your children, or the mandated 'best interests' standard of the court.

2 You will argue that nothing less than that accords with universal principles enshrined in children's rights laws and specifically in regard to The UN Convention on the Rights of the Child as signed and ratified by the US government. *See Chapter 6, International Law*

3. You are going to argue than anything less than that represents a deprivation of a vested constitutional liberty interest of the child and yourself.

In making these principle arguments, you will have to overcome the working bibles for the issues of divorce and custody, " The Best Interests of the Child", Freud, Solnit & Goldstein, or a garden-variety version of this book and Bowlby's Separation Anxiety. *See Chapter 2 for a Rebuttal to Freud, Solnit & Goldstein*

Your arguments depend on flawless logic. They depend on the use of statistical evidence. They rely as well on the psychiatric and psychological literature. The best way to overcome the court's inherent prejudice and gender discrimination is to adduce evidence not easily ignored by the court. For instance, regarding the best interests principle, you will cite and quote authorities that support shared parenting and reject sole maternal custody decisions. Some of these authorities exist in this book, while others exist in the literature. *See Chapter 1, 2, 3, 12 for some of the studies, Also, See References*

If the court ignores the evidence, than you will have solid grounds on appeal for reversal based on 'abuse of the court's discretionary powers'. And, of course, should the children subsequently show disturbances, then further applications to the court will have greater effect given your original argument.

There are two primary means to fight a case. You can instruct counsel (attorney-solicitor) or run the case as a pro-se litigant. I will deal with those options later in this chapter. For now, lets discuss the Shared Parenting proposition.

Shared Parenting and Full Joint Custody

Let me first dispel two common myths used to discourage joint custody from being implemented: Shared Parenting or full joint custody means an exact fifty-fifty split of the children's time and, a shared parenting order cannot work without the full cooperation of both parties or if one party objects to it.

The truth is that any number of variations exists to accommodate the unique circumstances of the family and a shared parenting formula organized to suit individual family needs. This means that in some cases, there will be a fifty-fifty split of the children's time while in others it might be sixty-forty. While in others it can be six months with one parent and six with the other, or another formula allows mother to have the children from Monday to Friday afternoon, and father gets them each weekend from Friday evening to Sunday evening or Monday morning. Parents can share vacation times, with one parent having the children over Christmas, the other having them for Easter. The permutations are endless.

The second misunderstanding is that, shared parenting orders do not work in the face of stiff maternal opposition. *See Ilfeld Study.* In fact, based on existing evidence, the very opposite might be the case. Shared Parenting Orders are, seldom shown to be worse than sole custody orders. Courts must face a challenge to prove that joint custody or shared parenting orders made over the objections of one party do not work!

If the deck is stacked against you why fight an un-winnable war? If all fathers follow that logic, children of conflictual divorce fall into the sole control of their mothers, with the consequences that I have reported. Fathers must start somewhere. Why not you! Your case might be the one that breaks new ground. These are your kids and nothing in the world is of greater importance to you. Third, even if you lose, you might get a better deal for the children. Do you want them to think you never loved them? Do you want them to feel abandoned?

Jurisdictions and Shared Parenting Escape Clauses

There are two types of jurisdiction. Those whose laws permit shared parenting orders and those that do not. Lets deal with the ones that do. Here, we come across the child and father's greatest single barrier. The phrases most often heard spit out by judges in the US and UK go like this,

'Although our laws allow for the making of shared parenting of joint custody orders, they are not generally in favor', or, 'although the law provides for the making of these orders, they are rarely made over the strong objections of one party (mother)'. *See Mnookin California Study for further information*

Sometimes these kinds of judicial comment come, after the fact, in summary, decision or in an opinion. Often they remain unspoken and lurk ominously in the background under the cloak of court policy. What normally follows from these power phrases is garbled nonsense about how conflictual ex-partners cannot co-operate to make joint custody work, how children are harmed by potential continuation of conflict and how shared parenting is not practical. Other clichés recited by courts are, how children require regulated and constant upbringing, and that the court needs to make a definitive decision in the matter to avoid future litigation. *See Freud, Solnit, Goldstein, See Rebuttal in Chapter 2*

Therefore, you must be prepared to rebut these unjustifiable rationalizations. For example: Where the court states or makes a silent assumption that a shared parenting order made over mother's objections will lead to countless future court appearances, your response is found in a study by Ilfeld (1982): "Does Joint Custody Work? A First Look at Outcome Data on Re-litigation" that dealt with the incidence of re-litigation in cases where joint custody was judicially mandated, often in the face of opposition by the mother, and showed that litigation was significantly reduced, not increased. *See References*

On the other hand, I know of no study coming to an opposite conclusion. Yet, I have never heard this study cited in argument, summary or rebuttal by a father's attorney. Obviously, if re-litigation reduced, there must have been a corresponding degree of increase in parental cooperation and acceptance of the court's order for shared parenting.

In other words, when courts act swiftly and strongly to make joint custody orders, the odds are that obstinate mothers will come to heel. They will temper their unresolved anger towards the father, adjust, and behave themselves in the interests of the children. If the courts indulge mothers, then hostility continues, and leads to one or two obvious consequences. First, there is definitely going to be continued litigation as father fights for his children and/or Dad in the end is going to give up, leading to the massive father absence we see today.

In fact, the argument can and should be made that, if sole custody must be awarded, it should be awarded to the parent most willing to lay aside their own personal interests in deference to the rights of their child to have a continuous and meaningful relationship to the other parent. This is the view of Dr. Jacobs and other responsible scientists. That being the case, an argument for father custody finds support from the research on the relative merits of sole paternal custody cited in the first chapter of the book.

As for the clichés about regularity originally fostered by Solnit, Goldstein and Freud, ample material has been included in the chapters on Psychiatry and Deprivation to fully rebut these old, erroneous ideas on child-care. Therefore, that important material is ripe for incorporation into your prosecution of the case for shared parenting. *See Chapter 2*

Every Family is Unique- or, is it?

Now, courts are often fond of stating that each case is as unique as are all families. Nothing is further from the truth of the matter. This prosaic declaration is merely truism. It is a devious prefacing comment used with the infamous 'best interests' guideline and the court's wide-ranging discretionary powers to construct a sole maternal custody award. Here is the probable context:

'Although our law permits us in principle to make shared parenting decisions, the individual circumstances (read uniqueness) of this case does not call for such a decision to be made.'

This typifies the judicial workaround in those jurisdictions where joint custody is on the books. Here is the formula: 'Every case and every family is unique' dogma plus the courts existing wide ranging discretionary powers plus an ill defined best interest standard equals the making of exclusive maternal custody decisions. It is a rather irresistible escape clause for biased courts.

The truth is that while individual families in all their superficial diversity, can be viewed as unique, they display even greater universal similarity in internal mechanisms. All families from Oedipus' to John Does' are subject to the exact same internal rules of conduct, affections, pressures, neurosis, jealousies, and conflicts. All families are alike and are not unique at all.

In making the shared parenting argument to a hostile court, you or your counsel MUST stress the fact that neither the case nor your family, are in any way 'unique' but are prototypical of the millions of cases marching through the courts. The issues for a parent seeking sole custody are, control, power and money, and perhaps retribution (*See Research Studies on Maternal Anger towards Fathers*). While for the other parent seeking shared parenting they are, the maintenance, indeed the very survival of parental rights and a continuing relationship to the children. The statistics, studies and professional sources provided in this book back the argument.

On another tier, courts will also seek to find that the 'physical' circumstances are such that it is in the 'best interests' of the child that custody be vested in 'one' primary caretaker. In one typical 'traditional' family example: Mother has acted as homemaker and 'nurturer', while father has gone to work and acted as 'provider'. *See Psychiatric Literature, Chapters on the Law.* Now you can understand the inclusion of what appeared to be irrelevant or merely theoretical historical material.

The court might also suggest that a child cannot split time equally between two parents, manage large geographical distances, or that having two different homes would be unsettling to him or her. The studies on joint-custody and two separate homes must come into play at this point and used in rebuttal. *See Chapter 2, Rebuttal to the Theories of Freud, Solnit & Goldstein, Modern Consensus on Joint Custody, and Importance of Father.*

The Use of Counsel

Lawyers are not stupid. They understand and accept the rules of the game...mothers win and fathers lose! My experience in the United

States and Britain confirms that lawyers are fully aware of the risk of confronting family court judges in too vigorous a defense of father. Judicial payback can be a swift killer of a legal practice.

You must also realize that a huge number of lawyers are incompetent, non-committal, and often harried by unrealistic caseloads. Often they cannot manage the attention to detail that is required, especially having to represent a father in a hostile jurisdiction.

However, there are lawyers who represent male clients to the fullest of their abilities and offer considerable support to them. Finding one is no mean feat! I have encountered many genuine and concerned lawyers who will go to the mat for a father seeking shared parenting.

Selection of counsel for fathers faced with a case in the United Kingdom (American fathers with Abduction cases included) presents special problems. Fathers face a divided legal system with solicitors responsible only for the general case management, organizing of affidavits, exchange of correspondence, and counsel known as barristers arguing the case before the court. Barristers are dependent on the solicitor for all the legwork and case preparation. A father is paying two lawyers. The barrister puts in separate fees set by his 'clerk of chambers' and submits his bill to the solicitor. The bill covers work including preliminary reading of the papers and report known as an 'advice', meeting of the client attended by the solicitor (another fee), preparation of preliminary argument, further reading of depositions and more meetings as well as significant charges for time in court (paid whether or not there are adjournments).

Aside from the dual fee problem, the client is one step removed from his courtroom representative. He never speaks directly to his barrister without the solicitor being present, and errors often occur because information passes continuously from client to solicitor to barrister. It is imperative that the client pay strict attention to case management and we will discuss this in this chapter.

Selection (finding the good lawyer)

Whether you are living in New York or London, the issues and the problems related to finding a lawyer are universal. I would advise trying the following options.

The Grapevine: Do you know someone who has been through it? (Most of us do) No one is better suited to making a recommendation than the father who has been down this miserable road.

Men's and Children's Advocacy Groups: Find them in the Yellow Pages, White Pages, Internet Websites and other media, or from friends and relatives. Try the local chapters of Children's Rights Council or if in England, Families Need Fathers or Equal Parenting Council

Internet Legal Links such as 'The Center for Children's Justice' ACFC, CRC, SCFC or DadsDivorce, *See Appendix D*

Meet with the prospective lawyer and ask probing questions. Have you represented many men? How long have you been practicing family law? What are your personal views on custody? What kind of strategy are you recommending to me?

Then up the ante. Do you have an expert witness who is fair, independent and willing to testify? Have you won any joint custody cases on behalf of men? Are you familiar with the recent psychiatric and psychological literature that favors a shared parenting approach? What strategy will you use?

Deal with financials and particulars of management. How much do you charge for your services? Can I see a sample of your brief writing? Will you handle my case directly or will you use associates and assistants? What are my chances of success in getting joint custody in this jurisdiction?

If you do not feel confident then dump him. In addition, Australian and English fathers have to discover which chambers and barristers the solicitor uses as this seriously affects the conduct and outcome of the case.

Wait a minute! Should I use a male or female attorney? It probably will not matter. Notions that female attorneys arguing on behalf of a male client carry more weight with the court are misguided. Equally, ideas that male lawyers will fight harder for a man client are also misplaced.

Instructions

Having appointed a representative, you want him to argue in the US for 'joint physical and legal custody' and in the UK for 'shared residence'. Again, do not be dissuaded by last minute attempts to get you to accept 'generous visitation' or 'access' while sole custody is vested in your former spouse. This 'acquiescence' will immediately reduce your rights in law and have serious consequences on your future legal rights and real relationship to the children.

Looking ahead; first she gets custody (full rights) and you accept visitation (de-limited or reduced rights), then for instance, at some point she meets another man and wants to move away with him and the kids. Recent case law (*See Case of Tropea v Tropea*) shows that the court will permit her to remove the children to a distant geographical location thus severely reducing access or making it a practical impossibility. *See Other Relocation Cases.*

But even if you are fortunate enough to survive the relocation issue, it is common for women to seek reductions in visitation schedules and generally to make the life of her former spouse a living hell when it comes to access to the kids. *See Appendix A US Census Statistics and Research Studies*

Unless the case is one of exceptional circumstances, do not attempt to discredit your former spouse and argue for paternal sole custody. First; that would be counter-productive given the slim chances for success, second; it is inherently wrong and injurious to the children, third; it deflects away from the principles and issues that are at the very heart of the matter, your children's right to meaningful parental relations with both parents.

On the other hand, should your former spouse give false, injurious testimony in her affidavit and on the stand, then instruct counsel (or solicitor) to challenge each claim or allegation, even if this should anger the judge (as it well might). If the judge angers, then you have no chance anyway but at least you get objections and answers to the allegations on the record to say nothing of disclosing possible judicial bias.

This is 'making a record', and is an important aspect of the conduct of a case and prospective appeal process. It is also part of a forthright defense (or prosecution) in a family relations case linking facts in evidence to accepted psychiatric and psychological literature (and expert testimony) as well as to the law.

Now that you have laid down the principle (shared parenting), it is vital that you define the general strategy. First ask; what is it that best promotes and underpins the principle of joint custody that you have offered to the court? What undercuts that argument? What arguments can you use to counter the negative argument?

Let me give an English example where the legal principles also apply to US cases (using state law).

England has national legislation governing proceedings involving the custody of children (The Children Act 1989). A barrister presents arguments based on that law, indicating that 'shared residence' (full joint custody) is and was the legislative intention behind the Act. He then represents that the court, bound by the Act's intent, must interpret 'The Best Interests of the Child' doctrine accordingly.

If the judge is reluctant (as he might well be) to accept that legal position, the barrister must proceed to provide the court with evidence that it was Parliament's intention when it passed the Act to have 'shared residence' (joint legal and physical custody) as the primary preference in custody cases. For example he might, produce parliamentary committee reports and working documents showing such 'legislative intent'. The judge may (disagreeably) accept this, but at the same time counter it. He might say that nonetheless, he still has wide ranging discretionary powers to make sole custody decisions dictated by the particular facts and circumstances of the case in the best interests of the child.

If you are an American father without the benefit of national law but are armed with a similar state statute (approximately 37 states allow for joint custody orders) you must use exactly the same strategies as your British counterpart. The issues are the same. From this point onward all, lawyers, barristers and pro se litigants alike have their cases re-defined by the court.

Now make a showing to the court that the case is not exceptional. You might argue: Your Honor, there is no evidence in this case to show that either parent has severe problems inhibiting their ability to parent. Judge, there is no evidence to show that either parent lacks the love and commitment to nurture. Your Honor, there is absolutely no evidence to show that the children do not love both parents.

This brings me to what I consider the most important aspect of defense or prosecution of the case for shared residency, the adduction of the psychological and psychiatric evidence.

The problem will be for you, your lawyer or solicitor to find an expert willing and able to testify. In the US, there are competent experts who will come forward. In the UK, most psychiatrists and psychologists are less likely to publicly support the position. US and UK courts will probably insist on the "joint' appointment of an expert acceptable to both sides, knowing that the likelihood of a truly independent psychiatrist being called will be very low indeed. Insist on calling your own expert.

Whether you are an American, English or Australian father makes no difference. You or your representative must be fully prepared to argue in a hostile environment against the expert witness. You need comprehensive knowledge of the literature that supports the shared parenting position as being in the best interests of the child. You must be able to articulate it in argument and, to use it posing nasty little questions in cross-examination of a hostile expert.

There is much more discussion on this vital subject in the section on *Witnesses and Evidence, Expert evidence, including a complete analysis of false reporting by experts*

In all cases, when dealing with the literature (some of which has been included in The Psychological Literature on the Child and other chapters, the destructive consequences on children of sole maternal custody decisions and subsequent loss of paternal ties must be stressed.

You must get this material into the record, and prove that (at the very least) if your children suffer paternal loss there is a substantial probability that your children will become dysfunctional in infancy, adolescence and adulthood. Argue that the research shows, removing the care of children into the sole hands of mothers leads to children suffering from a number of clinical pathologies and anti-social behavior. Use the statistics and studies provided in this book. *See Statistics Chapter I*

You or your attorney must make appropriate constitutional arguments (he'll just love that!), based on 'liberty interests', citing the long line of Supreme Court cases defining family and parental rights as protected interests. Although it seems a stretch, it is important to establish a legal link between the rights of cognizable classifications (divorced fathers and children of divorce) and international treaty law of the United States (The UN Convention on the Rights of the Child-The ICCPR). *See Chapter 6*

The UN Convention mandates courts of signatory nations (US-UK) to respect, foster and implement the child's human rights to have access based on a joint custody preference in it's best interests. *See Chapter 6, Dr. Quisumbing, Rep. Of the High Commissioner on Human Rights, UN.* Present contradictions in US and UK acceptance of the Convention (called reservations) prohibit the right to litigate based on it. *See Appendix C President Clinton Letter*

I have had success sneaking it by various US judges and into the record, even on the federal level. These arguments will most likely fall on stony ground, but make a part of the record for appeal. Whereas, on appeal argue that the US is bound to honor treaty law and cannot prevent litigation based on it. Insist your representative make the effort!

Be forewarned! Your former wife or girlfriend has long since de-personalized you and declared war. In this fight to keep your children, the first casualty will be the truth. So, do not be surprised by a sudden salvo of wild allegations questioning your character, motivation and parenting abilities. Charges of sexual abuse and domestic violence are a statistical reality despite the truth that the lion-share of such allegations are, when made during custody conflicts, almost a ninety percent certainty of being false. *See False Allegations of Sexual Abuse*

Radical feminist and other (lawyers-social workers) influences promote such charges, and they have become a commonly used and unscrupulous female tactic to gain immediate advantage in custody cases. Lawyers representing male clients must be aware and able to deal with the legal consequences of these allegations and counter them. You, the client, must be psychologically strong and able to deal with the infliction of pain they cause you and the children.

Do not 'voluntarily' leave the marital home and fight hard against 'expulsion' based on false allegations made before there is a proper court hearing with all parties present. Insist that such a hearing is criminal in nature and demands a jury trial (it won't happen but the argument must be made) to safeguard your rights.

Your opponent might try to get the court to write a pre-emptive order expelling you from your home before such a hearing takes place (US Orders of Protection-British Ouster Orders). They want to create an artificial and prejudicial 'de facto' control of the home and children by the mother. It will not matter to them that they are causing an almost incalculable magnitude of harm to the emotional lives of the children as Dr. Jacobs has alluded to in his television interview with me for "Wednesdays' Children".

Beware of the general problem of landing in a position in which you have to disprove a negative assertion. When did you stop beating your wife? When did you stop being a child molester and sexual abuser? If it occurs, voice your concern and objection to the court.

Overseeing and Management

Never, but never leave it solely to your lawyer! The constant supervision, oversight and management of your own case is no less a concern than was the appointment of counsel. It is commonplace for earnest and enthusiastic attorneys to lose sight of the case. Documents are misplaced, forgotten, or neglected. Lawyers fail to obtain depositions and affidavits on time. They do not return phone calls, follow-up on leads and information, or keep you posted promptly providing you with copies of inter-alia correspondence and legal briefs.

If you meet with your representative or hold conference calls (including the barrister or counsel) take notes on everything said, indicated and promised. You must ask intelligent and relevant questions. To ask probing questions, you have to read all of the papers in the case, searching out errors in facts.

The Pro Se Option

If hiring a lawyer is an expense that you cannot meet, or feel is unwarranted in light of the slight chances of success to get a joint custody or shared residence order-then go carefully. You are not alone! Round the world, nearly half of all fathers in conflictual cases go into family court on their own.

Do not take lightly the decision to represent yourself and the children. You can only make it after a careful weighing up exercise. Having said that, the principles remain the same as if you had engaged counsel. Just remember that you must take on all the legal burdens and responsibilities alone, running a risk that an unfriendly court might confuse your advocacy as counsel with your persona as parent. Be extremely disciplined in your approach, language and demeanor. Another disadvantage of running your own case is that you lack the experience, and technical expertise of a skilled attorney. On the other hand, you can put in far more work and attention to detail than the average attorney. Of course, you save thousands of dollars, money that you can use on behalf of the children.

Assistance of Counsel

However, you do not necessarily have to do it all alone. Try to get help from friends or support groups such as Children's Rights Council, Coalition for Fathers, Families Need Fathers, in the UK. One may have an activist or two willing to offer, 'non-attorney' 'assistance of counsel' (Next Friend) in the United States, and 'Mackensie Friend' in England.

Unfortunately, the vast majority of family courts will fight tooth and nail to prevent effective assistance of counsel, especially where it involves the 'friend' appearing in court alongside of the father. Some judges actually go bananas. There are two reasons for the courts' lack of sympathy; first, it violates the prime rule of the legal fraternity: 'thou shalt not infringe on our monopoly', and second; having a legally inexperienced 'lame duck' father in front of the bench unaided and unprotected, makes the process of eliminating him as an effective parent far less cumbersome.

Do not be intimidated, even though this will raise a distracting issue. There are historical precedents for non-attorney assistance to litigants. State charters from the earliest days of the Republic allowed such representation. Many people distrusted and disliked 'lawyers', often having a non-attorney 'friend' stand up for them in court. In fact, the origin of the word 'counsel' refers not to lawyers but to a non-attorney friend rendering 'assistance of counsel' to a defendant or plaintiff. There are even Supreme Court cases that underpin a due process right to have assistance of counsel by non-attorney friends.

Case Preparation

Take advantage of technology. Get on the Internet to access legal sites holding cases (the Supreme Court down to state courts) and state 'domestic relations' code. You can pull up cases on the monitor, review them and either print out or download into a directory on the computer. You can copy and past the data directly into your legal brief. This is a time saving methodology because it combines research with legal writing without leaving the desktop. The downside is that some state case law may not be available i.e. most recent decisions or those in states that have not yet gone online. Internet access is also useful for acquiring articles, reviews, and journals that might contain helpful information. *See Appendix D Internet Legal Resources*

Go to the Law Library. Pro se litigants are granted free admission to court law libraries. Some libraries accommodate the use of personal computers with scanners and some do not. The cost of photocopying documents in court libraries is extremely expensive. The downside is the physical limitations of transferring data into a usable format.

Alternative systems include the hiring of online services such as Westlaw, Lexis-Nexis and other similar law providers which is very expensive, or sneaking into university law libraries.

This book is your first resource. Use it. Select what you consider appropriate source material and quotations and get it into your legal brief. Use it in argument and examination of witnesses. If you have the time, read further material from the professionals whose contributions I included. *See References*

Transcripts & Filing Fees for Pro Se Fathers

Conflictual custody cases are seldom resolved in one court date. If you are a pro se father, make sure you get a copy of every court transcript. Written transcripts are prohibitively expensive. If you cannot afford to buy a copy, then file a motion to proceed **'in forma pauperis'** (poor persons relief) asking that the court excuse you from paying for transcripts and filing fees. You will have to provide an affidavit of means that satisfies the court.

Remember that you must have a copy of these transcripts available to you for subsequent hearings. Judicial statements, questions and interim decisions, as well as statements and evidence from your opponents from preliminary hearings might be vital for your defense and for a prospective appeal. You cannot function without the transcripts! Transcripts are an important part of the record.

Appeals

Appeals are made 'on the record' created by the proceedings, including the Opinion of the Court's findings of the facts and on the law. You cannot make fresh arguments. It is, as a rule, almost impossible to overturn a decision made by a judge based on his 'finding of the facts'. Therefore, most appeals are against his conclusions of law.

However, there is an exception to the 'finding of facts' premise. That is, the judge 'abused his discretionary powers' in making his finding by either grossly misinterpreting or disregarding the facts as presented on the record, or failed to arrive at a just verdict based on the evidence, in conjunction with the law, court policy, and general guidelines or principles applied in family law cases.

Courts of Appeal, whether they are British, American, Australian or whatever, are loathe to over-turn lower court decisions, and appeals are seldom upheld in family law cases.

Further Applications & Orders to Show Cause

Other avenues are open to you if you have lost your original custody case. A long-held maxim is that children's cases never truly end until the child's age of majority (18 or 21). From a strictly legal point of view, there is nothing to prevent any father from coming before the court with a fresh application(s) for either a change of custody or variance of the terms and conditions of the original custody order. For instance, these applications can argue a 'change in circumstances', or that mother has failed to abide by the original court order.

One American father, married to an English woman, trapped in the hostile confines of the British High Court, fought for over four years, eighty court appearances, at a cost to the British taxpayer of three quarters of a million dollars on their legal aid bill. In the end, he not only overturned the original court order, but he got full custody of his son (who had finally run away from mother's home). See the *Case of Stephen S.* The son, then age twelve, turned around and sued the guardian ad litem and The Official Solicitor for a denial of his legal rights.

A persistent father can set precedents. Fathers such as Stephen S. sometimes overcome the odds and get a result for their children. However, nothing disturbs the peace of the court more than a persistent and resolute father. Courts have been know to attempt to declare such fathers as 'vexatious' or 'nuisance' litigators' threatening them with severe sanctions for bringing future court applications, and making orders to control the ability of the father to initiate a legal action.

However, repeated applications made to the court, remains an extremely viable strategic alternative to the appeal process.

*Please note that many legal forms for Motions and Orders to Show Cause are obtainable over the Internet from sites such as Findlaw.

Enforcement of Visitation-Contempt of Court Orders

This brings us to the problems of court ordered access or visitation. One of the most vexing problems facing fathers and children is the laxity of family courts enforcement of their own paltry visitation orders. It is a vicious circle. Courts failure to act in the best interests of children starts first with their refusal to make joint custody orders. The court places the child into the hands of a parent intent on severing or curtailing the relationship between father and children. This traumatic circumstance is then, exacerbated by court refusal to make contempt citations against mothers who deny visitation, or to make them but fail to enforce fines or imprisonment.

All you can do is to return to the court as many times as it   is necessary to obtain your rights. This refers to the idea of 'changing circumstances' as a tactic. You might want to consider seeking a new paternal custody order based on your former spouses refusal to obey orders of the court and her denial of the best interests of the children.

Witnesses and Evidence

What are we looking for from witnesses? We are looking for witnesses who have direct and intimate knowledge of the relationship between you and your child. Someone who can substantiate your argument to the court that a.) You have been an ongoing and important parenting figure and b.) You have had a positive impact on the emotional life and development of your child. Their positive evidence might be that they have seen and heard father and child on a number of close occasions interacting in a loving and supportive manner. Their negative evidence might be that they have interacted directly with your child following paternal absence and have observed negative effects on the child of that absence.

The weight of witness evidence is measured according to the nature of the their relationship to the family and the child. For example: A passing acquaintance will carry less weight than a close friend or family member. A brief encounter in the street might count less than observations made over a three-hour dinner. A witness who has been an observer on a number of intimate occasions generally gives stronger evidence (unless extreme bias is shown).

Written, video-audio taped evidence from the children counts too. You can introduce evidence from your children in the form of writings (letters, notes, memos, child's drawings, video and audio tapes), any of which might go to either positive or negative proofs. If your former spouse has hurled damaging accusations at you, intending to either limit or destroy your relationship to the children, you should record the children's remarks on video-audio tape and get it into evidence. This is an uncomfortable process, but might be a necessary one. I do caution you not to induce the children to speak in your favor or against your spouse. They must not face pressurization or intimidation! Their feelings and thoughts must express themselves naturally!

Children's Evidence

The area of children's direct evidence is a veritable minefield. Such evidence, permitted in most jurisdictions is extremely limited in weight unless the child is 'of such an age as to know his or her mind and have the capability to express clear preferences as to which parent they wish to live with'. Generally, the age at which most courts will give credence to child testimony is about the age of ten years upwards. Some courts will not allow a child under the age of ten to testify. Some will.

However, that is not say that a child of even three years cannot express a valid opinion or their true feelings about the parental relationship. I believe a child of that age often expresses more accurate intuitive knowledge than the often heavily rationalized expressions of older children and adults. Some courts will permit very young children to testify. On the other hand, in adjudging the negative statements of young children about their fathers, courts must exercise caution due to the traumatic circumstances in involved. *See Parental Alienation Syndrome and Dr. Gardner. See False Allegations of Sexual Abuse*

For example: if mother has filed for divorce and custody, and has hurled accusations of either child abuse or domestic violence against the father the following scenario gets unleashed. First, the judge acts to order the father out of the home as an interim measure. *See Orders of Protection, Ouster Orders.* Second, the child is now under the sole influence of the mother, and subjected to her continuous pressure and barrages against the father. The child might react in two distinct ways. He or she might begin to feel that the father has abandoned, or is a bad person. *See Dr. Jacobs on False Accusations. See Dr. Gardiner on Parental Alienation Syndrome. See Case of David B. v Helen O.*

Alternatively, the child might begin to overly identify with the missing parent. All of these possibilities meet discussion in other chapters. *See Chapter 3 The Quest for Father.*

In another scenario where mother simply files for sole custody, the court will most assuredly grant her an interim custody order with visitation arrangements for the father. These are usually very limited, disrupting the normal contact between father and child. That, in turn can lead to the child feeling anger, guilt, remorse, fear and separation anxiety from the missing parent. In either case, the child's feelings might lead to exaggerations and distortions that make it impossible for the court to properly adjudge their testimony.

There are other problems related to taking evidence from young children including the circumstances of the testimony. I have seen and participated in too many cases in which social workers, law guardians and judges browbeat children for me to feel comfortable with this process. When young children give evidence, it must be in the most neutral circumstances possible, in a quiet room, with neither parent present. The person taking the evidence must be truly impartial while all interested parties must have simultaneous audio and visual contact with the process to ensure its fairness.

Unless considered as absolute necessity, I would advise that you should not call your children to give evidence. Force the court to acknowledge and operate under their own legal assumption (*See gender neutral standards*Best Interests*) that the child is part of a family triad and has a natural attachment and love for both psychological parents.

General Examination and Cross Examination

Although courts grant much greater latitude to a pro se, questions and phrasing must be as neutral as possible. There are essentially two kinds of witnesses, friendly and hostile. Broadly, the approach to both should be in the same manner. The art is in the construction of the questions. How well one leads to another, building without badgering, berating, leading or harassing the witness. What is it you want from this witness?

There are exceptions, especially where a witness is an obvious 'hostile' witness. However, you must have extremely good reason to believe that a fulsome attack can bear positive results, i.e. an admission of fact that favors your case. The court will allow you to lead this kind of witness to some degree. Remember the earlier caveat, if you are conducting your case as a pro se litigant, the court might confuse your manner as an advocate with your role of either plaintiff or defendant. This is unfair and wrong, but it might well happen. Be prepared. All too often, I have seen pro se fathers lose their composure under the pressure that the dual role demands.

Follow the general dictum: Do not ask a question if you do not know what the answer is going to be! There are exceptions to the doctrine, but you really have to know what you are doing to run on counter theory. There will be times when you follow the dictum, but have your hand bitten. If that happens, forget it and move on to another question.

Expert Testimony

Expert testimony is the most crucial aspect of any family law case. It is central to your attempt to adduce evidence supporting your contention that only shared parenting or joint legal and physical custody can do justice to the best interests of your children.

Family courts judges have precious little knowledge or training in the field of psychology, family nexus, and parent child relationships. Personal prejudices aside, they lean heavily on expert witness reports and evidence. I would advise you to carefully read and review the several sections and cases I have provided that analyze various Expert Psychiatric and Psychological Reports. These reports arise in ordinary custody proceedings, relocation cases and parental abduction cases.

Psychiatrists and Psychologists

There is widespread abuse of power by expert witnesses on behalf of those seeking to foster, maintain and promote exclusive maternal custody. Beyond my own anecdotal evidence, The American Psychological Association (1994) in its: "Guidelines for Child Custody Evaluations in Divorce Proceedings" sounds the warning:

"Psychologists provide an important service to children and the courts by providing competent, objective, impartial information in assessing the best interests of the child; by demonstrating a clear sense of direction and purpose in conducting a child custody evaluation; by performing their roles ethically; and by clarifying to all involved the nature and scope of the evaluation.

The Ethics Committee of the American Psychological Association has noted that psychologists' involvement in custody disputes has at times raised questions in regard to the misuse of psychologists' influence. Sometimes this has resulted in complaints against psychologists being brought to the attention of the APA Ethics Committee" (APA Ethics Committee 1985; Hall & Hare-Mustin, 1983; Keith-Spiegel & Koocher, 1985; Mills, 1984) and raising questions in the legal and forensic literature (Grisso, 1986; Melton et al., 1987; Mnookin, 1975; Ochroch, 1982; Okpaku, 1976; Weithorn, 1987).

Yet, another source confirming abuse and misuse of the expert witness position comes from Ronald Henry, an attorney representing Children's Rights Council at a recent conference sponsored by the international human rights organization, Jarosh-Flynn Family Fund:

"Child custody litigation has experienced an explosive growth in the use and misuse of experts", and he cautioned lawyers to, "look for the signs that the judge has abdicated decision-making authority to the expert", while he emphasized that the court must, "insist that testimony from proposed experts fully comply with the standards for admissibility set forth in the applicable rules of civil procedure."

Case Analysis of a Psychiatrist's False Expert Report

What do I mean by misuse of power and position?

One earlier glimpse of such misuse was the false reporting demonstrated in the re-location cases (*See New Zealand Re-location Cases*). To answer the question, I advise any father, with or without counsel, to read the analysis of the following psychiatric report with the greatest possible care and attention. This seminal case teaches you about the construction of false reports, tearing apart the coded language, slants, inaccuracies, prejudice and misdirection in these reports. We are fortunate to have the Report, but even more fortunate to have three highly respected mental health experts address parts of it.

The disreputable abuse of power by psychologists and psychiatrists is best described in Dr. Dora Black's blatantly biased reporting in a case that involved an English mother and an American father. The basic facts were as follows.

1. Mother had suffered from long periods of clinical depressions during the first two years of the child's life, during which times father had been primary caregiver.

2. Mother had kidnapped the child aged two (twice) from the family home in France and was now 'safely ensconced' in the friendly confines of The English High Court.

3. Father went to the English court asking for the return of his child and he publicly committed himself to a shared parenting position despite the mother's previous kidnappings of the child.

Included here are portions of the report by court appointed expert Dr. Dora Black, my comments, and critiques of her work carried out by her fellow psychiatrists Dr. Linda Cohen-Saffer (Israel) and Dr. John W. Jacobs (US), who reviewed the case more than one year later.

English lecturer and author (The Balancing Act) Dr. Judith Ryder also examined the report contemporary to the actual case hearing.

Case Summary

Dr. Black, in a key error, fails to inform the court that mother had abducted the child. Here is her summary:

Psychiatric Report of Dr. Dora Black

" X is a normal child, well-developed, but showing some signs of the strain imposed on her by her parents inability to agree where she should live...She should be based with one parent who has sole custody in view of her parents inability to agree, but she should have reasonable access to the other parent."

This is the setup. Two important points; Dr. Black deliberately ignores mother's act of international parental child abduction and it's affect on the child, falsely reporting the circumstances by classifying and downplaying them as, "parents inability to agree where she should live". She then announces her strategic approach to maternal custody prejudicially based on the erroneous material from Klein in 1922 through Bowlby to Goldstein in 1977. She continues:

"It is, therefore, important that both parents retain a relationship with her. In my view this can best be done by **mother having custody, care and control**."

This is the knockout punch. The doctor opts for vesting Sole Custody in a mother who has suffered bouts of serious depression, kidnapped the child twice, and acted to delimit and to eliminate the child's relationship to her father. Is she really saying that placing the child in mother's hands guarantee the maintenance of the child's paternal relationship?

Dr. John W. Jacobs puts things in perspective:

"The...relevant fact is that in March, Mrs. Y left Mr. Y, unannounced, and returned with X (child) to England. Though I am certain that Mrs. Y felt that she had good personal reasons for her move and for not informing Mr. Y that she was taking X from their joint care, by doing so she initiated a profound change in her family which is likely to have serious deleterious effects on her child, her husband and ultimately on herself...By moving back to England and removing X from regular quality access to her father, Mrs. Y compromised and threatened X's relationship to him, potentially traumatizing her child and her husband. The seriousness of this move, and X's loss of regular contact to her father, should be assessed as being equal to the trauma that would have been imposed upon X had her father taken her away from her mother in the same manner."

Jacobs, using the traditional professional language, has raised the scepter of mother biased misreporting and continues:

"Unfortunately in the documents listed above (particularly in that written by Dr. Black) I can find no reference to this fact that is that X has two parents to whom she is extremely attached, and that any attempt to deprive or limit her contact (abduction) with either parent is clearly not in her best interest. The desire by either parent to limit X's access to the other either represents an acting out of that parent's antipathy toward the other parent or a response to the threat of the loss of the treasured relationship to the child."

Rein:

Dr. Black in opting for sole maternal custody in what was essentially an abduction case, endorsed mother's unlawful and psychologically harmful actions in order protect the interests of the mother, while repudiating the best interests of the child in shameful, but typical fashion. Having done this she continues to describe the kind of access, she had previously described as 'reasonable', the victim parent should have to the child that is equally appalling in it's denial of the child's and father's rights: Dr. Black states:

"Father having reasonable (a court cliché that has no meaning) and hopefully, reasonably frequent access. This should not include long-staying access. If father wishes to take her back to France, it should be for a maximum of ten days until she reaches school age. More attention should be paid to ensuring that her trust in her mother is not undermined."

Rein:

Not only does Dr. Black endorse the kidnapping of the child by mother BUT insists that the emphasis be placed on "ensuring that her (child) trust in her mother is not undermined", when clearly the child can have no trust in a mother who kidnaps her and destroys her relationship to her father.

Dr. Linda Cohen-Saffer, having also reviewed Dr. Black's report, the case decision and much evidence, states:

"This woman (mother) seems to be using to her full advantage the tendency of the British Judiciary to favor maternal rather than shared or paternal custody/access. Mr. Y wants shared access and believes the child should see both her mother and her father. **It is apparent that no authority involved in this case seems to be thinking of the child's best interests, but only of the interests of the mother.** This child was, apparently twice abducted from her domicile home and country, by the mother. The question arises as to why the mother is now free from judgment?"

Dr. Jacobs continues the theme:

"In addition to depriving (child) X of the value of her relationship to her father, Mrs. Y, by removing X from the family home, has also threatened and deprived Mr. Y of the important relationship he has with his daughter. Though this certainly is not the court's major concern, it is an important part of this case because in the documents before me, especially the one written by Dr. Black, there is a profound lack of clinical understanding of the effects of this kind of threat and potential loss on Mr. Y. Dr. Black's understanding of this case seems to ignore this important material."

Dr. Jacobs relates the above to aspects of Dr. Black's report, which seem to attempt to find picayune criticisms of Mr. Y as an obvious ploy in rationalizing a sole maternal custody decision in what was essentially a maternal kidnapping case.

Moreover, Dr. Jacobs has more pointed criticisms of Dr. Black's professional work:

"Dr. Black makes a number of incorrect assumptions on which I would like to comment.

1. After stating that X "is attached to both her parents" (p.9) she then states that a child before the age of four years cannot maintain an attachment (to a parent) in the absence of the physical presence of the attachment figure "on an almost daily basis "(p.10). Clearly in the year before their interview with Dr. Black, X and Mr. Y had not even seen each other on such a frequent basis, but X, according to Dr. Black, remains attached to her father. This is because the bonds of paternity are strong for all children, and are probably extremely powerful for this child who was raised by her father (and mother) since she was born. Ignoring the evidence she reports in her statement, Dr. Black then goes on to contradict what she sees with her own eyes. She then suggests that these parents cannot share this child because it is not in the child's best interest...It is X who wants to see both her parents, and who does not want to have to chose between them...That Dr. Black takes up (parents cause) by siding with the mother for X's sake, seems unfair to this child."

2. "Dr. Black's assertion that Mr. Y is undermining X's confidence in her mother by returning X early to the mother's home (p.9) although he stays with the child until mother returns, totally ignores the real logistical problems of visiting fathers (this father had to travel from France to England for a one daytime visit), and worse, ascribes a malevolent motivation to Mr. Y without any evidence to support her view. To my mind, it is clearly biased...Mr. Y is to be congratulated that he is on time and not late. That he stays with X until her mother returns is a testimony to his concern for his daughter's well-being."

3. "Dr. Black makes a point of saying that X's behavior on returning home from time with father "is an indication that she is beginning to be traumatized by these long separations from her mother (p.9)" I can only assume that such a statement reflects Dr. Black's lack of familiarity with what is called the "switch-over phenomena" of child visitation... It is not though to be indicative of the trauma of missing the parent to whom the child is currently being brought, but represents instead the trauma of leaving the (visitation) parent who is about to be left... NO published expert on divorce suggests that such behavior should be cause to limit visitation (excepting radical feminists such as Dr. Black-Rein)."

4. "There is no evidence to suggest that visitations that take place in the next country are any more or less difficult for a young child than visitation that takes place in the next town. Before she is in school, X can safely spend ten days alternatively with either parent. **It is the absence of either parent in her life and the parents continued conflict which will ultimately cause the most harm to this child.**"

Dr. Jacobs concluded his report by stating that if one had to make a sole custody decision it must go to the parent (father): "who shows the greatest capacity to support X's relationship with the other parent. The parent who is most supportive of the other parent's co-parent function will clearly turn out to be the more psychologically mature parent and will act in X's best interest most often.

Finally, in settling the matter in this way the court will foster the diminishment of the threat to the other parent's relationship to the child. This in the end is the most critical aspect of the resolution of the case. Since the entire situation begins with an unauthorized, threatening removal of the child from one parent by another (mother)..."

In a rather terse summary and criticism of Dr. Black's psychiatric report for custody, Judith Ryder, Lecturer in Health Education, King's College, London and author of "Balancing Acts in Personal, Social and Health Education", stated the following principle points:

1. No attempt is made to specify what Dr. Black's criteria are for determining the child's best interests.

2. The report appears to assume the mother's case for custody, leaving the burden of proof on Mr. Y to show that he is a suitable parent. Is this because of Mrs. Y's de facto role as custodial parent (based on her abduction of the child) or because Dr. Black believes that a child's best interests are automatically better served by mothers?

3. The evidence adduced by Dr, Black to reach her decision against Mr. Y's case for custody (joint custody) is dubious on two levels: much of it is subjective or, worse, trivial; there is also great difficulty for an outsider in separating 'fact' from 'opinion' in the report."

Ryder concludes after hearty critique of the Black report:

"There is a distinct lack of balance here (in the Black reporting style). I would simply register my concern at the conflation of observation, interpretation, hearsay and value judgments in Dr. Black's report and at the danger of bias and subjectivity this entails. I am not prepared to accept such lack of rigour and obfuscation in my student's work and am, thus, surprised that Dr. Black appears to ignore such distinctions in the evidence she has to handle. When the issue at stake, the child's 'best interests', is so crucial, this is unhelpful and unprofessional."

Case Resolution:

Mother got sole custody of the child and delimited father's access to her. Father had only a 1-day out of 14-day access order to the child, although the family home was in France and the child was living in England (thanks to mother's abduction). Mother interfered at every turn including blocked telephone access. Mother put an answer-machine on twenty-four hours a day. Eventually, mother used a shrill alarm sound to prevent either the child of father from hearing one another, when the young girl learned to overcome the obstacle of the answer-machine. She refused contact over and again until matters reached a point where father lost all contact to the child and they have not seen each other in years. The child is now 13 years of age.

Everything that was done in this case by the English authorities, especially Dr. Black, was done to protect the special interests of first, a woman, second an English subject, with abject disregard to the best interests of the child, in the knowledge that events would lead inevitably to the above conclusion.

I have only touched on some aspects of this case. I only warn that it is typical of the pitfalls facing fathers in all jurisdictions when so-called experts investigate and make reports. I hope the analysis is of some benefit.

Guardian-ad-Litem

In your case, you might encounter a fair-minded guardian-ad-litem, though it is doubtful! What is a guardian-ad-litem? The court appointed guardian-ad-litem is another extremely dangerous expert on our list of possible sources of mother bias and mother oriented slanting of expert reports.

My experience in both England and the US, based direct involvement, interview and case research has convinced me that these so called child representatives are rarely if ever unbiased, and nearly always associate the interests of their child clients with those of the mother. *See case of David B v Helen O*

The American Bar Association gives you a general framework for the purported role of guardian-ad-litems:

"In general, because a minor in most cases cannot initiate or defend lawsuits without adult assistance, a court will appoint a guardian ad litem for a minor appearing in court in order to ensure that the minor's interests are adequately represented. While parents usually serve as the guardian, a guardian ad litem may be appointed if a parent or general guardian is unavailable, incompetent, or has conflicting interests. Any person, including non-lawyers, may be appointed to serve in the capacity of a guardian ad litem. Some states have mandatory training in order to qualify as a guardian ad litem, while other states have no training or standards. Various terms exist for guardian ad litems, including Court Appointed Special Advocate, law guardian, or next friend.

Guardian ad litems perform various functions depending upon the state and type of court. In general, they serve one of three purposes: (1) to protect a child's "best interests" (2) to be an independent fact-finder for the judge; or (3) to follow and advocate the child's wishes. The appointment of guardian ad litems is generally considered to be within the discretionary powers of the court. They are often appointed in adoption, child custody, child support, paternity, visitation rights, and child abuse cases. Guardians ad litem have also been appointed to represent the interests of unborn heirs who are beneficiaries to a trust, in cases involving wills and trusts, and when a child has an interest in an insurance policy or some other benefit." American Bar Association

Division of Media Relations and Public Affairs "Facts about Children and the Law - What is a guardian ad litem?"

Source: Donald Kramer, "Legal Rights of Children" vol. 1, 530-543 (2nd edition, 1994).

However, two prototypical cases summarize the corrupt approach taken under cover of neutrality by the guardian ad litem to child custody issues. The first is an English case involving an American father and British mother in a child custody/visitation case, the second an American case involving the kidnapping of English children from Britain to the United States by the mother (this case is also reviewed under Parental Abductions-Hague Convention).

Case of Stephen S and a Reversed Maternal Order

Father was an American citizen. Mother was a British national. The family was living in London when conflict in the marriage took place and the couple split apart. Mother demanded full custody of the boy child, and sought to diminish the contact between father and child.

The Lord Chancellor's Department, through The Official Solicitor's Office interposed a representative (as guardian ad litem) to act on behalf of the child. During a two-year period, the family logged more than eighty court appearances at a cost to the English taxpayers of two hundred thousand pounds. The Official Solicitor constantly sided with mother and her representatives on every issue of contact. One typical example of mother's intransigence was her refusal for no apparent reason to allow father to take the child to a jazz concert that the young boy wanted to attend. Naturally, the Official Solicitor sided with the mother, and the court refused the contact.

This and other events experienced over a prolonged period of time had caused the child an extreme amount of distress, turning him away from his mother Subsequently, he ran away from mother's home demanding to remain with his father. After four years of continued pressure on him and father, they returned to court and demanded a change in the 'residence order' in favor of father. The court reluctantly acceded to the child's demand, while the child turned around and attempted to sue The Official Solicitor and other professionals involved in the case.

Case of Parental Child Abduction, David B vs. Helen O

Involved a British father and a British-Nigerian mother who had married and resided in England, They had two children, a girl aged 8 and a boy aged 5, when mother departed London with the children ostensibly for a vacation. Father understood that they were going to visit Disneyland. In the event, mother traveled to New York with the children and refused to return them to England.

Father hired an attorney and attempted to recover his children using The Hague Convention on the Civil Aspects of International Child Abduction (ICARA) as controlling law. Mother had legal aid to contest the action and under New York State law, a guardian ad litem appointed to represent the independent rights of the children.

It is worth noting that mother had no green card or any other permission to remain in the United States. As the case progressed, the guardian ad litem acted continuously to frustrate the efforts of father to affect a return of the children, siding with mother on every issue.

Under the Hague Convention, the ONLY issue before the court is whether or not the children have been abducted, and if so, then custody matters are not heard, and the children must be returned to the jurisdiction in which they had been 'habitually resident' immediately prior to the abduction. For a more detailed understanding, the reader should review the material in *Parental Abductions*.

At various points, father and his attorneys, had no idea where the abducting mother and the children were, while the Board of Education and the guardian ad litem refused to reveal their whereabouts, even in camera, to the court. This was a serious violation of law (specifically of the Hague Treaty), as well as a contempt of court. However, the judge took no remedial action. Father's attorney told me that during the trial the guardian ad litem had packed the courtroom with supporters who catcalled, shouted, and derided the counsel for father, with no action taken by the judge.

Subsequently, I took over this case on appeal and later took it to the federal district court prosecuting under The Civil Rights Act 1984. What the father's attorney reported turned out to be true as I encountered similar tactics from Lawyers for Children (guardian ad litem), the Board of Education and The British Embassy, all of who refused to reveal the whereabouts of the children. The defendants (law guardian and a panel of New York State judges in particular) made strenuous efforts to get me dismissed as father's assistance of counsel placing pressure on the federal judge.

After eighteen months of battle, in the end, I was on the record, taken off and then allowed back on it during the trial. I won this case in an extremely bizarre 'chambers decision', off the record. After I had written a compelling memorandum of law, backed by a conclusive foreign law opinion, the judge informed The British Embassy that their client (mother) was about to have a Hague Convention finding made against her for parental abduction.

Though I will never know with certainty precisely what he said, mother and the children were 'secretly' placed on a plane back to London without either the father or myself being informed by the court, even as we awaited the judge's long overdue decision. Two things were clear-the judge had communicated ex-parte with the other side, and, the children returned to Britain with the assistance of the British Consulate in New York.

The postscript to this case was that it took the father over two years in the British courts, first to get even modest access to the two children, finally getting full control over the youngest child (boy). However, by this time, his relationship with his daughter lay in ruins due to the poison injected by the mother (parental alienation syndrome) and the girl remained in mother's control and in therapy.

Parental Child Abduction Cases

If you have read the chapter on abduction, you will be familiar with many of the problems facing parents trying to locate and have their children returned into their custody following an act of abduction by the other parent.

Be aware that if your child taken and abducted out of the United States, there are two sets of laws to deal with the abduction. One is criminal and the other is civil. *See Chapter 4 Parental Child Abductions*

In these cases, you must take the following steps immediately:[45]

Immediately contact the US State Dept., Office of Children's Issues. They handle all outgoing cases of international parental child abduction.

File a missing person's report with local police and the FBI.

Go to your family court and get the judge to make an order for the return of the children, granting you interim custody if possible.

Discover, whether or not the children have been taken to a Hague signatory nation. If so, The Hague Convention on the Civil Aspects of International Child Abduction comes into operation.

If not, look to Bilateral Treaty Law between the US and the other country. There may or may not be a provision for child abduction or kidnapping that can be applied. You may be able to use the criminal statute on child abduction to obtain the return of the children and prosecution of your spouse under bi-lateral laws. *See Laws on Child Abduction*

Failing that, you will have to apply to the family court of the country in question.

In cases involving the abduction of children to other US states the following steps must be taken immediately:

File a Missing Persons Report with the local Police. If they are reluctant to file the report, insist that they must do so as this is

---

[45] Never, but never go to the country where the child is being held and submit to their jurisdiction. You would be acquiescing to the case being heard in their courts.

federally mandated. If they still refuse, call up your state branch of The National Center for Missing & Exploited Children and enlist their support. Take the matter directly to the District Attorney.

Get The National Center for Missing & Exploited Children to list your children as abducted and supply them with recent photographs. Ask them to inform the FBI of the abduction

Go straight to your local Family Court and get a custody order and an order for a return of the children back into the jurisdiction.

One excellent resource for victim parents is Maureen Dabbagh's "The Recovery of Internationally Abducted Children", McFarland & Co, 1997, especially useful for getting help on non Hague Convention cases.

Support Groups, Lobbies, and their Limitations

There are numerous so-called fathers and children's rights groups in countries all around the globe. They exist in Slovakia, France, Australia, Canada, US, England and others. Paradoxically, while anathema to radical feminist extremists, judges and legislatures, they are rather peripheral, ineffective, splintered, disorganized, under financed and without real influence or power. Have I stated the position clearly enough?

However, for tens of millions of fathers thrust into the inferno of divorce and custody proceedings, they remain a viable means of obtaining some useful information, and companionship. Perhaps, they help fathers to keep their mental equilibrium through crisis and catharsis.

Having held positions in two such organizations in diverse international jurisdictions, I am perhaps in a better position to judge the merits and drawbacks of these groups than almost any other writer on the subject. The first father's rights, or children's rights organizations came into existence as early as 1972, representing a reluctant admission by some men of the developing problems related to family dissolution and loss of their paternal function. In the main, they have proven ineffective in attempting to address the complex imbalances caused by radical feminist ideas and changing behavioral modes related to gender and family issues.

One of the principle reasons for these organizations continued ineffectiveness is the lack of key financing necessary to lobby for change. Without funding, they cannot maintain full time employees, services to members, offices, help-lines, advice centers and law libraries. They cannot endorse and support political candidates who are willing to pursue policies that agree with their constituent's views and needs.

The Women's Movement was by contrast, enabled by virtue of its access to state and federal funding. One clear example of the problems related to under funding comes from recent experience. The Children's Rights Council, an organization devoted to the principle view that the best parent is both parents, failed to send a National speaker to key New York State Senate hearings in 1997 on Joint Custody. In my correspondence with President David Levy, he painfully pointed out that the organization lacked financing and could afford only one full time paid employee in Washington.

This and other groups also find that there is a severe limitation on raising capital from amongst their memberships. For the most part, men who are members, are in the midst of costly custody battles, and have little free money for contributions, while most are not high capacity earners.

While money remains a primary problem, there are other difficulties. These difficulties connect to the very nature of the male custody dilemma and the kind of men who normally take up leadership positions. Some of these, might be well intended, but are often lacking in leadership skills and the energy necessary to press forward in areas of direct action. Others simply use their positions as a means of self-gratification or as a means to create a subsidiary livelihood.

Beyond that, there is a deep chasm amongst the leaders and organizations arguing for children's justice and men's rights. Having experienced and observed this phenomena first-hand, I can only report that divergence of views, strategies and tactics, make any sort of concerted effort impossible. Some want to sue judges whereas others attack domestic violence laws. Of course, many focus on child support issues, rather than the more fundamental ones. What they fail to comprehend is that child support issues are the 'back end of the horse', an artifact of the original custody issues. If the custody issues receive just treatment (meaning shared parenting), than child support problems will resolve themselves.

There is an utter lack of consensus on how best to concentrate attempts to reform the legal system. For instance, one organizational spokesman so fears the federal government in general, that he extends his fears to an irrational rejection of national children's rights legislation. He is so rapped up in irrelevant states rights debates, that he loses sight of the fact, that, the states have abused children of their civil and human rights.-not the federal government.

Another carries his American xenophobia forward to reject the possible impact of international children's rights law. Why? Because he cannot accept any proposition suggesting, that control can rest in any authority other than the US government. He cannot accept the idea that the people of the world know more about liberty, than Americans do. How can these foreigners teach us about the law, or civil liberties? Thus, The UN Convention on the Rights of the Child remains an avenue of redress both unexplored and unimplemented.

The bodies of children and fathers litter the playing field. The fragmented efforts of individuals and organizations are just that and doomed to aborted actions and failure. What all of these organizations and leaders fail to appreciate is the fact that efforts must have focus. Given the economic limitations, the numbers involved over diverse jurisdictions, time and effort constraints, as well as other roadblocks, it is important for resources to channel into viable directions.

Simple logic dictates that all groups work to one common goal and attack one primary source of injustice, not fifty, or one hundred and fifty. The flow of energy should be the same for British, Australian, German and American fathers. At the very least, each should focus on national legislation. Where possible, each should contribute to the national incorporation of international law affecting children's rights. Once that is accomplished, the battlefield will shift to the judicial process of each country for the challenge of abuse of national and international law. This kind of challenge will carry far more force.

Finally, when it comes to these palpitating blood issues, men lack the organizational commitment to one another failing to see and act on the broad issues. I have often heard from fathers that, 'I would like to do more, but I'm in the middle of my own case.' Men, unlike women, do not have a group survival instinct. Men have not learned from the historical experience of the women's movement.

Out of Court Settlements

Of course, it is possible to avoid custodial conflicts, if the parties can negotiate between themselves or with the assistance of a counselor, or with cooperating attorneys. There are millions of cases managed and resolved in this way. Kudos goes to those parents who set aside personal agendas in order to consider the best interests of their children.

There are important fundamentals to bear in mind when negotiating an out of court settlement. Principle amongst them is that unlike most other law cases, a family matter can be re-opened many times until the age of majority of the children. For example; Mother and father agree to joint legal custody of the children, but mother is the principle caregiver. Father sees the children for x amount of the time. Some time later mother meets another man and wishes to remarry and to re-locate to another state, province, or country. Or, mother decides to move in with her family, or take up a job somewhere else. Despite the fact that the parties have made this agreement, mother can and will return to court seeking the relocation order she desires. Accordingly, the latest interpretations of law in numerous jurisdictions make clear that the court will rubberstamp her decision.

Now, if father had an ironclad agreement that called for both joint legal and physical custody, he would stand on much firmer ground in arguing against the relocation of his children to another geographic area.

I would put into the language of the settlement a clear acknowledgment of the literature, the precise reasoning of both parties agreement on shared parenting as being in the best interests of the child, and a provision that no future events and relationships can alter the parties' agreement without the express consent of the other party.

However, it must be noted that an out of court settlement covering financial arrangements such as child support is assailable by mother on many grounds, one being changing circumstances. It is further noted, that mother has acquired an extra legal reach through The Interstate Child Support Act, giving access to federal as well as state courts. Additionally, due to a theory known as 'Comity', financial orders are given credence by the courts of one national state in the courts of another nation state and are covered by local statutes.

In summary, if I were the father involved I would on no account accept any agreement that did not fully endorse shared parenting in principle and fact, nor from my position as a children's rights advocate could I accept anything less.

The Use of Pre-Nuptial Agreements

One practical means to preempt problems generated by divorce and custody actions, when a mother seeks to eliminate the rights of children and fathers, is the use of pre-nuptial agreements.

These agreements, although not holding a guarantee of family court acceptance, especially when one tries to project future directions of court policy in diverse jurisdictions, offer at least principle evidence of a contractual intent to guarantee the provision of shared parenting to children in the event of divorce.

The initial problem is lack of male recognition of the potential problem. In matters of love and marriage, men have proven themselves completely naïve, lacking information, foresight and knowledge of what is taking place at present in family relations. They might, as well, be fearful that introducing such an agreement into the romantic relationship might sour the romance, create distrust and suspicion. They might be right in this appraisal, but it might be better to be safe than sorry.

Part II

Chapter 9

The Historic Development of the Family

To fully understand modern family disruption we need to trace human development of sexual regulation, interpersonal gender relationships and child nurturance over a long time. In ancient Rome the family model transposed into a monogamous patriarchal system. This system regulated female sexual behavior under cover of protection, ensuring nurturance of offspring and continuity of economic resources. The system had legal codification.

In exchange for their sacrifice in the name of family (a lifetime of protection-provision-nurturing), men as husbands and fathers had permission to treat their wives and children as chattel, as property. In other words, men had ownership over women. Men even had the right to sell or put their wives and children to death if it pleased them.

During the time of the Emperor Constantine, the state began to intercede to delimit these rights of men setting historical precedent for modern state intervention in family matters (Irving et al 1984).

Although there is little documented evidence of widespread oppression of women or infanticide, no one in contemporary society would endorse a family system in which children and women might remain without rights and status. We are a human and civil rights conscious society. We celebrate the rights of the individual without regard to race, religion or gender. Historically, the position of women and children viz. a viz. the family remained largely unaltered at least until the middle to end of the nineteenth century. Male law courts began to address the inequity of a situation in which women found themselves protected but enslaved within marriages and treated as their husband's chattel.

Following the important British Act of 1839 (discussed elsewhere), by the turn of the century, the British Parliament passed the Guardianship of Children's Act of 1905. This Act radically changed the approach law courts would take in dealing with matters of divorce and custody. The Act basically declared that men and women coming before the court would come as equals and that the interests of children would take preference over those of the parents in deciding custody matters[46]. Decisions in US courts roughly paralleled those of Great Britain and the new doctrines gradually became enshrined as black letter law[47] in both countries. Women and children had rights.

From 1900 through the Industrial Revolution

Along with this important first legal change in the status of women, came other reformations of the traditional family structure that had great and lasting significance. The modern world had undergone one earlier industrial revolution and now headed for a second one. It had immediate impact on family life and affect on its social, psychological and political dynamic.

Here one must bear in mind that before industrialization families lived and worked more or less together. The family environment was interactive, close and offspring were nurtured by both parents, albeit it in different ways. The Industrial Revolution changed that. Men forced

---

[46] Paramountcy of the child's interests
[47] Judge made law built up over time

out of the home and away from agrarian endeavors moved into the factory workplace in order to provide for their families. This marked the time when the term "Provider" entered the social and psychological vocabulary describing men as both husbands and fathers.

"When the preference was for male workers, women assumed increasing responsibility for child rearing and domestic chores. Fathers became unavailable to their children and changed from influential agents of socialization to economic providers only." (Huntington 1986, Lamb 1981)

Simultaneously, women acquired the description of exclusive "Nurturers" of children. The early developmental child psychiatric literature reinforced these overstated and stereotypical characterizations of both men and women within the revised family structure. Therefore, these limited characterizations gained conceptual legitimacy.

The establishing of family gender related stereotyping, though not of great significance at the time, came to play a major role in the lives of children of later generations and would be manipulated by the feminist cultural elite. However, even though psychiatrists had erroneously perceived and defined family relationships, these relationships continued to function in relative balance within normal boundaries. In the context of stable relationships, absent of separation and divorce issues, conditions and events did not exist to cause traumatic or substantial alterations to the essential structure.

Clearly, church and state frowned upon divorce. Further, historical psychological and social imperatives worked against its incidence. From a legal perspective, the relatively sparse numbers of divorce and custody actions were traumatic, publicly embarrassing and difficult for many to obtain. Most families had little practical recourse but to work at resolving marital problems or to remain conflictual and accept a degree of dysfunctionality. Divorce was fault based and determined on objective, not subjective evidence.

Change was on the way.

The Social Revolution of the Sixties

In order to grasp the fundamentals of contemporary family breakdown, gender conflict and threat to our children's health and best interests, we need to look for causative factors. None can possibly be of greater significance than the social revolution that took place in the nineteen sixties. An event or series of events can trigger changes to essential structures.

In an exciting epoch of radical social reorganization, containing new visions, challenges, hopes and rising expectations, we discern the prime catalyst or triggering events for the family drama unfolding over the past thirty years[48]. Dr. Dorothy Huntington later observed that there had been fundamental shifts in family constructs growing out of the sixties culture:

" A gradual realization that attainment of women's rights depend on changes in men's roles led to an understanding that increased paternal participation at home and with children was not only desirable but essential."

Thus revealed was a twin phenomenon, rising feminism (liberal feminism) and concomitant recognition of the importance of paternal influence. Lamb's observations (1983), confirmed Huntington's view:

"The acknowledgement and recognition of paternal influences on child development occurred-probably not coincidentally-at a critical point in the lives of the civil rights and women's rights movement."

These developments force us to re-trace our steps back to this uncompromising era. We need to review the changes taking place while keying on those agents and agencies interacting with other dynamic forces to produce the effects on family structure and children that so trouble our consciences today.

Typically, the period saw a youthful rebellion from traditional family values. An almost unconscious collective recognition demanded a time for a voyage of discovery through experimentation and self-examination. The sixties generation was led beyond the portals of blind faith and obedience into the open, uncharted spaces of

---

[48] See Rummel's theory of The Conflict Helix, Chapter 10

a radical new life style. Simultaneously, in America, Britain, France and Germany, tens of millions of young men and women began to express a rapidly developing set of fresh ideals. The base of information access expanded enabling a free movement of these new ideas. A universal, international collective was born, with the various multi-cultural groups forming into one earth shattering youth movement.

What began as rather timid, innocent and youthful rebellion became a culture of alternative lifestyle. What changed things?

For one thing, there was an unjust war beginning in Asia. Involvement in Viet Nam began slowly with the selective support of a local fascist regime in South Viet Nam. Significant numbers of apologists and self-interest parties rationalized intercession as necessary in order to protect democracy from the threat of worldwide communist aggression. Youth, however, began to question the premise and the raison d'etre of those who argued for United States involvement.

A doctrine was invented known as "The Domino Theory". This doctrine explained why South Viet-Nam needed protection by America. It's simple logic declared that if one nation fell to the communist hordes, then another and another would go until the whole world fell to this red menace. American public opinion controlled by government agencies and powerful vested economic interests bought it. That is all but the now rebellious and suspicious youth movement.

Without a doubt, the sixties generation grew increasingly hostile to this 'limited' war in Vietnam. Between 1960 and 1964, while that involvement was taking place, another battlefield formed at home. The sixties generation, along with informed and motivated elder colleagues, were disgusted by the legal, social and economic suffering faced by black Americans. In the southern states, race discrimination and civil rights deprivations flourished. This dehumanizing injustice prevailed despite the fact that an Act of Congress enacted (first in 1865, and then again in 1871) (The Ku Klux Klan Act), set out protections for the constitutional rights of black Americans. Black Americans lived lives relegated to a sub species of human being, not entitled to equal rights, due process and to the protection of our esteemed constitution.

Individuals, groups, organizations formed to pressurize the American legal and governmental system into enforcing existing law and restoring the rights of this important minority group. The youth movement joined with CORE, NAACP, American Civil Liberties Union, religious leaders, and artists. They marched bravely into the South. They staged demonstrations, rallies, sit-ins, and helped to lobby politicians and government leaders. By 1964, after President Kennedy's untimely death, Congress had passed the revised version of The Civil Rights Act 1964 and federal agencies acted aggressively to end segregation, bringing prosecutions under the new Act.

Viewed from the perspective of an informed, inquiring, and already rebellious generation, the signals sounded clear. "All was not for the best in the best of all possible worlds" and rebellion had turned into revolution.

As the Viet Nam war gathered force, prodded on by the military-industrial complex grown bold by lack of serious mainstream opposition and ever- rising profits, millions of sixtiers forged a powerful opposition coalition. Some of it organized and some of it based on the new collective consciousness. This coalition of youth voiced an angry, militant advocacy against the Vietnamese War and all it represented. How did all this operate to change male-female relations?

Changes in Male-Female Perceptions

Coincidentally, there was an entirely different side to the revolution that was taking place. Social, political and economic injustice in America and an unseemly war in Asia had stirred a whole generation into political action. Moreover, their disquietude preceding these events had already stirred them into revision of their value systems rejecting those of their parents.

Whether a part of cognitive reality evolved over time or merely the child of circumstances, young men's views of women had shifted dramatically. I rather expect it was a combination of both unconscious transition and thoughtful revision of earlier thinking. After all, young men now worked side by side with women. The genders mobilized as equals against political repression, denial of civil liberties, and a war in Viet Nam. During these periods of interpersonal contact, intensely focused on non-gender related or sexual issues, they inevitably had their perceptions of one another altered. Sixties women had become sharers of their male counterpart's political and social experiences, goals and aspirations. The new commonality of interests had severed the bonds of the old sexual and gender stereotypes.

Another important factor in the fast paced social-sexual revolution of the period was the invention of "the pill" giving women the confidence to express their sexuality without fear or concern about unwanted and fettering pregnancies. Not only did they discover a new confidence but with it came a rather invigorating freedom. Gone were the accoutrement of petticoats and braids, prissiness and feigned coquettishness. Petticoats gave way to mini and micro mini skirts. Men were beginning to burn draft cards and women their bras. Women, freed from the shackles of past constraints could and often did approach men initiating flirtations and sexual relationships. Long-term predicates became as un-necessary as did guilt and social pressure. Young men, far from fearing or being suspicious about the changing attitudes and habits of women, embraced the new zeitgeist and surely benefited from it's more obvious effects.

For the most part, a gender revolution was taking place that was a micro system ensconced within the larger framework of the sixties socio-political revolution. Initially, and for a considerable period of the decade it was restricted to university campuses and the more cosmopolitan urban centers where intellectuals and artists lived. However, just as the decade progressed so the effects spread wider. It reached into the hinterlands of Iowa, the little towns of New England and even into the South. It infused itself into the minds and spirits of a much larger consensus of women.

The principles promoted by the sixties generation in relation to human dignity, freedom, equality and justice had naturally extended to the protection of minorities and those not empowered. It is, therefore, hardly surprising that one such extension would be the formation of a women's liberation movement. Inspired by the writings of Simone DeBouvoir and Betty Friedan, the politics of recent experience and self-discovery, women sought to overcome obstacles (whether real or imagined) in more mainstream areas of American life. It is equally unsurprising given the climate of the times that sixties men naively sounded their approval and lent their moral and practical support to the women's movement.

The Nuclear Family 1965-1984

The sexual liaisons formed by the sixties generation at the end of the decade were inherently different to those formed by previous generations given all that had been experienced. The floodgates of change had been thrown open. The dam had burst. Relationships formed between men and women based on a new concept-mutuality.

The Women's Movement gained national and international prominence as a potent political, economic and social force, later spawning a strident, hawkish and effective feminist minority lobby. Just as women had proved assertive and organized lobbyists in the early part of the twentieth century fighting for the right to vote, they would now do so once again. However, now, having the benefit of the sixties experiences they were far better placed to organize, lobby, and pressure for public policy changes as well as reach out to their millions of sisters informing their opinions.

Feminists argued that although an educated minority of them had scaled the heights of male injustice and domination, millions of other women were still in the control of a male dominated society. To them, religious dogma, social mores and vestigial psychological dynamics still enchained the majority of women. They rejected past models of family life in which women had been restricted to or had limited themselves to stereotypical roles and called upon their 'sisters' to join them in the fight against patriarchy.

There can be little doubt that marriages pushed forward under the new construction of 'mutuality' steadily moved millions of more conservative women to form similar unions. What followed was a radically altered family unit. The traditional family had given way to the nuclear and then to the post nuclear family. The primary change to the structure flowed from the premise that men and women were equal, relationships with men were 'negotiated' and based on mutuality.

The old notions of man as hunter-gatherer and woman as nurturer/homemaker were no longer relevant to a modern and allegedly enlightened society. The perception of these rejected ideas was that they were neither equitable nor productive. For the purposes of this book, what impact does a new structure have on family law? Let me review the situation. There is now mutuality in relationships. Earlier twentieth century developments saw women winning important legal concessions in the arena of custody processes. Mid-twenties psychiatric literature began to describe men as mere 'providers' and women as biological 'nurturers'. The question now arises as to whether or not the conclusions previously drawn in the psychiatric literature during the industrial revolution were either essentially false or had been overtaken by events and modern revision of the family dynamic proffered by women's leaders. The answer was and is that the psychiatric investigators were in serious error and events had indeed overtaken their previous work.

Another question also arises as to whether or not the common law and codified legal rights favoring women in family court scenarios remained on the table. It would seem obvious from all available evidence that women's codified and common law rights have remained in place. Nevertheless, the question of the marginalized role and reduction of rights for men in marriage becomes a rather complicated and enduring enigma. This is especially so in light of two factors: modern women's drive for equality within the family and expression of other life goals outside of the family and their encouragement of male nurturing. If women were no longer exclusive nurturers and men no longer exclusive providers, then what were they?

The quintessential element of the optimized post nuclear family structure seems to have been, at least superficially, that the roles of men and women were somewhat more flexible and interchangeable.

Each capable, at least in theory, of nurture and provision of means leading to presumed shared responsibilities and equal self-expression. Women, having gained control over their bodies and reproductive function, could regulate the timing and number of offspring. Men enjoyed freedom from immediate paternal pressures and from their burdensome 'sole provider' role. At least in theory, the new family structure began with a sense of mutual independence, freedom, equality and with far greater social and economic mobility.

The past stabilizing, although inhibiting, influences of church, state and social behavioral codes were clearly on the wane. Unions between men and women founded now on mutuality rather than on the habitual compulsion and almost ritualistic fatalism of past generations. The sixties had produced a generation of women whose educational opportunities had vastly increased and whose visions of life had encompassed far more than those of their predecessors. Clearly, they sought to combine mating and childrearing with previously described 'male pursuits'. They sought to expand their horizons in a search for a greater meaning to their lives. The past model man and husband was considered arcane and disposable. Women called for men to become more 'sensitized' to the needs of women and lauded the male who was a caring-sharing man, one in tune with the modern woman. The Charles Atlas model male was as dead as the notion of man as a hunter-gatherer.

In parallel, the feminist movement, riding on the back of the black minority's sudden and dynamic social progress, sought redress and reformation from a socio-political and economic system which had, in their view, excluded them. Just as the black minority pressed for equal educational and employment opportunity, women too began to press for change and space for self-expression in the workplace. Now, the abstract of the new family model began to take shape in earnest. Women were entering the workplace.

Another factor in the equation was the formidable growth in the federal and state governments commitment to minorities. One manifestation was financial support in adjustment to recent political, legal and social developments. From the mid-sixties on a multitude of grants had become available. Perhaps these grants initiated out of national guilt, perhaps as a sop to disenfranchised groups. Moreover, government economic involvement marked a quantum leap from the so-called welfare state to the affirmative action 'rehabilitation' state. While these grants and other funding primarily focused on assistance to black Americans, they initiated a conceptual revolution leading rather inevitably to the funding of other 'so called' minorities or classifications. The Women's Movement became a net beneficiary of other government interventions and funding.

The grants and funding gave women's groups the opportunity to not only disseminate information, informing and misinforming a wider public and to argue for a change in consciousness, but allowed them to create an extremely powerful lobby at all levels of government. These early developments have come to play an important part in aspects of the dilemma we face today.

In order to understand the complex dynamics of our modern social and interpersonal maelstrom, we need to chart the growth and direction of the post nuclear family over a long period. We have to red flag all visible changes both to family models and to male-female relationships. As remarked earlier, the traditional family unit had, historically remained intact, predictable, and relatively stable. What would happen to men, women and our children, given the challenges thrown up by this radical departure from what had been the normal value system? We know for a fact that the incidence of separation and divorce from between the turn of the century through the mid-sixties had been stable and of little statistical significance. We know, therefore, it had no real societal effect. Would marriages structured in the new style 'mutuality' be as stable? No! Would children suffer a myriad of disorders subsequent of divorce? Yes!

In retrospect, women's urge for freedom from past constraints and injustices carried them forward without regard to the consequences of their acquired liberty. To paraphrase Eric Fromm, women really 'escaped from freedom' as so called liberation led to both inner contradiction and problematic relationships with men inside of the new family model. The altered societal and family structure affected women in two ways simultaneously. Women became more independent, self-reliant, critical and self-expressive, while over time they became more isolated, alone, suspicious, selfish and fearful.

Moreover, the introduction of confused intellectual feminist rhetoric and concepts, has only exacerbated matters for the family and women as one can see from the following comments:

"For many women," says feminist Dr. Alice Rossi "the personal outcome of experience in the parent role is not a higher level of maturation but the negative outcome of a depressed sense of self-worth, if not actual personality deterioration."

"The heart of woman's oppression," says Shulamith Firestone, "is her childbearing and childrearing roles."

Thus, feminist thinkers equate parenting, giving birth and nurturing with measures of loss of self-esteem, depression, and those roles considered as sources of oppression. Dr. Rossi and Ms. Firestone are paradoxically denying both the nature of woman and her source of power. While these two radical feminists assign such negative values to women's experience and natural bio-chemical roles, the reader will see elsewhere in this book that when convenient, radical feminists paradoxically reverse their position and assign extremely positive values to nurturing. This is especially true in a climate of divorce and non-marital separation.

As one can see, the negative aspects of post nuclear family models resides in the notion that freedom from perceived psychological and societal oppressiveness was not enough in itself to avert the devils from internal contradictions. Women's freedom from perceived oppression was one thing, their freedom to, another thing. The external evils were easy for women to target but, judging by Rossi and Firestone, feminist thinking has failed to resolve the contradictions arising from their so-called liberation. Nor does it wish to.

One of the most salient facts about post nuclear family structure is that along with the new freedoms of women came a reduction in their commitment to their relationship within the marriage. This was not immediately evident except for noting that special law courts came into creation to deal with steeply rising (though little noted) numbers of divorce and custody issues. Statistical analysis of the divorce figures over time confirms this sudden lack of commitment to marriage. *See Chapter 10 Graphs on Divorce & Lone Parenting*

There are numerous factors governing the behavior of women after the liberation of the sixties, including control over their reproductive function, educational opportunity, growing economic and employment power. Significantly, their reliance on men and commitment to their husband-fathers fell proportionally to their increase in status and empowerment.

Contradictorily, just as their ultimate reliance on their spouses decreased, they simultaneously made role-changing demands on their men as partners and co-nurturers of their offspring. Inevitably, by the early nineteen eighties the divorce statistics reflect the strain on the psycho-dynamics of post nuclear family structure and we observe dramatic increases in the divorce rate in most industrialized countries. It is not difficult to construct a hypothesis suggesting that women's new freedoms had actually lessened any necessity for them to make long-term pro-creational relationships work. It made it more or less predictable that almost any stress or conflict within the marriage would end in summary separation and divorce. Women's freedom came without any accompanying sense of responsibility or comprehension of its affect on men or their children.

In lamenting our collective failures to form lasting relationships, Laurie Lee has stated it most lyrically and succinctly:

" Perhaps the main cause of our failure still lies in our attitude to love itself-that it is good only so long as it pleases, and that as soon as it drops one degree below the level of self-satisfaction it is somehow improper to attempt to preserve it. This is the natural expression of that contemporary fallacy- the divine right to personal happiness, the rule of self-love, to be enjoyed without effort, at no matter what cost to others. Whoever gave us this right to be merely happy and what makes us think it so enlightened an idea? In claiming the sanction to withdraw from any relationship the moment our happiness appears less than perfect, we are acting out a delusion, which denies all but the most trivial kind of love. Worse still, it makes a paper house of marriage, flimsily built for instant collapse, haunted by rootless children whose sense of incipient desertion already dooms them to an emotional wasteland. Indeed the interpretation of rights that allows the jettisoning of children in furtherance of their parents right to happiness, not only cancels that happiness but makes more than reasonably certain that the next generation will be denied it too."

If you rent a house, you can easily pack the bags and depart. When buying one you throw your life savings into it, your hopes and dreams. Marriages for women were becoming house rentals rather than home purchases.

All that was now required to complete the cycle of disassociate marital relationships was an external validating and enabling system. Divorces had been difficult to obtain within the 'traditional family structure' as I have previously pointed out. However, by the early nineteen eighties, under the increasing power and influence of the feminist organizations, pressure was being placed on the legal system to initiate family law reform. This reform made it easy for women to get divorces, acquiring sole custody and economic benefits along the way. The so-called male establishment had slowly been yielding ground in a number of areas, including women's ease of access into the family law section of the legal profession. Feminists had been successful in lobbying for legislative change and handed a virtual fiefdom in the newly formed 'family law' area. These developments occurred in parallel, confirmed in two rather important countries at roughly the same time. One example can be found in the revised divorce law of New York State in 1966 and 1980 and in The Divorce Law Reform Act 1984 of England, Northern Ireland and Wales. *See The Impact of Contemporary Divorce Law Reform.*

The legal criteria for obtaining divorces was severely simplified and eased. One or other of the parties no longer had to establish proof of dastardly behavior, merely unreasonable behavior, irreconcilable differences or mutual consent. Gone were the onerous jury trials, public scrutiny and private detectives and in came the new breed of specialist mother oriented divorce lawyers and accountants, psychologists, social workers and welfare agencies. Although Attorney Barbara Sobal points out that in New York State, one can still have a jury trial on the grounds[49], this is not common practice and in any

---

[49] New York State Domestic Relations Law ("DRL") Section 173

event does not apply to the issues of custody. *See Reform of the Legal System*

The direct consequences of this law reform was an immediate escalation of divorce percentages leaping up to 25% and more and the creation of a new and profitable 'cottage industry' making multi millions off the pain and suffering of children. *See Graphs on Lone Parenting and Divorce in Chapter 10*

While the observed affects of recent law reform also included the visible increase in women who were becoming the initiators of divorce and custody actions, no doubt because not only were they now coming to courts as equals, but were actually gaining economic advantage and protection under the law in respect to the division of marital assets. Both anecdotal evidence and controlled research shows that women are the initiators of the vast majority of divorces. *See California Study, See Dr. Cornec*

The covert consequences of these developments were that we were beginning to foster a generation of tens of millions of children who no longer lived in intact, two parent homes, and who, invariably would suffer from the psychological affects of an enforced, court fostered father-absence.

The Post Nuclear Family 1984-Present

If the period from 1965 to 1984 had seen a dramatic increase in the numbers of divorce and custody actions, past family displacements would now escalate into an avalanche of family turmoil. Divorce figures reached proportions that no one had or could have predicted when the traditional family unit had transmogrified into the post nuclear family unit. Rates of divorce during the period of 1984 to the present have risen to a conservative estimation of between 40 to 60%, especially in large urban centers in America and Europe. Further, informed professional predictions amongst the psychiatric community envision that these rates will literally go off the scale, with a probability that each man and woman will end up marrying three times in their lifetimes.

Numbers are not the only unfortunate changes undergone by our post nuclear family. However, they do reflect one area of impact of catastrophic developments in the psychodynamics of gender relations. Deteriorating relations between women and men have led to marital problems causing separation and divorce.

A recent study conducted by sociologist Edward Laumann at The University of Chicago found widespread sexual dysfunction amongst our population with more than forty percent of women reporting very little interest in sex and inability to have an orgasm, while thirty three percent of men had similar difficulties. The author stated that he was "stunned" by the results that were based on a sample of 1,749 women and 1,410 men between the ages of eighteen to fifty nine (Journal of the American Medical Association, Anne Landers column September 20th 1999). I take the view that the gender schism is at the root of this finding on sexual dysfunction and that it will continue until conditions exist that might reverse the trend.

While difficult to pin down with precision it seems apparent that somewhere between 1970 and the eighties attitudes of women toward men became increasingly hostile in fact and theory. Perhaps, in large measure, this was due to the influence of militant cultural-radical feminist organizations. Their strident rhetoric and propaganda had ingrained formidable anti-male views into the collective consciousness of significant numbers of women.

Women, bombarded by a plethora of books, press articles, TV coverage, magazines, lobbying and by peer pressure, began to cross an invisible line. On the one side stood a genetic imprint allowing for positive relations with men and on the other a world in which general perceptions of males suffered negativity to such an extent that the chances for healthy concords with men would prove impossible.

Braver, S., & O'Connell, D. (1998), Taking on myth 6: Who leaves the marriage...and why it matters. In Divorced Dads: Shattering the myths (pp. 125-145). New York: Tarcher/Putnam, reported:

"Three social changes that have increased women's propensity to divorce include the establishment of no-fault divorce laws, women's financial independence and presence in the work force, and **the women's movement**. While men have increased their roles as fathers and husbands, women's tolerance for their husbands' failings has decreased."

How did this shocking state of affairs reveal itself? To an aware observer, the answer was and still can be found in both in language and events, studied separately and taken together. Traditionally, at least through to the middle-sixties, there had always been a rather benign and gently oversimplified male-female 'war of the sexes' often playfully illustrated in our more common cultural literature.

Male Scapegoating & Media

This mock war was humorously described and memorialized in the cinema by films such as "Battle of the Sexes" and produced a host of heroes-heroines such as Alec Guiness, Doris Day and Rock Hudson. The common perception of the male was as endearingly philandering, childish and impractical, while the portrayal of women was as nurturing, practical and patient. The models were always stereotypical and in the end, the sexes resolved all conflicts forming into stable family units producing progeny. Thus, the movie models conformed to pre-seventies society psychosexual ideals. One truly amusing example that took mock conflict to an extreme was "How to Murder Your Wife", starring Jack Lemmon and Virna Lisi.

However, by the nineteen eighties the popular cultural language and real events caused an enormous reversal in attitudes. We went from scherzo to fugue in the flash of a microsecond with no bridge between the two. Unflattering terms, never before used to describe men, now entered the scene, encouraged by a feminist establishment whose political agenda had run amok. A new agenda seemed focused on regaling and denigrating all men. From a linguistic analysis, terms such as 'oppressors', misogynists', 'patriarchal', 'domineering', 'discriminatory', 'insensitive', 'violent', and 'condescending' indicated a changing landscape. Such slanders represented a few of the epithets hurled at the male population. As a society, we went from innocent stereotypical depictions of male-female relations and marriage to a brutal portrayal of men all lumped together as perpetrators of child and sexual abuse, kidnapping, domestic violence and as lacking in fidelity. While women continued to enjoy universal representation symbolizing mother earth, the good nurturer, loyal wife and victim of male oppression and betrayal.

Typical for more recent film industry trends, in "Striptease" the heroine (Demi Moore) goes before a family court judge demanding custody of her son against the wishes of an evil, gangster husband. Remarkably, against all real life statistical proofs, the judge grants custody to the father making her a victim who rises to overcome male oppression and control. She says to the judge, "My husband is a criminal. I hardly think that makes him capable of raising our son." The judge replies, " Oh and a mother without a job is better?" This deliberate prevarication of the film i.e. that a male judge will grant custody to a criminal father over an unemployed good mother is simply preposterous but, illustrates the use of media as feminist propaganda. Only in "Kramer v Kramer", 1987, have we ever seen a major Hollywood film in which father earns custody over mother (unrealistically of course), and as the film implied, that was an exceptional event. Of course there was "Armageddon" in which mother deserted the family, while Bruce Willis raised his daughter. That is an exception to the rule!

I would challenge the reader to make a random selection of say 100 movies made over time during the past twenty years. See the portrayal of each of the genders in films whose theme or sub plot involved family, husbands and wives or children and divorce.

My research shows that for every 100 films in this subject area approximately 98 of them will be anti-male and pro-female at various levels of intensity. Women in these films are almost universally described as nurturing, open, peaceful and victims of male violence, discrimination, domination and insensitivity. Hard-line feminist language, thinking and actions in communications media cannot be underestimated in its effect because with growing political, social, economic power and with greater access to the communication media, their voices were and are heard far and wide.

The National Fatherhood Initiative (1999, March), Fatherhood & TV: What does prime time network television say about fatherhood, reported:

"This article examines how prime time network television presents fatherhood, with a focus on frequency of father appearance, father portrayal, and whether some networks are more father friendly than others. The sample was limited to shows, which aired on the five major networks CBS, NBC, Fox, WB, and ABC between November and December 1998. The sampled shows met three criteria: a father was a recurring character; the father-child relationship was the focus of the show; and the children were 18 years old or younger. The shows were then evaluated for five dimensions of responsible fatherhood: father involvement with family activities, father engagement with the child, father guidance as a role model for his children, father competence, and family and father role the father's top priority. The study found that of 102 shows, only 15 featured fathers as a recurring character.

Furthermore, on Saturday evening, when most families are watching television, no shows featured fathers during prime time hours. Fathers were invariably married or single, custodial fathers; non-custodial fathers, who in reality make up 40 percent of all fathers, are absent from prime time television. The study found mixed portrayals of fathers. Of the 15 father-including shows, four gave positive portrayals, four negative, with the remaining seven portraying positive fathers who were deficient in some fathering area. Only 40 percent of the shows portrayed competent fathers. Involved fathers were portrayed as incompetent men, while competent men are portrayed as uninvolved fathers. The researchers found that the WB network had the most shows with positive portrayals of fathers. The researchers stress that television, as an instrument of mass media, needs to do more to promote responsible fatherhood."

Leaning heavily on the language of the black experience, borrowing and transposing terms, counting on America's guilt about race relations as well as the past war in Southeast Asia these radical feminists benefited from a wave of misplaced national sympathy and guilt. They seized the moment to seek unwarranted power and undue influence in the corridors of the establishment and in the minds and hearts of women.

The complex psycho-dynamic balance of gender relations was being turned on it's head without even the slightest shred of comprehension, first, that it was happening at all, and second, of the affect on the future of male-female and family relationships. The deep-seated hatred and condemnation of 'all men' promulgated by the radical feminists would slowly erode the already shaken foundations of mutuality developed by the sexes as an aftereffect of the sixties experience. The creation of universal negative stereotyping and scapegoating of men would ultimately allow for the de-personalization of men as husbands and fathers within the post nuclear family. This made divorce a far greater, more attractive option, and its terms harsher than one could imagine in respect to our children.

If all men were inherently bad and all women were universally good, one could only conclude that in the particular the dissolution of their marital relationships was predictable and inevitable. Having drawn that conclusion, it follows that the offspring of the marriage were far better off in the care and control of the 'good' mother than in the care of the 'bad' father. Armed with false moral rationalization, women seeking and obtaining divorces did so with an enmity that had been notably absent in the period immediately following the sixties revolution. Sitting astride this moral imperative was the existence of an extremely aggressive cottage industry. This industry consisted in part of family lawyers spurring their female clients on to conflictual divorce actions while reinforcing their client's subjective and destructive views.

Correspondingly, millions of men implored by the feminists in their more tantalizing propaganda to 'become caring-sharing new men' and who had tried to cooperate now lay fallen in states of total confusion and de-moralization. The very demands on them by their spouses to change their consciousness and to be co-nurturers of their children, once met, would now act to psychologically disable them in the post nuclear family divorce. The modern literature on the affect of divorce and loss of paternal function confirms that men can suffer a number of pathologies (Jacobs 1986). Wives, in obtaining divorces in huge numbers, sought not merely the lion-share of family assets but sought importantly the murder of their spouses as parents to their children. Psychiatrist Frank Williams notes that:

"Psychological parentectomy develops in the minds of mothers..."

He notes amongst the causes a boyfriend or stepfather influence over the mother and financial pressures influenced by " judges awarding higher child support payments to mothers whose children are with them most of the time". He also mentions the negative influence of mental health professionals stressing the need for structure and stability in the post-divorce life of the child. He recognized that "when a mother...takes steps to toward erasing the presence of a father, " her underlying motive may in part be expressing her chronic, unresolved anger with the father" and finishes by stating that:

"The negative aspects of such parental (read mother) anger on children of divorce have already been illustrated in the psychological literature (Kelly 1981, Derdeyn 1983)"

It is evident that the law in fact (not theory), once reformed in favor of the rights of women, had not equally recognized nor addressed the changing structure of the family relationship and role of fathers in the post nuclear family unit. The law had failed in practice to maintain balance in its approach to family matters. Children of divorce handed over to their mothers in sole custody lost their fathers and fathers had little or no access to their offspring.

Until recently, the trauma and affect on these men of the loss of cherished paternal relationships gained little recognition or study. While I do not intend to deal extensively with this aspect of divorce and custody, I simply note that a number of psychiatrists have concurred with what Dr. Jacobs described as 'Involuntary Child Absence Syndrome' (Jacobs 1986) which occurs precipitated by divorce and custody situations in which father loses contact and rights in respect to his children. *See Chapter 11, Consequences of the Destruction of Intact Families, The After effects*

However, the research and psychiatric literature from the mid-seventies onward did begin to deal with the affects on children due to separation and divorce and demonstrated that the loss of a parent in a two-parent home, was the single most devastating effect a child could suffer. For a variety of reasons as I will show later, this research was largely ignored. *See Chapters 2, 3*

Moving out of the eighties and into this decade, the divorce rate had continued to spiral out of control. This does not even take into account the huge numbers of non-marital families that separate and escape the statistical net. The original post nuclear family had undergone a metamorphosis into the non-intact post nuclear family and now into the statistically significant ' female-headed single- parent family unit'. Two decades of cumulative anti-male propaganda had made a generic attack on men both politically fashionable and complete.

County, state and national divorce courts are burdened with caseloads that far exceed their capacity to deal with the issues of family dissolution and the numbers of children living their lives absent of their fathers has mounted into the tens of millions. *See ABA Statistics.*

The Children's Rights Council had once estimated that five million American children did not see their father within 18 months of separation or divorce. As of 1994, out of a population of some seventy million children in the USA there were officially about 12 and a half million living in single parent homes, 11 million of them with their mothers. These figures were extremely inaccurate and seriously underestimated the actual numbers involved. This is similar to the divorce figures not accounting for the dissolution of millions of long-term child bearing relationships. Present estimates have reached an incredible 22 to 28 million children living in single-parent homes.

As the statistics prove, women in increasing numbers have moved steadily to reduce, limit or severe the ties between their former spouses and the children and have rejected all father's pleas for joint custody or shared parenting after divorce. *See Appendix A*

Organized Feminist Opposition to Shared Parenting

One glaring example of the new female intransigence to male participation in the post-divorce parenting of children recently came to my attention. There is at it happens one particular anomalous county (Monroe County, PA) within an American State which normally acts to grant sole custody to mothers, that defies the system and opts in principle for a shared parenting approach. One day, while perusing the local newspaper (The Pocono Record) I saw a FrontPage photo and accompanying headline showing an angry mob of women picketing the courts demanding a reversal of their joint-custody policies in favor of sole custody.

One of the most disturbing aspects of this development has been the formation of notions that serve to rationalize the existence of non-intact matriarchal single-parent family units as somehow natural and appropriate in contemporary life. Any number of support systems have sprung up to bolster the acceptance of these families headed by mothers which include everything from media propaganda to supporting day care centers and complete social services assistance. These agencies encourage and continue the present appalling conditions of family life for our children. Increased public spending policies are encouraged by radical feminists and it has become politically incorrect to question or challenge feminist ideals promoting the superiority of women and accepting the validity of female single parenting.

To give but one example of this, I had a few years ago been invited to give evidence and a report to the New York State Standing Committee on the Family when it was considering reform of present divorce and custody law that would have made joint custody or shared parenting a presumption in law. Of the 12 invited sources to speak before the committee, eight were from feminist or feminist driven organizations. These groups opposed the bill. Some of the opposition came from The Women's Bar Association who presented absolutely no reasonable evidence to support their case for sole maternal custody. While the Women's Shelter Organizations made particularly specious arguments that due to the incidences of sexual, abuse and domestic violence women and children would be at risk if the law were changed. The following ludicrous pronouncement by the director of the Michigan Domestic Violence and Treatment Board was the same as those offered by women before our committee:

"Imposed joint custody is particularly dangerous to battered women and their children. As said in her testimony opposing change to the law based on satisfying the oft recited best interests theory, and not special or anomalous cases where domestic violence or abuse might be in issue, the arguments of these feminists were not only spurious and irrelevant but an insult to reasoned debate. I recently came across an article from radical feminist Gloria Woods, President of Michigan NOW, "Father's Rights" Groups: Beware Their Real Agenda" in which the worst aspects of this approach are demonstrated conclusively by Ms. Woods:

"Michigan NOW opposes forced joint custody for many reasons: it is unworkable for uncooperative parents."

However, it is she and her constituents who are uncooperative, refusing to consider children's desperate interests over their own selfish feminist aims. In addition, of course she offers no accredited evidence that shows joint custody does not work when mother protests. See incidence of Re-Litigation and Joint Custody. However, lets get down to what she is really all about:

"It is dangerous for women and their children who are trying to leave or have left violent husbands/fathers;" The precise argument made by her colleagues at the New York hearings inviting us to agree that all men are violent and women must leave them. She raises the specter and arouses fears of widespread domestic violence as a means to defeat humanist 'in principle' approaches over a wide spectrum of child custody issues. If NOW and Ms. Woods were sincere, they would not set their gender policies before the needs of children, knowing full well that anomalous cases are dealt with by a variety of laws sufficient to the purpose of protecting 'alleged' victims of domestic violence. She really opposes the principle of joint custody because in her words:

"It ignores the diverse, complicated needs of divorced families; and it is likely to have serious, unintended **consequences on child support.**"

Unfortunately, the first part of her claim lacks support from 30 years of research and is without the adduction of evidence. Moreover, the crunch comes at the end, MONEY, being the real hidden agenda. The bottom line to NOW'S opposition to joint custody or shared parenting is nothing more than protecting the monetary benefits that accrue to women, while defeating the well established psychological needs of their children. This is in line with radical feminist goals and objectives to establish de facto matriarchy as illustrated by radicals Glendon and Fineman, who without directly commenting on income sharing, have suggested that the first principle at divorce ought to be "adequate provision for children". They favor a "division between the adults that ought to follow the provision for children even if that imposes a greater hardship on the non-custodial parent (father) than on the custodial one (mother)."

The first principle, it seems to me, ought to be provision of the legal and psychological rights of the child. Glendon and Fineman put money first and above the emotional well being of the child. Their views also assume that there will be no shared parenting with sole custody vested in mother. Glendon, M.A., "Family law reform in the 1980's". Louisiana Law Review (1984) 44:1553-73. See note no. 4, Fineman, p. 177.

For that reason, Fineman is critical of an exclusive reliance on an equal division that reflects marital contributions and prefers an emphasis, like that of Okin and Rutherford, on the custodial family's continuing needs. (Carbone 1994) That means mother's lifestyle is going to be 'financed' by the departed father, while he has no legal rights to his children and they have none in respect to him. This is radical feminism at its very best!

It is not surprising, therefore, that feminists reject father's rather desperate pleas for shared parenting derivative from a rather simple and overt agenda. Most fathers seek protection of their children's emotional health and their own parental identity. Psychiatrist Frank Williams who writes on the need to de-escalate custody wars, which he says is rooted in the struggle to maintain parental identity and states:

"Attorneys and judges can choose between two major approaches to custody wars. They can emphasize the children's need for ongoing relationships and access to both parents, or they can stress one-parent superiority. If they choose the latter, they create a "winning parent"...This author concurs with those in the legal-judicial fields who emphasize the value of the both parents approach as most likely to serve the best interests of children and parents of divorce (Foster 1983; Williams 1983)"

That then is the 'hidden agenda' of fathers referred to in Ms. Woods threatening title, "...Hidden Agenda".

Paradoxically, she ignores even her own constituents who complained that:

"Often have we heard custodial moms wish that their children's father would share the parental responsibility?"

However, ignoring her own evidence, Ms. Woods warns them against this attitude, and produces no evidence either statistical or confirmed research findings of widespread male domestic violence against mothers.

Similarly, her compatriots addressing the New York legislature made only subjective appeals to the committee based on the inappropriate anecdotal evidence of a few individual cases. Here is the embodiment of their peculiar logic:

John is a man.

John is a sexual abuser of his children.

John beats his wife.

All men are sexual abusers and beat their wives.

Their ludicrously ill-informed opposition works directly against the interests of the lion share of our children. It provides insight into the private political agendas of anti-male radical feminist groups and the pressure produced on legislators to turn 'a blind eye' to the ongoing human tragedy befalling tens of millions of innocent children. Those agendas extend from the influence brought to bear on legislators into public forums through the media of TV, Radio and Newsprint. Access to information opposing their views, is often denied to the American and Western European peoples. Feminist media control exercises on a scale unprecedented since the regimes of Hitler and Stalin.

We have the outrageous claim of NOW'S Michigan President to serve as an example of feminist disinformation and outright lies:

"The truth is that in 90 percent of custody decisions it is mutually agreed that the mother would be sole custodian. According to several studies, when there is a custody dispute, fathers win custody in the majority of disputed cases."

Is there truth to her first claim? To which studies does she refer? As to the latter, I have reviewed national and international statistics showing that fathers' chances of getting either joint or sole custody are nothing more than non-existent. Women hold between 90 to 92 percent of all custody over children. Worse still, almost 40% of men face prohibition from obtaining ANY access to their children. As to the former, Ms. Woods refers to superficial statistics claiming that 90 percent of cases settle without trial and are rubber stamped by the court. However, that is misleading. It is not the same as proving that in those ninety percent of cases the father actually agrees. Moreover, the figures do not tell us how many of those cases eventually either end up back in court or resolve into cases of 'enforced father absence'. Finally, even if her figures were accurate, that measly ten percent comprises tens of millions of children on a global basis, over time, left in outright despair and fatherless.

While if all this was true, why would NOW feel so threatened by joint custody as a presumption in law? The fact is that sole maternal custody is seldom mutually agreed and that many men simply give up rather than face un-winnable custody battles (Thompson 1994). As to her outrageous claim about men winning disputed custody cases she cites no statistics or specific research. She seriously misleads by suggesting that men "win custody in the majority of disputed cases". The statistics prove quite the opposite. Fathers almost never win sole custody. Ms. Woods depends not on reasoning but rather on false argument, prevarication and on an inappropriate accusative style when she states:

"The legislature's determination to impose joint custody on parents in conflict is a frightening proposition for many women and places them and their children in harm's way."

The only interpretation one can give this hysterical, nonsensical and self-serving statement, is that she and her cohorts own the rights to children and will not tolerate the notion that children have a right to both parents. It seems that women can initiate conflict through a refusal to cooperate with shared parenting and then claim that this presents the "frightening proposition" described by Ms. Woods. Thus, joint custody transforms itself in the matriarchal radical feminist world to mean "children in harm's way". She and her fellow radical feminists conveniently ignore all modern research and studies proving that in damage control situations such as divorce and custody, the least detrimental alternative is the one that guarantees equal rights and continuous ongoing access of the children to both parents.

If my experience of the New York State Senate was dispiriting, then my reaction to a blanket refusal of networks and cable TV to assist with the finishing and airing of a program I had made, "Wednesday's Children", on Parental Child Abduction was also depressing. This program, made on a tiny grant with the co-operation of The US State Department, Justice Department, a leading woman attorney and a highly respected psychiatrist included as well three fathers who had suffered the unprincipled loss of their children due to child abduction. It was refused even a cursory review by Lifetime Television the Women's Network. One female executive told me privately that it was not 'politically correct' because it portrayed women in an unfavorable light. I have shown a rough-cut version at a recent conference on parental child abduction and women in the room were in tears!

Chapter 10

Social Contracts, Misandrism & Family Transitions

Social Contracts, Misandrism and Family Transitions

The traditional characteristics of the family unit were transposed by the sixties revolution into the nuclear and then post-nuclear family structure. Post-nuclear families have more recently become female-headed single-parent families.

Having discussed the manner in which our legal system now functions to deprive children of their most important resource (father)), we need to see how all the individual threads of social, anthropological, psychological, bio-chemical and genetic realities are intertwined. Those forces have caused a radical shift in social organization, family structure, gender relationships and, inevitably, on our children's' lives.

There are also three fundamental external influences, social, political and economic. These too are relevant to the conduct and evolutionary direction of family models. We have seen how the rapid fire changes of the sixties social revolution had drastically altered perceptions of male-female roles in monogamous child-bearing relationships. However, those early drastic changes were, initiated within a spirit of almost absolute optimism and led to the 'mutuality' inherent in modern relationships. This new style replaced the more rigid role definitions of each sex that had dominated over thousands of years of human development.

The Balancing Act

Some social scientists are fond of discussing human interaction in terms of an ongoing balancing act between needs, instincts and drives of one individual in relation to another, particularly the 'loved other'. This also applies to the individual in relation to the collective society. This balancing act can operate on groups or classifications in relation to other groups. Each group may have special interests, needs, rights and aspirations. Earlier in this book I reviewed some of the developments spawned by the sixties social revolution. This included the rise of the women's liberation movement and powerful feminist organizations. Here I want to discuss the problems that have arisen in terms of extant social contracts, the balancing act and more recent radical feminist objectives.

Social Contracts

It is arguable that Rousseau's analysis of "The Social Contract" is applicable to micro-models of male-female interpersonal relationships as well as to larger societal units such as tribes and nations. The development of the male-female social contract called marriage is traceable back to our ancestral roots. Survival drives (our prime directive) and natural selection determine the nature of this contract.

If Margaret Mead is correct in her assessment that somewhere in ancient history agamous relationships ended and man became an integrated and socialized parent within a structured family unit, then it is worthwhile looking for the reasons underlying this absorption. As Amneus also noted:

"Fatherhood in the sense of major male participation in reproduction is only a few million years old. Fatherhood in the sense of male headship of families is only a few thousand years old."

Man, unlike lower orders of mammals and other species of life, has a more complex and long-term system of nurturance of offspring. An obvious fact missed by the first researchers on attachment and child development. *See Chapter 2 Bowlby, Freud, Solnit & Goldstein*

"The relations arising out of the reproductive functions, which constitute the only analogue of social relations to be found in the animal world," says Briffault:

"...differ conspicuously from those generally connoted by the term "family." That term stands, in the tradition of civilized societies, for a group centering round the interests, activities, and authority of a dominant male. The husband is the head of the family; the other members of the group, wife and children, are his dependents and subordinates. The corresponding group arising out of the reproductive functions among animals presents no trace of that constitution. It consists of the mother and her offspring. The male, instead of being the head and supporter of the group, is not an essential member of it, and more often than not is altogether absent from it."

The analogue to human experience in pre-historic times comes from within those societies whose unique circumstances promoted agamous relationships over patriarchy. Dr. Farrell clarifies the point:

"All of history was focused on survival issues, whether there was a God or Goddess culture. There is one difference: many of the Goddess cultures arose in cultures like Crete, Tahiti, or central Malaysia, where there was adequate food, adequate water, and no fear of attack. The survival needs were taken care of, so you didn't need men to do the protecting."

The Marriage Contract

The history of the patriarchal marriage contract is therefore, nothing more than a corollary to the social contract. It seems to come from the human prime directive drive for successful reproduction, security, survival and prosperity.

The contract represents a balancing act of competing interests, mutual self-interests, rights, expectations and goals, all of which fluctuate between degrees of peaceful co-existence, cooperation, tension and conflict. The differentiation between the matriarchal style of the animal kingdom and man's patriarchal system that Briffault refers to (with Farrell's exceptions) is arrived at not through intellectualization but rather through necessity. It derives from man's primitive drives and instinctual or intuitive understanding of his condition and purpose.

In sharp contrast to radical feminist interpretations of the patriarchal family social contract which implores us to believe that man has somehow empowered himself at the expense of women, man has in reality exchanged his historically precedent personal, sexual and other freedoms for controlled regulatory behavior dedicated to the preservation and survival of the species.

In marriage, he takes on huge life-long burdens that include not merely the recent pejorative description of 'provider' but the psychological responsibility for nurturing and inculcating his offspring with those qualities that enable them to grow and prosper. He exchanges sexual promiscuity and no paternal responsibility for a life of close family attachments and fidelity. Is this then the mark of an oppressor? That is his sacrifice. What is his reward? It might be elevated status, or personal security, a sense of social purpose and guarantee of sexual loyalty from his wife and satisfaction of his normal sex drives?

What sacrifices does the woman make and what does she gain in return? First, she has her most compelling bio-chemical need to reproduce satisfied thus following the prime directive. At the same time, she ensures life-long protection of herself and offspring, provision of means, shelter, nurturance, safety, from other predatory males and warfare. She also gains lifelong companionship continuing after sexual attractiveness and reproductive function go into decline. What she sacrifices is her sexual promiscuity and subordination (more theoretical than factual) to the male, elevating his status and providing him with a controlled outlet for his sexual energies. Thus, it is clear that both genders make sacrifices. In the modern context Dr. Farrell has commented on feminist views of the traditional family unit:

"The fundamental mistake of the feminist movement was to take the female area of sacrifice, raising the children, and call that sacrifice, and take the male area of sacrifice, raising money, and call that power." "The Myth of Male Power, an interview with Warren Farrell" (Hoff, M.E.N. Magazine 1993,1997)

Survival of the species is the historical essence of the marriage contract. Another perspective of marital interpersonal relationships comes from an oblique source borrowed and applied to modern family dynamics.

The Conflict Helix Theory

We can look at family and gender relations from another perspective. According to the political scientist Dr. R.J. Rummel ("A Catastrophe Theory Model of The Conflict Helix, With Tests"):

"Macro social field theory has undergone extensive development and testing since the 1960s. One of these has been the articulation of an appropriate conceptual micro model--called the conflict helix--for understanding the process from conflict to cooperation and vice versa.

Conflict and cooperation are viewed as distinct equilibria of forces in a social Field; the movement between these **equilibria is a jump, energized by a gap between social expectations and power, and triggered by some minor event.**"

What happens when there is a major event? What happens when there is even a series of minor events leading up to a major event? What affect might this have on gender relations and the balancing act inherent in family structures predicated on psychosexual, economic and social needs? In Rummel's model of 'The Conflict Helix', he states the following:

"Even without so radical a change, the balance of powers and associated structure of expectations usually will become more incongruent in time, as what the parties want, will, and can do will diverge from that originally supporting the structure of expectations.

Whether sudden or gradual, however, the result is to cause a gap between expectations and the balance of powers. This gap creates tension and a force toward conflict; the greater the gap, the more pressure toward restructuring expectations in line with the change in interests, capability, and will; the more this pressure, the more likely some trigger event will disrupt the outmoded structure of expectations, precipitate a jump in cooperative, peaceful behavior to conflict and, if the status quo be involved, possibly social violence or war."

Rummel's theory applied to larger social fields are applicable to the observable events and behavioral shifts of the sixties social revolution. These sowed the seeds for radical changes to the equilibria of forces within the traditional family model, altering female expectations and perceptions of control and power.

Moreover, in principle this is not necessarily destructive as Rummel points out:

"The process of jumps between successive equilibria within a situation, of social contract is a winding upward in mutual learning and adjustments. **As long as the major conditions of a relationship remain fairly constant, this process leads toward longer lasting and deeper peace,** interrupted by shorter and less intense social conflict."

However, just as the sixties had produced the radical change that Rummel described as a conditional event of the helix, it also produced forceful agencies that threatened those "major conditions of a relationship" upon which marriages depended, for constancy and ultimately for healthy survival:

"A sharp change in these conditions can set this process back, or even shear the conflict helix, and cause the whole process of mutual adjustment and learning to begin anew.

What changes will have this affect will depend on the parties involved. Between husband and wife, it might be the first child or the mother-in-law moving in."

Moreover, we have observed, over the past thirty years a consistent dissembling of traditional family units and gender warfare. We have also observed the intended imposition of a matriarchal family system promising further conflict, de-stability and corruption of the process of natural selection we so depend on for survival as a species.

The Rise of Radical Feminist Misandrism

The sharp change in conditions that Rummel warns of is best characterized by the transposition from "The process of jumps between successive equilibria within a situation, of social contract...winding upward in mutual learning and adjustments" into a process where reason gives way to radical ideas that rather than seek 'adjustments', blindly obliterate the social marriage contract itself. We have the radical feminists to thank for this.

It began with early feminist stirrings of the nineteen sixties best characterized by Betty Friedan's rather plaintiff description of women as being Sleeping Beauties:

"I think it will not end, as long as the feminine mystique masks the emptiness of the housewife role, encouraging girls to evade their own growth by vicarious living, by non-commitment. We have gone on too long blaming or pitying the mothers who devour their children, who sow the seeds of progressive dehumanization, because they have never grown to full humanity themselves. If the mother is at fault, why is it not time to break the pattern by urging all these Sleeping Beauties to grow up and live their own lives? There never will be enough Prince Charmings, or enough therapists to break that pattern now. It is society's job, and finally that of each woman alone. For it is not the strength of the mothers that is at fault but their weakness, their passive childlike dependency and immaturity that is mistaken for "femininity." Our society forces boys, insofar as it can, to grow up, to endure the pains of growth, to educate themselves to work, to move on. Why aren't girls forced to grow up--to achieve somehow the core of self that will end the unnecessary dilemma, the mistaken choice between femaleness and humanness that is implied in the feminine mystique?"

Mrs. Friedan's critical view of women was closer to "...the fault dear Brutus is not in our stars, but in ourselves", than to cries of male exploitation. This was feminism, not cultural or radical feminist thought.

But, as Professor Amneus points out in "The Garbage Generation":

"Ms. Friedan's Sleeping Beauty feminism was an unwelcome derogation to American women because it came close to the truth, still more unwelcome because it threatened the free ride they had no intention of giving up."

He went on to state:

"Small wonder that the **Playboy/Feminine Mystique/Sleeping Beauty** pitch was discarded by feminists as an unsuitable basis for a popular movement and that it is today as extinct as the trilobite.

The idle sex-toy doll-housewife pampered by an overworked husband is unmentioned in the literature of post-1960s feminism. The Sleeping Beauty has been replaced by the Slaughtered Saint, tyrannized over, oppressed, brainwashed, beaten, enslaved, exploited, crucified, impaled, racked and harrowed, flayed, trampled and hung in chains by remorseless, inhuman, fierce, sadistic, exploitive, brutal alcoholic male despots, beasts, marital rapists and so forth.

It is useful, though, to remember that the initial thrust of feminism was that "The problem seemed to be not that too much was asked of [women] but too little."

While I have reservations about some of Amneus' conclusions, for the most part I find myself in agreement with the main thrust of the argument. The facts do support the contention that early feminist goals certainly transposed into an extremely negative and hostile long-term campaign against men, as men, husbands and fathers. That, in turn, gave rise to the prevailing misandrist attitude governing present gender relations, the circumstances of marriage as well as the means and manner of divorce. One discernible consequence that radical-feminist misandrism has had on women, along with other identifiable phenomena, is the reported data on who initiates divorces. Dr. Wallerstein reported in "The Impact of Divorce on Children (1984)" that:

"Although the adults who were married to each other by and large did not disagree about the sad state of the marriage, they did disagree strongly about the decision to divorce. Mostly, the divorce was sought by one member of the couple and opposed by the other. In the California study, as well as in other studies across the country, **the divorce was sought by more women and opposed by more men.**"

My own interviews with divorcing men, carried out in England almost ten years later, confirmed that the disparity had reached huge proportions. Women initiated over 90% of the divorces, and in some cases, men admitted to commencing proceedings only because their spouses were preparing to act. They felt compelled to act first in order to retain any legal rights to their children.

One can speculate on whether or not women could accept the 'sleeping beauty' concept of feminism or had to conceptualize an enemy, an external force (man-husband), in order to construct a dynamic popular movement. The fact remains that the invective aptly described by Amneus has become a part of feminist vernacular. At the very least, this reflects moribund changes in feminist and female patterns seen in the escalation of female initiated divorces. It extends to female opposition to male influence on children. This, of course, has a serious impact on the rights of the child. One example of more recent departure in language comes from a radical feminist, Mary Daly:

"...feeding on the bodies and minds of women, sapping energy at the expense of female deaths. Like Dracula, the he-male has lived on women's blood...The priests of patriarchy have eaten the body and have drunk the blood of the Sacrificial Victim in their Mass, but they have not wished to know **who** has really been the Victim whose blood supported this parasitic life.

The insatiable lust of males for female blood has resulted in a perpetual blood transfusion throughout the millennia--a one-way outpouring into the veins and arteries of the bloodthirsty monster, the Male Machine that now can continue its obscene life only by genocide. If the Machine dreams, it is of a future filled with megadeaths. The total vampire no longer needs even to speak of blood, which is after all visible, measurable. It drinks instead in quantities calculable only through the highest mathematics...It is men who have sapped the life-force of women."(Amneus 1996)

What we do know about human nature is that it is often far simpler and effective to focus on real or imagined external evils, "taking aim against a sea of troubles and by opposing end them" than to resolve internalized conflicts that possibly date back to early childhood. No doubt the politics of experience taught the most ardent of feminists to focus their campaign for women's liberation on grounds similar to those of the civil rights and anti-war movements.

As the intensity and rhetoric increased, so it attracted increasing numbers of more unsettled, sexually immature, emotionally dysfunctional and or sexually divergent women into the arena. These women have had private agendas that are decidedly anti-male and misandrist. They have managed to supersede and superimpose their ideas over the early feminists and more rational feminist thinkers.

According to the dust cover of feminist Lynne Segal's book:

"She argues against the exponents of the new apocalyptic feminism, among whom are Mary Daly, Andrea Dworkin and Dale Spender, which says that men wield power over women through terror, greed and violence and that only women, because of their essentially greater humanity, can save the world from social, ecological and nuclear disaster."

How, one asks does all of this translate into social, political and economic pressures to eliminate fathers from being parents to their children? Why have men almost universally failed to understand the process unfolding before their very noses?

One might accept the view of Polonsky(1984) that the attitudes of people (in this case women) link to their behavior. If that view is accepted, then it becomes a compelling argument that the invasion of the women's movement by misandrist radical feminists, with disproportionate influence and access to mass communication media, led to a general attitudinal change. That attitudinal change altered not only by female behavior but also by the passive reactive behavior of men. As the influences of misanthropic radical feminists inured themselves into women's thought and behavior they inevitably became prevalent. This, in turn, led to the development of a belief system related to their behavioral style. As Polonsky points out:

"Once attitudes about the behavior have changed, even more diverse behavioral alternatives are permitted, and this in turn can lead to further attitudinal changes."

What we have witnessed over the past thirty years is an indoctrination of women into acceptance of a belief system fostered on the grounds of sexual politics. This has divided men and women. The issues are often falsely present as 'matriarchy versus patriarchy' and contrived to create a power struggle between the sexes. Amneus reports:

"The matriarchal family pattern is being restored by the welfare system, by the feminist/sexual revolution, by women's growing economic independence and by the legal preference for mother-custody following divorce."

Writing of the educated and economically independent women created by women's liberation, Elizabeth Nickles and Laura Ashcraft say:

"The Matriarchal woman who finds that her relation with a man is undermining her sense of self-esteem will not consider it necessary to cling to the relation for the traditional reasons, and she will have the self-sufficiency to stand on her own."

It is abundantly clear that the radical feminists have been empowered over the past thirty years turning mere pseudo-intellectual thought into effectual behavioral changes. This is because the so-called patriarchy that they so despise has literally handed them the means to realize a substantial reversion to the failed family system of the Neolithic period. That was a time when, in their view, men were not much more than peripheral to the process of pro-creation/nurturing.

The means to this end were and are still economic. Without the enormous amount of funding, through federal and state grants, private foundations, IRA's, charities, and the like, radical feminists could not have disseminated their message. They could not maintain organized efforts to lobby for legislative change favoring women and allowing for greater economic independence. They could not manage to appoint misandrist judges. Nor could they gain strategically important access to positions of power and influence further effecting belief systems, attitudes and behavior.

The legal preference for mother-custody is part of the imposition of matriarchy pointed out by Amneus and nothing more than an artifact of the economic process in which so called male society granted access to women inside of the legal profession. This is particularly true within the practice area of family law. Women dominate here and effectively change open and covert court policy. Complaisant older male judges fully cooperate with the newly installed radical feminist female judges to reinforce anti-child, anti father views reflected in present court practices.

One such judge in New York, Gangel Jacobs, was so obvious in her dismissive and abusive views of men as parents that it forced her removal from the bench. Unfortunately, not before she had done untold damage to the lives of many children and their fathers. *See Peter Nicholls case*

Circumstances were ripe for radical feminist rhetoric, absurd intellectualizations about female superiority, male-female gender roles and of 'natural' family structure, to translate into action. Armed with the ludicrous psychoanalytical literature based on the assumptions of traditional family structure that no longer existed (Bowlby), they were in a position to have an almost absolute control over the mechanisms of divorce and custody process. Their power is extensive enough to ensure the easy defeat of legislation aimed at protecting the 'Best Interests' of our children by incorporating shared parenting into the law. Raggio, Lowell, Halverson, Kydd, Divorce in New York (1987) wrote:

" The welfare of children and of the public is overlooked when an issue becomes man against woman, woman against man. For example...men's groups have attained a measure of success in pushing for a statutory preference for joint custody. **They won in the New York State Legislature, only to be thwarted by the success of the women's lobby in obtaining the Governor's veto.**"

The legal position steadily deteriorated until:

When I was invited to speak before that same New York State Legislature several years later in 1995 arguing for joint custody as a preference and as a means to reduce the staggering number of parental abductions, the Standing Committee on the Family would not even act to present a proposed shared parenting bill to the floor. Predictably, the bill subsequently saw burial in committee by a chairwoman known to have strident radical feminist views.

So, having created social peer pressure on women, and having gained a large measure of political influence and control in strategic areas, radical feminists empowered themselves to create economic pressure on men using the court system as an ally. And as Raggio cautions rather meekly in Divorce in New York (1987):

"It is not surprising, and it may be natural, for organized pressure groups and lobbies to seek to retain unnatural but accustomed advantages, without regard to the best interests of children, the public, or themselves.

The women's movement, notwithstanding the words of caution voiced by Betty Friedan, has valiantly fought sexual discrimination, but it also fights for special advantage and preferential treatment."

Radical feminist utilization of family law (as a means to obtain full and sole control over our children) links as much to economic self-interest, as to Amneus' reasons for the return to matriarchy. Nevertheless, in a sense, Amneus is not wrong. If we accept Polonsky's views, a natural by-product of the cycle would be the implementation of a new normative thinking leading us inexorably towards universal matriarchy.

To illustrate the real affect and incredible impact of radical feminist thought taken together with their successful drive to divorce law reforms of the late sixties and early nineteen eighties (that we discuss in detail (Chapter 5, sub chapter: The Impact of Contemporary Divorce Law Reform), there are three graphics which make plain and frightening reading. You will note the similarity in results between the U.S. and British graphs and the timeframes involved.

Divorce Rate Graph

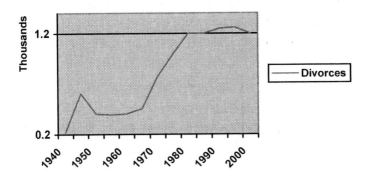

Figure 1 US Graph shows the staggering effects that divorce law reform commencing in 1966 has had on the state of marriage.

Children Living with Parents Graph

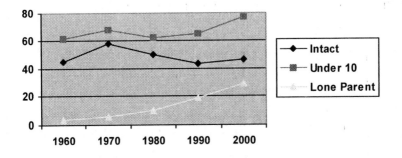

Figure 2 US Graph shows the effects of divorce rates on the make-up of contemporary families, as two parent families decline and female -headed single parent families accelerate leaving us with over 28.8 million US children without their fathers.

Family Breakdown Trend Graph

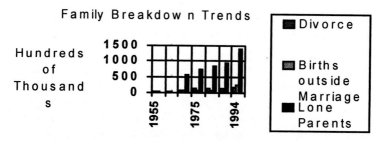

Figure 3 English Graph shows the impact of divorce law reform on the wild escalation of lone parenting figures, births outside of marriages and divorces.

Along with these horrific statistics, we observe other complex and subterranean changes in behavioral styles and patterns. Some of these become apparent in the divided family loyalties and confused gender defense exhibited in an email sent by one mother (grandmother) to Mother's United Dreambook:

Monday December 28th 1998 01:09:57

Your Name: Debra

Your Comments:

I ran across your website while "surfing" on the subjects of custody & visitation. **My daughter-in-law is having problems with her son's biological father (to whom she was never married). At the same time, our son is having problems with his ex-wife who was given custody of his two daughters** (four & two years). There is evidence of abuse & neglect and she has taken the children into hiding before. Therefore, **I find myself on both sides of the courts (fighting for both mothers & fathers).** I love the way you have your website put together. I really enjoyed it.

Debra"

This is a prime example of a woman hopelessly confused and unable to comprehend the contradictions of her own psychological predicament:

" I find myself on both sides of the courts fighting for both mothers and fathers".

This is not the truth. In reality she supports **mothers only** but for the solitary unhappy fact that it is her own son who is threatened with loss of his relationship of his two daughters. She defends her son against his former wife, not fathers and she supports his new wife against her former boyfriend who is demanding the self-same access to his kids. Thus, we have a classic case of double standards!

Man portrayed as woman slayer, destroyer, oppressor, threat to world peace, social progress and to all humanity (except of course for a mother's son), can be easily de-personalized. The logical progression of misandrist radical feminist goals starts with his immediate expulsion from family models. It moves toward his establishment as 'non citizen' slave, defined merely by production of semen and drone-like economic ties to the repudiating female mother.

Indeed, we now have evidence that it begins much earlier, as one of the most horrifying aspects of radical feminist misandrist posturing is the rather gruesome indoctrination of male toddlers and youths into believing that they are already sex offenders, violent, abusive and dangerous to women.

In her article:" The War against Boys" Christina Hoff Sommers, a philosophy professor at Clark University and author of "Who Stole Feminism? How Women have Betrayed Women" reports:

"When a Worcester mother came to pick up her son from school a few weeks ago, the teacher told her he had been made to sit in the "time-out chair." He had violated the behavior code by hugging other students. "He's a toucher," the teacher said. "We are not going to put up with it." The mother was startled, not by her son, who she knows to be loving and who, indeed, likes to hug, but by the school for punishing him. Her son is three years old."

This insane radical feminist campaign against men as innocent children of age three years is part of a long-term process reported on by Christina Sommers:

"What the mother does not know is that for the past 10 years, feminist groups such as the American Association of University

Women, the Ms. Foundation for Women, and the NOW Legal Defense and Education Fund have been successfully lobbying the federal government to impose strict harassment codes in the schools. In August, the U.S. Department of Education's Office of Civil Rights (OCR) issued a 26-page guideline on the subject of "peer harassment." That guideline specified no age limits."

Thus a healthy, normal, three year old boy "who hugs" becomes a sexual harasser of young girl children who need to protected by lunatic radical feminist government civil servants such as Norma Cantu, an Assistant Secretary of Education who explains:

"What our regulation anticipates is that sexual harassment could occur at **any age**."

Coming from a responsible official, this is a rather bizarre statement. What psychological damage will this bizarre point of view cause young and innocent male children?

According to a critical and enraged Dr. Sommers:

"**The little boys are casualties of a movement that scapegoats men and boys and seeks to protect women and girls from what Gloria Steinem calls the "jockocracy." Feminists like Patricia Ireland and Steinem sincerely believe that ours is a sexist society that wages an "undeclared war against women" (Susan Faludi's subtitle to Backlash). Such feminists think most adult males are incorrigibly sexist, and that boys must be retrained --- the earlier the better.**"

Is it surprising that women, like Steinhem, whose early childhoods show family disturbances, have distorted or subjective views of men quite possibly tainted by that experience? Is it surprising that they transfer those views onto young boys? What is that background? Simply this as reported in an article on Steinhem:

"As a child, Gloria and her family traveled constantly with her father's antique business. Steinhem was home-schooled, by her mother, until the age of ten, when her parents split up. Gloria and her mother settled in Toledo, where her mother's bouts of depression worsened to the point that young Gloria was forced to run the household through most of her high school years." ("In Excelsis Deo:

Gloria Steinem shows us what 65 should look like", by Arthur Greenwald.)

Ms. Steinhem's apparent adult problems are evident in her hatred of men and accords with the literature on the possible affects of childhood traumas revolving around marital discord, loss of a male parent and life with a depressed mother who becomes the child in the relationship[50]. Studies show that:

"Daughters in single mother homes have more negative attitudes toward men in general and their fathers in particular." (Pg. 146, 2, lines 5 - 8) "Interparental Conflict, Relationship with the Noncustodial Father, and Adolescent Post-Divorced Adjustment" - Gene Brody and Rex Forehand, University of Georgia, Journal of Applied Psychology, Vol. 11, No. 2, April - June 1990.

As for her mother's depression and its impact on the child, let us consider the fact that:

"55.3% of children living with divorced mothers and 59.2% of children living with remarried mothers suffer from anxiety or depression. "National Center for Health Statistics"

Hardly earth shattering news given some of the known affects on children living in female headed single parent homes where mother is depressive and passes on the depressive style behavior to the child genetically or by learned behavior[51].

These matters, addressed in other chapters, illustrate the dangers of radical feminist women like Ms. Steinhem having carte blanche to inflame opinion and influence important public policies. Policies based not on reason but on rather subjective, intemperate and distorted views derivative of their own unfortunate life experience.

The Indentured Servitude of Men

The institution of slavery is not dead. It lives and breathes through the Machiavellian influence and power of the radical feminists, who,

---

[50] See Chapters 2 and 3, female depression, mothers, cycles of deprivation
[51] See Professor Laden on Depressive Patterns

contrary to early feminist thinking, seek definitive economic advantage from the institution of divorce.

As Professor Amneus observed:

"In l963 the subsidization of ex-wives by ex-husbands was said to be contemptible; today the feminist party line is a demand for "support rules that aim at equalizing the standards of living of the two parties after divorce" and that divorced women "have earned the right to share their **husbands'** income for the rest of their lives and to maintain a standard of living that is equal to theirs"--so that even though the man is no longer a husband, and even though Betty Friedan had told wives to be ashamed of themselves for expecting to be subsidized for the trifling services they perform, the man deprived of these services should continue to subsidize the woman who withdraws them."

In the light of recent common experience, a number of things become clear. We understand how divorce law reform in England and the various American states between 1967 and 1984 comes into play. We can immediately see that divorce for women becomes an attractive and practical option. At the very least, we see how the perceptions of advantages in divorce factor into the situation. It is an alternative to remaining in a long-term relationship with a man she no longer has a use for except as a continued provider. He now subsidizes her private lifestyle for a lifetime without incurring any benefits to himself or his children. Although feminist language and legislative intent seem to indicate an equitable distribution of the marital assets, this is not the case in reality. Once mother gets sole custody, she receives a disproportionate amount of assets and ongoing financial support. The real motivation is as Amneus points out:

"Feminists believe that the patriarchy ought to subsidize its own destruction by paying women to create fatherless families. According to Martha Sawyer, a PhD candidate at Howard University, the **costs of these fatherless families should be paid by "the most advantaged category, monied white men."**

Ex-husbands bear huge and unmanageable financial burdens. They have to support the matriarchal family home and a separate home as well as the individual costs of living of their own. Additionally they incur the costs of having to maintain contact to their children, when this is even remotely possible, including travel fares, the cost of day trips, food, shelter and other expenses generated by the visitation process. Of course, while this is the case, mother often moves on to a second liaison with a man who also supports her, and courts steadfastly refuse to consider her additional income as relevant to former husband's maintenance and child support burdens. Although studies conflict on this point, logic dictates that if father finds a new relationship, he faces obstacles in acting to support it because of his prior commitment. In other words, mother is free to form positive relationships and father is without the means to do the same.

Whatever the intellectual or psychological rationale may be for vesting sole custody in mother, it is obvious that by doing so, she becomes a net **beneficiary** and father with few or no legal rights, becomes a net **debtor**. Is this a form of slavery?

The concept of slavery implies a set of legal rights and obligations on both parties absent a contract, and husbands or former husbands were parties to a contract apparently with legal rights and obligations, the abstract differentiation is of little significance in the context of divorce. Of course, in English common law there is a contract known as a **Slave-Contract.** That is an unenforceable contract, which arbitrarily places one party in an inferior and inequitable position to the other party.

In fact, divorced men (the lion-share of divorces being initiated by women (Wallerstein (1984), Cornec, 1994, Rein (1996), become victimized by this contemporary 'economic' enslavement. Unlike even the outlawed Slave-Master relationship, they have no rights at all.

Men, after divorce, become indentured servants of their former spouses subject to recently developed onerous 'child support' and 'maintenance' laws. Laws that include financial penalties and prison sentences without jury trials[52] should they fail to meet the imposed economic burdens of divorce even where in specific cases they do not have the means to comply.

---

[52] See Imputation of income and civil contempt of court proceedings

Notwithstanding the cries and disinformation flowing from radical feminists that huge numbers of men seek to evade child support payments, the statistics invite us to draw an opposite conclusion. It is clear from them that when men have custodial or visitation rights respected, there is a high degree of compliance. *See Appendix A. See Braver & O'Connell.*

Conversely, most problems of child support only arise in circumstances following obliteration, or, seriously impairment by mother and the courts of custodial and visitation rights.

While on the one hand, divorced fathers are divested of custody of their children with little or no rights to have meaningful and ongoing contact, on the other hand, they are forced into a virtually perpetual economic servitude. This is the very essence of a **slave contract**.

Interestingly, the so-called patriarchal system that radical feminists complained of did not contain similar practical treatment of wives. Moreover, divorce was of no statistical significance, having little real impact on the lives of women. In one particular case that I am familiar with;

Case 1

Father and mother divorced, and naturally with father thrust into the role of non-custodial parent, while the family court made orders to include his maintenance of the mother and child support for the children. As it turned out, the man lost his job and could not find employment. For the next two years, while he was on social welfare, the court constantly, at the prompting of the mother and her lawyers, sought sanctions against him for failure to meet his financial obligations. Despite the fact that evidence taken showed that he was on welfare and had no cash reserves, the court 'imputed' income to him that he did not have, several times held him in civil contempt and jailed him. As he had no money, and legal aid was not made available to him as is normal in family law cases dealing with financial orders, he turned to a father's rights advocate with legal experience to assist him. The court refused to allow the assistance of counsel[53] provided and jailed the man once again.

What we learn from this case is that the civil family court has draconian powers of arrest in most national and international jurisdictions. It can arbitrarily hold a defendant in 'civil contempt' imprisoning him for up to six months in jail without a jury trial[54], and he seek freedom by 'purging' the contempt. That means paying up! If he does not have the money, he remains in jail, facing another contempt hearing and sentence.

This raises the issue as to whether or not debtors prisons, outlawed since the early part of the century, have been re-established in the guise of civil contempt proceedings. These proceedings threaten to place men into prison for failure to pay a debt, without jury trial, on subjective evidence, and the inherent power of the court to impose prison time in lieu of payment. In regard to subjective evidence, we learn that a family court judge has the power to 'impute' income, which means that the court does not have to conform to normal rules of evidence in determining it's decision. The imputation of income is a process in which the judge merely states his or her belief that the defendant has the money. This takes place often even in the face of production of records that prove the opposite and I have personally known cases where the man has brought to court his tax forms, pay slips, and accounts, only to be imputed and sent to prison.

The essence of the matter is simply this; first, the legal system has dynamic social and political pressure applied to grant full custody of children to their mothers, second, father is 'parentectomized', removed from his parental rights, and forced into indentured servitude.

---

[53] Over 50% of fathers fight custody and support cases as pro se litigants, without legal counsel
[54] 18 months in England, Northern Ireland & Wales

The Legal, Psychiatric and Social Welfare Money Tree

Clearly, women are the perceived beneficiaries. However, who, apart from mothers, has an interest in continuation of the current family law system?

The lawyers, judges, welfare agencies and mental health professionals all can claim a share in the participation and dividends that flow from the money tree of divorce and custody. Ever since the divorce rates began to spiral upwards in the nineteen eighties, they have been an integral part of a multi-billion dollar a year industry that consumes personal wealth and drains the public coffers; leading Dr. Jacobs to comment:

"Make no mistake, a number of people profit from divorce and custody cases, judges, lawyers, welfare workers and even myself as a psychiatrist, making millions of dollars each year, not me personally, but all these people."

According to an Associated Press story on the glut of lawyers in New Jersey, numbers rose from 8,963 in 1960 to 56,768 in 1994 and projected to reach 76,100 by the year 2,000. A mainstay of these practices is the work generated from divorce and custody matters. One attorney, Francis Monahan, a member of the Ad-Hoc Committee to Review the Impact of the Large Number of Lawyers in New Jersey, said:

"Competition for revenue also could tempt unscrupulous practitioners to milk their clients, especially in divorce cases, instead of seeking a quick and amicable settlement."

As more and more men refuse to accept the loss of their paternal rights and relationships to their offspring, cases often tend to get stretched out over numbers of years, with repeated court appearances, lawyers letters, applications made, hearings held, reports made and costs escalating. This is the emerging pattern. It ensures the paychecks of judges, lawyers, social workers, psychiatrists, psychologists and law guardians.

Despite the efforts of maternal sole custody advocates like Freud, Solnit and Goldstein to make all case decisions final, their colleagues on the money tree have resisted such naive temptations, so that the general approach in child custody matters is that they can be revisited on numerous occasions over time until the children reach an age of majority. You need not be a rocket scientist to calculate the costs of ongoing legal conflict. Let me explain by example how the system works. Let us take the social service involvement, in New York State. New York family court law demands that the child have independent representation by counsel, or more explicitly, by a law guardian. The Law guardian is court appointed. Law guardians such as the feminist driven Lawyers for Children, depend at least in part on grants for their primary funding. When assigned to a case, the system picks up the charges for their services. Every case the law guardian gets attracts matching funds by federal and state grants. In other words, they have a vested institutional interest in holding on to cases. As the case continues over a number of years and results in numerous court appearances, the child representation continues and the law guardians profit from such continuation. Imagine a typical case involving two young children ages five and 3, in which father is consistently denied access and does not relent in his attempts to redress the wrongs. That case never ends. Thus ensuring that the law guardians have money rolling in forever, as the child/children remain on their books.

What might happen if we juxtaposed a radically different pattern into the process, if the courts (except in anomalous cases) faced a federal standard that favored a joint custody approach? What would happen to the money tree? Here is one possible scenario:

A Theoretical Case

A husband and wife come before the family court judge and are in conflict over who is to have custody over their two children. She is demanding sole custody and he is fighting for joint custody. Each makes their arguments and produce evidence. The judge even hears the opinions of the children.

Judge's decision (greatly simplified)

You folks come in to my court and have conflicting views on who is to have the custody of the children. I am going to make this process very easy on you and the children. As we all know, I'm bound to make my decision following the best interests of the child principles and guidelines that Stewart Rein has set down and our state legislature has enacted into law. Now, I've heard you both giving evidence, taken into account the views of the court appointed psychiatrist and the children themselves, heard your witnesses, and reviewed the facts of the case...and I conclude first that, there is nothing unusual in the case that warrants extreme measures being taken by this court. There are no circumstances other than the ones I expect to find when hearing a conflictual interpersonal matter involving the painful breakdown of a marriage...having said that, bearing in mind our judicial mandate preferring joint custody to any other approach, I intend to make such an order. And I would advise both parties that although you have the right of appeal, that it is unlikely that such an effort would meet with success, and that any further continuation of this conflict will be injurious to the health and well-being of the children.

Once I have made this joint custody order, there will be other matters to consider. We will have to sort out the division of the time that each of you may have with the children, in what circumstances that might occur, and how we shall apportion the assets of the marriage so that neither party has an unfair and unrealistic burden placed upon them, while the interests of the children are upheld and protected. I am going to hold a special hearing to decide on these matters, and I am now informing counsels to prepare the necessary papers to assist me in this process. I want to make it perfectly clear that I am going to take a gender-neutral approach, and I am going to make certain that each parent will have ample quality time with the children. Both parents must make sacrifices, as both must contribute financial support to the children. We are no longer dealing with a normal intact family and there might now be hardships placed on both parties and the children due to this marital breakdown. Assets and income have to provide two homes for the adults, where formally they did for one home.

Now, I want to give you both a firm warning. The court will not only frown on any interference with the process of shared parenting and access by the children to both parents, but it will act swiftly to take any appropriate action it deems necessary if it finds that either of you has disobeyed the order of this court. This action might include a summary judgment of sole custody to the injured party. On the other hand I want to warn both parties that this court will not tolerate frivolous motions or applications to alter our custody decision, so that if either party attempts to bring false allegations against the other aimed at upsetting the balance, that too might result in a summary decision of sole custody to the injured party. In respect to the former matter I warn counsel that they too will be held accountable for their actions, that costs, fines and contempt may be found against them.

Sounds like a fantasy, but following the work of Ilfeld's study on the incidence of re-litigation in cases of judicially mandated joint custody (even in conflictual cases) this approach is the one to be followed on social policy grounds and because it would substantially reduce the enormous amount of private and public assets wasted in the present process.

Returning to the money tree, just as we have explored the economics of middle-middle-class to rich wives who profit from divorce, there is another group of women who had been deceived into thinking they would benefit, but as part of a lower classification (lower-to-lower middle-class) find in fact that the cupboard is bare. For them, the branches of the 'money tree' while flowing from the same trunk are of a different shape and texture, bearing the fruits of massive state expenditure and opening of the public coffers. To get some basic idea of the real economic impact of divorce on society I want to give the example of my own figures, submitted in my briefing paper to The Right Honorable Michael Portillo, Chief Secretary to the British Treasury in 1994, taken from official government sources in The United Kingdom. *See Chapter 11.*   The figures represent comparable data on a broad scale in parallel to the American experience. State involvement includes social services, day care centers, housing benefits, legal aid, medical services, schools, civil servants, legislation, grants and subsidies, all in addition to the previously accounted for custody case claimants (judges, lawyers, mental health professionals, social workers and guardians) and runs into billions of dollars/pounds annually.

Divorce has become a multi billion-dollar/pound growth industry that, based on present trends, is sure to escalate in future.

Chapter 11

The Consequences of the Destruction of Intact Families

Consequences of the Destruction of Intact Family Models

The breakdown of the institution of marriage and therefore, intact family models, has dragged us down as a whole society. We have accepted the inevitability of divorce as we do summer storms and the changing seasons. We have followed Lemming-like over the cliffs into a sea of trouble. We have marched to mysterious drums that fail to beat in real time. We have watched as families have been transposed from one composition (whole) into another (nuclear) into another (post-nuclear) and finally into the most degraded form imaginable, the single-parent maternal unit.

This book looked at family problems from the child's perspective. I have tried to analyze the causes and effects on them of the last hundred years of social, political, psychological and legal policies. These policies have robbed tens of millions of children of their proper birthrights, their bonds to father, self-esteem and childhood

ontological security as well as their chances for a healthy adulthood
What are some of the knock-on or secondary effects of divorce and
father absence on the family and society?

Implications of the Replacement of Intact Families by Female Headed
Single-Parent Families

I had an opportunity to meet with then Chief Secretary to the
British Treasury, The Right Honourable Michael Portillo in 1994. He
asked me to provide him with a Briefing Paper on the financial aspects
of divorce. During my research I was astonished to discover the real
economic impact divorce had on both individual families and on the
nation. The first given was that the family courts of England, Northern
Ireland and Wales were consistently ignoring the legislative intention
of <u>The Children Act 1989.</u> They were universally making sole maternal
custody decisions over the shared parenting preference of the Act. The
second given was that England had instituted **no fault divorce** and I
then asked the question: If divorce has been made simple and the
divorce rate has skyrocketed to 40% and the type of order made in
respect to custody has been sole residence, leading to over one million
to one and a half million children with no fathers.............. What are the
consequences of the above formulations?

The results showed the following Areas of National Impact

1. Destruction of the family and family values

2. Disruption to the lives of millions of men, women and children

3. Massive economic repercussions for the Treasury and the
Taxpayer burdening the Legal Aid System, Income Support, Child
Benefit, Housing benefit

4. Predictable financial hardship on children, reduction of
educational performance and opportunity, and therefore a
generational loss of productive citizenry

5. Increased juvenile crime, mental dysfunction and vastly
increased spending on Police, Courts and Detention facilities

6. Economic implications secondary to the primary affect in respect to the reduced individual capacity of divorced persons to spend monies in the market place:

Luxury goods such as cars, boats, electronic equipment

Entertainments such as movies, shows, sports

Consumer goods and services

Essential life items such as clothing, food, transportation and heating/lighting

7. Increase in unmarried teenage mothers, undesirable pregnancies and further cycles of deprivation built on the tenuous foundations of single parenting and creating further burdens on the state in respect to item 3

The figures I obtained from the Legal Aid Board bore out the argument that the current treatment of both divorce and custody issues had led us to the point where the system is about to implode on itself. The ease of divorce has served only to encourage its realization. The initial disassembling of the family and the prevalence of sole residence orders (over the strenuous objections of fathers), together with subsequent difficulties in gaining contact, has led to a continuous stream of repeat applications in custody cases. This places an enormous burden on the states' resources, while leaving its wards without their fathers.

English Legal Aid Disbursements Civil Legal Aid Bills Paid & Expenditure 1992-1993

Number of cases Matrimonial Proceedings	Children Act
135,802	23,919

Total Cost: Pounds Sterling 227,690,473.00

While the staggering cost to DHHS Social Services was as follows:

Costs to the Dept. of Social Services

Income Support

Housing Benefit

Note: According to the Guardian Newspaper, November 10, 1993 the lone parent cash bill was 66,000,000 per week

Number of lone parents claiming income support for the year 1992 was 985,000 consisting of over 90% mothers   * 1993 1,400,000 90% mothers

Total Cost: Pounds Sterling 3,432,000,000

As part of the Brief, I had conducted lengthy interviews with a sampling of fathers who were members of FNF Inc., a father's rights group, and discovered the following process that seemed typical of custody battles:

Implications drawn from typical circumstances as reported by FNF membership

The mother goes straight on to Legal Aid

The father commences the action with cash assets

The mother often leaves the matrimonial home taking the children

Council provides accommodation for mother and children

The mother tries to obtain ouster order and father resists

If mother loses, council continues support

If mother wins, father is now homeless

The father rents accommodation

The mother applies for financial relief

CSA (Child Support Agency) assess father

The father now has disbursed his cash assets to solicitors and counsel

The father now on Legal Aid with very small assessment

Assortment of Direction Hearings, Welfare Report, Expert Evidence

Court for Residence/Contact Applications

Re-litigation over a prolonged period due to contact abuse or changing circumstances

That represents a typical scenario in conflictual cases. One can draw conclusions as to what happens both to individual assets of the family, and the knock-on effects on the state coffers. The US experience and statistics mirror that of the English experience.

Statistics released to me by The Right Honourable Peter Lilley, Minister of Social Services in England showed that as of 1994:

1, 500,000 Children without their fathers

1, 400,000 Lone (female) parents on Income Support (welfare)

DSS Figures on Expenditures were:

Lone Parent Income related Benefits increased from 1 billion pounds in 1978/9 to 5.6 billion in 1993

Total Benefits on Lone Parents had increased from 1.75 billion in 1978/9 to 8 billion pounds in 1993/4

These figures are astounding and come about because of government policies that accept and encourage marital breakdown by offering divorce on demand, while removing men from the family by making sole maternal custody orders.

The After Affects

There are of course a number of important secondary or knock-on effects indexed to the breakdown of traditional family models through divorce and installed policies of sole maternal custody. Just as psychological cycles of deprivation come to exist in this invidious process, external effects are frequent and long lasting. These effects are more difficult to define. I touched on some of these in the preceding sub-chapter. But, reduced financial capacities of men and women in the aftermath of divorce impact not only the children in the short term, but on their long term educational and economic opportunities.

Taking an overview, they bear directly on how and to what extent the national economy functions.

I have until now carefully avoided discussing fathers per se, though one can hardly ignore one half of the population. This segment is responsible for the lion-share of all national wealth. Dr. John Jacobs comments on one devastating knock-on effect, stemming from father's suffering involuntary child absence syndrome, is detailed by:

"In another study by Greif (1979), 40 middle-class divorced fathers were examined who differed widely in the amount of regular contact they were allowed with their children. Twenty-three of the men developed physical symptoms following marital separation that included weight loss, ophthalmologic and dental problems, hypertension, rheumatoid arthritis and headaches. The fathers who experienced more of what Greif called, "child absence" manifested more signs of depression, including depressed mood and difficulty sleeping, eating, working and socializing." (Jacobs 1986)

Passage of time only exacerbates the problems encountered by fathers. In another study that followed fathers three years after divorce, these men reported experiencing loss, dysphoria, sadness and struggle regarding their role as the non-custodial parent. (Tepp, 1983)

I know of only one study that followed the work-productivity of such men enmeshed in non-custodial positions and it clearly showed that their work fell off meaningful levels. Reason dictates that leaving fathers in a position where they suffer from involuntary child absence engenders serious symptomologies and loss of productive work life. Loss of productivity of significant numbers of men is then, affecting the national economy, reducing output and wealth. While coming full circle various symptomologies in divorced men effects their ability to function and impacts directly on their financial contributions to the child.

So what do we know about the consequences of the destruction of intact family models?

We already know that women fare much better in the aftermath of divorce than do men. The Braver & O'Connell study explored this very point:

"Women were more satisfied with the terms of divorce because they were more likely to get the settlement they want and because they felt they had greater influence in the divorce process than men. The study found that 67 percent of the mothers received the custody arrangements they wanted, as opposed to 15 percent of fathers. Father's dissatisfaction was rooted in feelings of powerlessness in the process...The study found 3 times as many mothers felt the system favored mothers as felt the system favored fathers." (Braver & O'Connell (1998) "Taking on Myth 5: Emotional Issues of Divorce In Divorced Dads", Tarcher/Putnam)

We know that children do much worse in non-intact single parent families than those in intact families.

We know that divorced men, cut off from their children, suffer from a loss of companionship and parenting known as Child Absence Syndrome (CAS).

We know that the economic resources of the non-intact family are halved, expenditures increased substantially and income reduced.

We know that there are increased public costs related to supporting non-intact female-headed families and pressures placed on social services, housing benefits, welfare and subsidiary agencies.

Are there any other consequences?

Repudiation of Human Rights and Liberation

The chronicle and expose of our collective mismanagement of interpersonal gender based relationships and child issues details a serious backsliding in our evolution. By far, one the most profound consequences of family breakdown not quantified nor measured is the loss of our fundamental understanding and respect of the human rights of all people, regardless of gender, race or religion.

It is interesting that I have had to write an exacting reference work replete with quotes, statistics, theories, historilogical reviews of the literature and arguments. All that was required was good old-fashioned commonsense, intuition and conscience. We do know right from wrong. We understand universal concepts of justice and morality. Not everything is grist for the relativist mill.

A general view on what radical-feminism has produced in society must conclude that it has forced us to repudiate the advances we have made as a civilized society. We have lost our comprehension of and adherence to human rights principles. What a sad commentary it is, that, women led by radical feminist extremists seek to produce the same effects on men and children that they had themselves experienced and fought to reverse. How can women of conscience even consider replacing an unjust and arcane patriarchal system that treated children and women as chattel, with one in which men and children become chattel?

The women's movement, stroked by radical elements, is as guilty as the Nazis were in formulating plans and strategies nothing short of a sophisticated form of male ontological genocide. Universal denigration of men and persistent 'scapegoating' is a similar propaganda technique to the one used by the Nazis against the Jewish people. It eventually dehumanized them to the point where they became 'things' not 'persons'. Once scapegoated, men, like the Jewish people under fascism, are so depersonalized that they can metaphorically be enslaved, beaten, experimented on and burned in the crematoria without remorse, regret, doubt or guilt. [55]

There is a remarkable similarity in the approach of the radical feminists, using the mythologies of the superiority of female power rooted in the archaic societies predating successful organization of the family, with the Aryan myths used by Hitler. Hitler's use of mythology linked contemporary German failures to the debasement of their bloodline by the Jews. The intellectual analogy centers, not on the specifics, but on the scapegoating strategy.

The very same radical feminists that scream the loudest for the unique inclusion of women in human rights treaties and special consideration under the law are the first to dehumanize men repudiating their human and legal rights. These women demanding 'special considerations' from our American Constitution calling for an

---

[55] See Chapter 1 De-Personalization of fathers

amendment recognizing their special status and implied need for protection, are the very last to recognize, respect and argue for the rights of children.

What kind of women's liberation movement can assert itself with moral right and authority where it fails to recognize and respect the rights of others? The liberation that some of us had envisioned following the sixties revolution was not one restricted to one particular group or classification. Liberation meant each one of us regardless of gender, sexual persuasion, race, religion, ethnicity and nationality.

What radical feminist organizations have managed to do is to pervert the goals and aspirations of the intellectual culture that wished to foster a new society balancing interests and rights on a universal basis. The society we envisioned was one providing means to what the constitution describes as the goals of life, liberty and pursuit of happiness. It is therefore, nothing short of ironical, astounding and outrageous that the radical feminists should become oppressors and violators of our children's human rights.

Chapter 12

Conclusions

Conclusions

What consenting adults do or do not do to one another is no concern of mine. However, what does matter is what happens to children when we form presumably lasting pro-creational relationships. That is and will always be my primary concern.

I have tried to weed out the myriad psycho-dynamics and other factors leading us down a darkened corridor into a world of abortive interpersonal relationships, gender divisions, and chaos. Those consequences are born for this and future generations of our children. I wanted to divide the material to make reading and comprehension more convenient for the uninitiated. Further, I hope that I provided professionals with a logical approach to the facts and problems.

There are, at the end of the day, a few conclusions that we can draw. The first one is that we are dealing with a problem on a scale of such enormity that, unless there is immediate action taken, children in this and following generations are doomed.

The first issue we confront is how, in the short term, to halt the present trend of fatherless children. The follow up issue is how to restore balance to enabling gender relationships, family models and society, thus averting future disasters in human relations.

291

Matriarchy vs. Patriarchy

There are but two essential choices left to us when dealing with the human tragedy of family deconstruction. This circumstance leaves children vulnerable, deprived and dysfunctional given the imposition of radical feminist ideas promoting a society based on a matriarchal hegemony.

On the one hand, we can continue the process and watch helplessly as the human race spins out of control in a mad rush towards collective regression. On the other hand, we can immediately act to reset the social balance that has maintained us through the ages.

For Professor Amneus and others who have correctly observed and criticized the present disastrous consequences of matriarchal influences driving policies and practical realities, the answer lies in father custody and reversion to patriarchy. He sees the issues as clearly being a fundamental choice between patriarchy and matriarchy. Amneus reasons:

"The application to the problem addressed in the present book is this: If mother-headed homes generate most of our crime, delinquency, illegitimacy, educational failure, drug addiction, infantilism, gang violence, sexual confusion and demoralization--as they demonstrably do--why should not our society adopt policies which make fathers heads of families? ("Garbage Generation")

Perhaps, the forced choice scenario represents one of our worst intellectual nightmares. It places us in an intolerable position somewhere between the proverbial rock and a hard place. Boxed into black or white, good or bad, we catapult from one extreme position to another equally extreme position. We will never find a balance or harmony in these intellectual games.

As I see it, we have two separate problems: the nature and composition of family models (patriarchy-matriarchy, intact or fragmented) and second, the custody of children in divorce situations. Based on all the existing evidence, intuition and commonsense, I argue in this book for shared parenting in the circumstances of divorce as being in the best interests of the child. Sole custody decisions whether favoring maternal preferences based on misplaced assumptions (an artifact of past stereotyping) or even older assumptions favoring father (ancient past) are inherently flawed.

However, as the evidence suggests, if we cannot formulate and implement social policies making joint legal and physical custody (shared parenting) the law, then I would reluctantly argue for sole custody to be vested in father because of the present effects of sole maternal custody on our children and the manner in which women exercise their control. Given that:

"37.9% of fathers receive no access/visitation" (pg. 6, col. 2, 6, lines 4 & 5) "Child Support & Alimony: 1989 Series P-60, No. 173, Issued September 1991 Pages 6 & 7 of the 1989 Census" - Current Population Reports

"Between 25% - 33% of mothers denied visits" (pg. 451, col. 2, 2, lines 11 - 14) "Frequency of Visitation by Divorced Fathers: Differences in Reports by Fathers and Mothers" - Sanford H. Braver, Ph.D., Sharlene A. Wolchik, Ph.D., Irwin M. Sandler, Ph.D., Bruce S. Fogas, Ph.D., Daria Zvetina, M.Ed. American Journal of Orthopsychiatry

"40% of mothers reported that they had interfered with the non-custodial father's visitation on at least one occasion, to punish their ex-spouse". (Pg. 449, Col. 2, 1, lines 3 - 6 citing Fullton, 1979) Frequency of Visitation by Divorced Fathers: Differences in Reports by Fathers and Mothers - Sanford H. Braver, Ph.D., Sharlene A. Wolchik, Ph.D., Irwin M. Sandler, Ph.D., Bruce S. Fogas, Ph.D., Daria Zvetina, M.Ed., American Journal of Orthopsychiatry

Overall, approximately 50% of mothers "see no value in the father's continued contact with his children" (pg. 125, 4, lines 1 and 2) "Surviving the Breakup" - Joan Berlin Kelly and Judith S. Wallerstein

"Unilateral abuse of parental custodial power is more common in court ordered sole custody situations." (Pg. 4, col. 1, 1, lines 17 - 20) "Child Custody and Parental Cooperation" - Frank Williams, M.D., Dir. Psychiatry - Cedar-Sinai - Presented to the American Bar Association, Family Law Section, August 1987 and January 1988

"Feelings of anger toward their former spouses hindered effective involvement on the part of the fathers. Angry custodial mothers would sometimes sabotage father's efforts to visit their children" (pg. 442, Col.

1, 1, lines 23 - 27) "The Effect of the Post Divorce Relationship on Paternal Involvement: A Longitudinal Analysis" - Constance R. Ahrons, Ph.D., and Richard B. Miller, Ph.D., American Journal of Orthopsychiatry, Vol. 63, No. 3, July 1993

"Mothers may prevent visits to retaliate against the fathers for problems in their marital or post marital relationship" (pg. 1015, Col. 2, 2, lines 5 - 8) "Family Ties after Divorce: The Relationship Between Visiting and Paying Support" - Judith A. Seltzer, Nora Shaeffer, Hongwen Charing, University of Wisconsin, Journal of Marriage & the Family, Vol. 51, No. 4, November 1989.

"Our research indicates that most fathers and children who are separated from each other face barriers to continued interaction" (pg. 675, Col. 1, 1, Lines 2 - 5) "Children's Contact with Absent Parents" - Judith A. Seltzer, University of Wisconsin - Madison and Suzanne M. Bianchi, U.S. Bureau of the Census

"The former spouse [mother] was the greatest obstacle to having more frequent contact with the children" (pg. 281, Col. 2, 1, lines 1 - 4) "Increasing Our Understanding of Fathers Who Have Infrequent Contact With Their Children" - James R. Dudley, Professor, University North Carolina, under a grant from Temple University, Family Relations, Vol. 4, No. 3, July 1991

"Unfortunately, some angry women attempted to use the child's symptomatic behaviors as proof that the visits were detrimental to the child's welfare and should therefore be discontinued, distressing the unhappy children even more" (pg. 126, 2, lines 1 - 5) "Surviving the Breakup", Joan Berlin Kelly and Judith S. Wallerstein, Basic Books

At the same time, I expect a new set of observable syndromes consequential to this type of custody arrangement. Having said that, research shows that where men have sole custody decisions, women's access as the non-custodial parent has been far better respected and maintained.

As for the question of patriarchy or matriarchy, for a number of reasons, I cannot envision a return to the patriarchal system of the past. Nor can I accept any proposition that supports the continuation of the imposition of a fierce and dehumanizing matriarchal system over men and children.

Where then do the answers lie?

One possibility outside of Amneus' conclusion on re-institution of patriarchy is immediate modification of the old patriarchal family model. We can redefine family order as neither patriarchal nor matriarchal, including a set of checks and balances of interests, rights and responsibilities. One method open to us is revision of marital and divorce laws, but especially the marriage contract itself. Since we have become a society dedicated to narrow self-interest (as individuals and as sub-cultural groups) and our law is in reality a property rights law (paying lip serve to human and civil rights) then lets reduce the complexities of interpersonal gender relationships to the level that we understand. Lets do a deal. One means to that end might be the introduction of private contracts (pre-nuptial agreements) or state documents (marriage contracts) setting out the terms and conditions of marriage with specificity. This would do away with the present slave contract arrangement signed by men in total ignorance of its consequences.

State Action to Support Intact Families & Protect the Rights of Children

One Irish psychiatrist, writing from the point of view of the child, suggested that marriages involving children should be irrevocable. Husbands and wives can take on mistresses and lovers, develop separate interests, pursue private objectives but otherwise maintain one home and joint care of the children. Perhaps, an extreme solution, but based on a rather valid point; that while men and women as consenting adults might be free to enhance or torment one another, they have a solemn obligation to the children they produce together, that is spiritual, moral and binding.

As I have suggested, it is conceivable that the state can seize the initiative here. Present marriage contracts have two major characteristics. First, they rely on symbolic value, and second, they can be broken with impunity. Finally, based on present interpretations and practice, they favor one party's social, economic and psychological interests over the interests of other parties (one active party father-and one who becomes a later silent party-child).

As parental rights are constitutional rights, the federal state should enact a national marital law that includes a uniform marriage contract applicable and enforceable in all states. The federal state should also enact legislation similar to but much clearer than The British Children Act 1989 in which the rights of the child are clearly recognized in accordance with international law (The UN Convention on the Rights of the Child), defined and balanced with those of its parents (A Children's Bill of Rights). This federalist intervention might best guarantee concerns of due process and the equal administration of justice in all jurisdictions. That might eliminate the habitudes and vagaries of justice for parents and children determined by local prejudice. It is not in the interest of children that a New York child might enjoy one type of custody decision standard, while another child living in Louisiana or Texas faces a different standard.

Wide ranging judicial powers in child related matters must be severely restricted. Rules and evidence must approximate those in other areas of civil and criminal law. Judges must be re-trained before sitting on domestic relations cases. Immunities normally granted should be either completely removed or having 'qualified' immunity reduced (judges, social workers, guardian ad litems, psychiatrists and psychologists) making them accountable. Child proceedings ruled by sub-judicae hearings must be open to the public.

Some might ask, whether or not the state should intervene in a meaningful way. Does it have a moral obligation to safeguard children? Does it have the right to act on their behalf and in their best interests?

In my view, it does have such an obligation and right, but only if it acts with equity.

State Abstention from Sexual Regulation

Failing pro-active state involvement, one radical but rather interesting idea might be to obviate the need for the state to regulate sexual function or family matters altogether. In this scenario, a departure from two thousand years of family law, men and women would be free to have sexual relations en passant, intermittent, co-habitat ional and long-term with production of children, absent of any state involvement, regulation, rules or laws. Arguably, given the present state involvement regulating marriage, divorce and custody seen as completely inadequate and unjust, it cannot claim to perform a justifiable function.

The possible ensuing anarchy might not be worse than the state's presently imposed systematic chaos and abridgment of children's and male rights. It could lead to a renegotiation of gender relations based upon a social contract that is not a 'slave' contract. Obviously, there is an argument that if the state cannot act with equity and sensitivity, then it should quit the business altogether!

Civil Disobedience and Passive Resistance

Failing state abdication of its authority to regulate sexual function, marriage and divorce, and if the State refuses to act properly to ensure the rights of all of its citizens, one faces a difficult situation. Just as Gandhi ultimately forced the British from India, using civil disobedience and passive resistance as a strategy, perhaps the only means for men (on behalf of their children) to achieve justice is for them to employ similar tactics. Imagine how the wheels of family law would grind to a screeching halt, if men failed to attend 'star chamber' courts, and simply ignored all attempts to strip them of their rights and the rights of their children using smoke and mirror legal process to give such deprivations the appearance of lawful action. What would happen if men were willing to go to jail? What would happen if millions upon millions of men joined hands chaining themselves to railings (just as had the suffragettes) and blocked entrances to family law courts? What would happen if they all simply stopped working?

The Betrayal of the Child

The matter is not complicated. We have all betrayed the child. Some of us have followed a path of mean spirited self-interest. Others have followed in ignorance. There are those who have seen and understood but have remained either silent, or too cautious, or fearful that a telling of the truth might interfere with their prestige, their tenure, their credibility, their income and lifestyles.

The psychologist Ross Thompson demonstrates the trepidation that professionals exhibit when writing on the inequities of present child custody decisions. If one were to take him literally, one would conclude that he is a feminist dupe. However, I do not, and reading between the lines, I understand his style to represent the fear that he faces when making a politically incorrect judgment and argument for following what he knows to be the child's best interests.

"Fathers figure prominently in a child's post divorce life, whether they are involved or disinterested, **but concerns about inadequate child support, non-custodial fathers who fail to visit, and the economic plight of single mothers have together raised policy questions about how better to enfranchise fathers with the rights and responsibilities** of parenting and ensure them a continuing and meaningful role in the lives of their offspring." (Thompson)

Is it the MONEY issue again (on behalf of feminists) that fosters his plea for father to be "enfranchised"? On the other hand, is it from the child's perspective that the evil of 'disenfranchising father', takes prominence? "The most important reason for thoughtfully considering the experience of fathers in divorce is to advance the welfare of children." Is he associating the welfare of children with MONEY, or is he concerned about the emotional well being of children?

"This discussion seeks to advance that goal by describing the experience of fathers in divorce, **not to advance a "father's rights" perspective.**" Is it necessary for a mental health professional to disassociate from fathers seeking the restoration of their parental identities and relationships to their children, in order to argue as he does for shared parenting? Not when father's rights perspectives express nothing more than he suggests as appropriate in stating, "Because both parents assume meaningful but different roles and relationships with offspring, custody decisions might better focus on maintaining relationships with each parent rather than just the "primary" one." Dr. Thompson concludes,

"At its best, joint custody presents the possibility that each family member can "win" in post-divorce life rather than insisting that a custody decision identify "winners" and "losers"

As for the rest of us, we have lacked the will, moral backbone and the organizational skills to protect our children. We have allowed feminist inspired hypocrisy and deceit to rule in singing songs of praise to children whose lyrics have no meaning, writing charters enshrining their best interests that are scrawled in sands that await the incoming tide, defending them against physical diseases while allowing their minds and spirits to suffer in stoic silence.

The Best Interests of the Child: The Least Detrimental Alternative

The title of this sub-chapter is mere parody of the infamous work authored by Freud, Solnit and Goldstein. Their text remains the bible on child welfare used by mental health professionals, social workers, guardian ad litems, lawyers and judges, as the means to obliterate the best interests of children. I can only implore men and women of sensitivity and good judgment to begin to undo the damage caused by adherence to a doctrine interpreted in such a way as to rationalize sole nurturance of divorced children by mothers.

Any external attempt to redefine the family as consisting solely of mother and child is a fruitless denial of the inherent conditions of human existence. When men and women, acting on ancient impulses and the prime directive of human experience, come together, forming a family unit predicated on procreation, a complex helix forms that cannot be dismissed or ignored, even in divorce.

Previous descriptions of 'the family' that spoke of dyads have missed an intuitive truth, that families are multifaceted and interchanging triads. There is no two, there is, three! This is a fact that is unaltered by separation and divorce. While the balance of interests, needs, and interactions are affected, the essence of the relationships remains the same, especially from the child's perspective.

I write in the hope that we will come to understand, as Dr. Alice Miller stated,

"For some years now there has been proof that the devastating effects of the traumatization of children take their toll on society. This knowledge concerns every one of us, and-if disseminated widely enough-should lead to fundamental changes in society..."

Finally, I judge it appropriate to end this book with the words of a young girl. She is but one of the tens of millions of children worldwide victimized by the consequences of divorce. When I interviewed her, she responded with immediacy, insight, and sadness. I asked her what she thought is best for children in the aftermath of divorce. She answered, " Joint custody and that parents should remain in the same locality." I then asked if families should stay together. She replied, " I think that parents should swallow their grief. They should try to get along and stay together until the kids are grown."

I can do no more than to leave you with that child's perspective.

END

Appendix A:

US Government Statistics

From the US Bureau of the Census; Child Support and Alimony: 1993 Series P-50, No 173.

37.8% of fathers have no visitation rights.

54.9% of fathers have some visitation rights but little enforcement

7.3% of fathers have joint custody (shared parenting)

Fathers with joint custody (shared parenting) paid 90.2% support

Fathers with visitation rights paid 79.1% support

Fathers with no rights paid 44.5% of ordered support

86% of fathers who did not pay support did not have visitation!

A federally funded study (Survey of Absent Parents- by the Urban Institute and the University of Chicago for the Office of Child Support Enforcement) previously had reported that "there were substantial differences between custodial and parents in terms of reported levels of payment".

Percentages of men who have visitation rights as a percentage of total fathers.

Category of Men/Visitation %of NCP's

No visitation rights: 37.8%

Visitation rights: 54.9%

Joint Custody: 7.3%

Total: 100%

<u>*Category of Men/Visitation*   *% of NCP's paying support*</u>

No visitation rights: 37.8% * 44.5% = 16.8%

Visitation rights: 54.9% * 79.1% = 43.4%

Joint Custody: 7.3% * 90.2% = 6.6%

Total: 100%   66.8%

This means that 66.8% of all fathers pay support in full to a total of about 75% of all child support owed in dollars

Appendix B:

Ankenbrandt v. Richards

From the Legal Information Institute and Project Hermes

NOTICE: This opinion is subject to formal revision before publication in the preliminary print of the United States Reports. Readers are requested to notify the Reporter of Decisions, Supreme Court of the United States,

Washington, D.C. 20543, of any typographical or other formal errors, in order that corrections may be made before the preliminary print goes to press.

SUPREME COURT OF THE UNITED STATES

No. 91-367

CAROL ANKENBRANDT, as next friend and mother of l. r. and s. r., PETITIONER v. JON A. RICHARDS and DEBRA KESLER

on writ of certiorari to the United States court of appeals for the fifth circuit

[June 15, 1992]

Justice White delivered the opinion of the Court.

Petitioner Carol Ankenbrandt, a citizen of Missouri, brought this lawsuit on September 26, 1989, on behalf of her daughters L. R. and S. R. against respondents Jon A. Richards and Debra Kesler, citizens of Louisiana, in the United States District Court for the Eastern District of Louisiana. Alleging federal jurisdiction based on the diversity of citizenship provision of 1332, Ankenbrandt's complaint sought monetary damages for alleged sexual and physical abuse of the children committed by Richards and Kesler. Richards is the divorced father of the children and Kesler his female companion. On December 10, 1990, the District Court granted respondents' motion to dismiss this lawsuit. Citing In re Burrus, , 593-594 (1890), for the proposition that "[t]he whole subject of the domestic relations of husband and wife, parent and child, belongs to the laws of the States and not to the laws of the United States," the court concluded that this case fell within what has become known as the "domestic relations" exception to diversity jurisdiction, and that it lacked jurisdiction over the case. The court also invoked the abstention principles announced in Younger v. Harris, (1971), to justify its decision to dismiss the complaint without prejudice. Ankenbrandt v. Richards, No. 89-4244 (ED La. Dec. 10, 1990). The Court of Appeals affirmed in an unpublished opinion. Ankenbrandt v. Richards, No. 91-3037 (CA5 May 31, 1991), judgt. order reported at 934 F. 2d 1262.

We granted certiorari limited to the following questions: "(1) Is there a domestic relations exception to federal jurisdiction? (2) If so, does it permit a district court to abstain from exercising diversity jurisdiction over a tort action for damages? and (3) Did the District Court in this case err in abstaining from exercising jurisdiction under the doctrine of Younger v. Harris, [supra]?" 502 U.S. (1992). We address each of these issues in turn.

Lower federal courts have invoked the domestic relations exception upon which the courts relied to often decline jurisdiction. The seeming authority for doing so originally stemmed from the announcement in Barber v. Barber, 21 How. 582 (1859), that the federal courts have no jurisdiction over suits for divorce or the allowance of alimony.

In that case, the Court heard a suit in equity brought by a wife (by her next friend) in federal district court pursuant to diversity jurisdiction against her former husband. She sought to enforce a decree from a New York state court, which had granted a divorce and awarded her alimony. The former husband thereupon moved to Wisconsin to place himself beyond the New York courts' jurisdiction so that the divorce decree there could not be enforced against him; he then sued for divorce in a Wisconsin court, representing to that court that his wife had abandoned him and failing to disclose the existence of the New York decree. In a suit brought by the former wife in

Wisconsin Federal District Court, the former husband alleged that the court lacked jurisdiction. The court accepted jurisdiction and gave judgment for the divorced wife.

On appeal, it was argued that the District Court lacked jurisdiction on two grounds: first, that there was no diversity of citizenship because although divorced, the wife's citizenship necessarily remained that of her former husband; and second, that the whole subject of divorce and alimony, including a suit to enforce an alimony decree, was exclusively ecclesiastical at the time of the adoption of the Constitution and that the Constitution therefore placed the whole subject of divorce and alimony beyond the jurisdiction of the United States courts. Over the dissent of three Justices, the Court rejected both arguments. After an exhaustive survey of the authorities, the Court concluded that a divorced wife could acquire a citizenship separate from that of her former husband and that a suit to enforce an alimony decree rested within the federal courts' equity jurisdiction. The Court reached these conclusions after summarily dismissing the former husband's contention that the case involved a subject matter outside the federal courts' jurisdiction. In so stating, however, the Court also announced the following limitation on federal jurisdiction: "Our first remark is--and we wish it to be remembered--that this is not a suit asking the court for the allowance of alimony. That has been done by a court of competent jurisdiction. The court in Wisconsin was asked to interfere to prevent that decree from being defeated by fraud.

"We disclaim altogether any jurisdiction in the courts of the United States upon the subject of divorce, or for the allowance of alimony, either as an original proceeding in chancery or as an incident to divorce a vinculo, or to one from bed and board." Barber, supra, at 584.

As a general matter, the dissenters agreed with these statements, but took issue with the Court's holding that the instant action to enforce an alimony decree was within the equity jurisdiction of the federal courts.

The statements disclaiming jurisdiction over divorce and alimony decree suits, though technically dicta, formed the basis for excluding "domestic relations" cases from the jurisdiction of the lower federal courts, a jurisdictional limitation those courts have recognized ever since. The Barber Court, however, cited no authority and did not discuss the foundation for its announcement. Since that time, the Court has dealt only occasionally with the domestic relations limitation on federal court jurisdiction, and it has never addressed the basis for such a limitation. Because we are unwilling to cast aside an understood rule that has been recognized for nearly a century and a half, we feel compelled to explain why we will continue to recognize this limitation on federal jurisdiction.

Counsel argued in Barber that the Constitution prohibited federal courts from exercising jurisdiction over domestic relations cases. Brief for Appellant in Barber v. Barber, D.T. 1858, No. 44, pp. 4-5. An examination of Article III, Barber itself, and our cases since Barber makes clear that the Constitution does not exclude domestic relations cases from the jurisdiction otherwise granted by statute to the federal courts.

Article III, 2, of the Constitution provides in pertinent part:

"Section 2. The judicial Power shall extend to all Cases, in Law and Equity, arising under this Constitution, the Laws of the United States, and Treaties made, or which shall be made, under their Authority;--to all Cases affecting Ambassadors, other public Ministers and Consuls;--to all Cases of admiralty and maritime Jurisdiction;--to Controversies to which the United States shall be a Party;-to Controversies between two or more States;--between a State and Citizens of another State;--between Citizens of different States;--between Citizens of the same State claiming Land under Grants of different States, and between a State, or the Citizens thereof, and foreign States, Citizens or Subjects."

This section delineates the absolute limits on the federal courts' jurisdiction. But in articulating three different terms to define jurisdiction--"Cases, in Law and Equity," "Cases," and "Controversies"--this provision contains no limitation on subjects of a domestic relations nature. Nor did Barber purport to ground the domestic relations exception in these constitutional limits on federal jurisdiction. The Court's discussion of federal judicial power to hear suits of a domestic relations nature contains no mention of the Constitution, see Barber, supra, at 584, and it is logical to presume that the Court based its statement limiting such power on narrower statutory, rather than broader constitutional, grounds. Cf. Edward J. DeBartolo Corp. v. Florida Gulf Coast Building & Construction Trades Council, Inc., , 575 (1988). Subsequent decisions confirm that Barber was not relying on constitutional limits in justifying the exception. In one such case, for instance, the Court stated the "long established rule" that federal courts lack jurisdiction over certain domestic relations matters as having been based on the assumptions that "husband and wife cannot usually be citizens of different States, so long as the marriage relation continues (a rule which has been somewhat relaxed in recent cases), and for the further reason that a suit for divorce in itself involves no pecuniary value." De La Rama v. De La Rama, , 307 (1906). Since Article III contains no monetary limit on suits brought pursuant to federal diversity jurisdiction, De La Rama's articulation of the "rule" in terms of the statutory requirements for diversity jurisdiction further supports the view that the exception is not grounded in the Constitution.

Moreover, even while citing with approval the Barber language purporting to limit the jurisdiction of the federal courts over domestic relations matters, the Court has heard appeals from territorial courts involving divorce, see, e. g., De La Rama, supra; Simms v. Simms, (1899), and has upheld the exercise of original jurisdiction by federal courts in the District of Columbia to decide divorce actions, see, e. g., Glidden Co. v. Zdanok, , 581, n. 54 (1962). Thus, even were the statements in De La Rama referring to the statutory prerequisites of diversity.

Jurisdiction alone not persuasive testament to the statutory origins of the rule, by hearing appeals from legislative, or Article I courts, this Court implicitly has made clear its understanding that the source of the constraint on jurisdiction from Barber was not Article III; otherwise the Court itself would have lacked jurisdiction over appeals from these legislative courts. See National Mutual Ins. Co. v. Tidewater Transfer Co., , 643 (1949) (Vinson, C. J., dissenting) ("We can no more review a legislative court's decision of a case which is not among those enumerated in Art. III than we can hear a case from a state court involving purely state law questions"). We therefore have no difficulty concluding that when the Barber Court "disclaim[ed] altogether any jurisdiction in the courts of the United States upon the subject of divorce," 21 How., at 584, it was not basing its statement on the Constitution.

That Article III, 2, does not mandate the exclusion of domestic relations cases from federal court jurisdiction, however, does not mean that such courts necessarily must retain and exercise jurisdiction over such cases. Other constitutional provisions explain why this is so. Article I, 8, cl. 9, for example, authorizes Congress "[t]o constitute Tribunals inferior to the supreme Court" and Article III, 1, states that "[t]he judicial Power of the United States, shall be vested in one supreme Court, and in such inferior Courts as the Congress may from time to time ordain and establish." The Court's cases state the rule that "if inferior federal courts were created, [Congress was not] required to invest them with all the jurisdiction it was authorized to bestow under Art. III." Palmore v. United States, 401 (1973).

This position has held constant since at least 1845, when the Court stated that "the judicial power of the United States . . . is (except in enumerated instances, applicable exclusively to this court) dependent for its distribution and organization, and for the modes of its exercise, entirely upon the action of Congress, who possess the sole power of creating the tribunals (inferior to the Supreme Court) . . . and of investing them with jurisdiction either limited, concurrent, or exclusive, and of withholding jurisdiction from them in the exact degrees and character which to Congress may seem proper for the public good." Cary v. Curtis, 3 How. 236, 245. See Sheldon v. Sill, 8 How. 441 (1850); Plaquemines Tropical Fruit Co. v. Henderson, (1898); Kline v. Burke Constr. Co., (1922); Lockerty v. Phillips, (1943). We thus turn our attention to the relevant jurisdictional statutes.

The Judiciary Act of 1789 provided that "the circuit courts shall have original cognizance, concurrent with the courts of the several States, of all suits of a civil nature at common law or in equity, where the matter in dispute exceeds, exclusive of costs, the sum or value of five hundred dollars, and . . . an alien is a party, or the suit is between a citizen of the State where the suit is brought, and a citizen of another State." Act of Sept. 24, 1789, 11, 1 Stat. 78. (Emphasis added.) The defining phrase, "all suits of a civil nature at common law or in equity," remained a key element of statutory provisions demarcating the terms of diversity jurisdiction until 1948, when Congress amended the diversity jurisdiction provision to eliminate this phrase and replace in its stead the term "all civil actions." 1948 Judicial Code and Judiciary Act, 62 Stat. 930, .

The Barber majority itself did not expressly refer to the diversity statute's use of the limitation on "suits of a civil nature at common law or in equity." The dissenters in Barber, however, implicitly made such a reference, for they suggested that the federal courts had no power over certain domestic relations actions because the court of chancery lacked authority to issue divorce and alimony decrees. Stating that "the origin and the extent of [the federal courts'] jurisdiction must be sought in the laws of the United States, and in the settled rules and principles by which those laws have bound them," the dissenters contended that "as the jurisdiction of the chancery in England does not extend to or embrace the subjects of divorce and alimony, and as the jurisdiction of the courts of the United States in chancery is bounded by that of the chancery in England, all power or cognizance with respect to those subjects by the courts of the United States in chancery is equally excluded." Barber, supra, at 605 (Daniel, J., dissenting). Hence, in the dissenters' view, a suit seeking such relief would not fall within the statutory language "all suits of a civil nature at common law or in equity." Because the Barber Court did not disagree with this reason for accepting the jurisdictional limitation over the issuance of divorce and alimony decrees, it may be inferred fairly that the jurisdictional limitation recognized by the Court rested on this statutory basis and that the disagreement between the Court and the dissenters thus centered only on the extent of the limitation.

We have no occasion here to join the historical debate over whether the English court of chancery had jurisdiction to handle certain domestic relations matters, though we note that commentators have found some support for the Barber majority's interpretation. Certainly it was not unprecedented at the time for the Court to infer, from what it understood to be English chancery practice, some guide to the meaning of the 1789 Act's jurisdictional grant. See, e. g., Robinson v. Campbell, 3 Wheat. 212, 221-222 (1818). We thus are content to rest our conclusion that a domestic relations exception exists as a matter of statutory construction not on the accuracy of the historical justifications on which it was seemingly based, but rather on Congress' apparent acceptance of this construction of the diversity jurisdiction provisions in the years prior to 1948, when the statute limited jurisdiction to "suits of a civil nature at common law or in equity." As the court in Phillips, Nizer, Benjamin, Krim & Ballon v. Rosenstiel, 490 F. 2d 509, 514 (CA2 1973) observed, "[m]ore than a century has elapsed since the Barber dictum without any intimation of Congressional dissatisfaction. . . . Whatever Article III may or may not permit, we thus accept the Barber dictum as a correct interpretation of the Congressional grant." Considerations of stare decisis have particular strength in this context, where "the legislative power is implicated, and Congress remains free to alter what we have done." Patterson v. McLean Credit Union, 172-173 (1989).

When Congress amended the diversity statute in 1948 to replace the law/equity distinction with the phrase "all civil actions," we presume Congress did so with full cognizance of the Court's nearly century long interpretation of the prior statutes, which had construed the statutory diversity jurisdiction to contain an exception for certain domestic relations matters. With respect to the 1948 amendment, the Court has previously stated that, "no changes of law or policy are to be presumed from changes of language in the revision unless an intent to make such changes is clearly expressed." Fourco Glass Co. v. Transmirra Products Corp., , 227 (1957); see also Finley v. United States, , 554

(1989). With respect to such a longstanding and well known construction of the diversity statute, and where Congress made substantive changes to the statute in other respects, see note, we presume, absent any indication that Congress intended to alter this exception, see ibid.; Fed. Rule Civ. Proc. 2, Advisory Committee Note 3, 28 U. S. C. App., p. 555, that Congress "adopt[ed] that interpretation" when it reenacted the diversity statute. Lorillard v. Pons, , 580 (1978).

In the more than 100 years since this Court laid the seeds for the development of the domestic relations exception, the lower federal courts have applied it in a variety of circumstances. See, e. g., cases cited in n. 1, supra. Many of these applications go well beyond the circumscribed situations posed by Barber and its progeny. Barber itself disclaimed federal jurisdiction over a narrow range of domestic relations issues involving the granting of a divorce and a decree of alimony, see 21 How., at 584, and stated the limits on federal court power to intervene prior to the rendering of such orders:

"It is, that when a court of competent jurisdiction over the subject matter and the parties decrees a divorce, and alimony to the wife as its incident, and is unable of itself to enforce the decree summarily upon the husband, that courts of equity will interfere to prevent the decree from being defeated by fraud. The interference, however, is limited to cases in which alimony has been decreed; then only to the extent of what is due, and always to cases in which no appeal is pending from the decree for the divorce or for alimony." Id., at 591.

The Barber Court thus did not intend to strip the federal courts of authority to hear cases arising from the domestic relations of persons unless they seek the granting or modification of a divorce or alimony decree. The holding of the case itself sanctioned the exercise of federal jurisdiction over the enforcement of an alimony decree that had been properly obtained in a state court of competent jurisdiction. Contrary to the Barber dissenters' position, the enforcement of such validly obtained orders does not "regulate the domestic relations of society" and produce an "inquisitorial authority" in which federal tribunals "enter the habitations and even into the chambers and nurseries of private families, and inquire into and pronounce upon the morals and habits and affections or antipathies of the members of every household." Id., at 602 (Daniel, J., dissenting). And from the conclusion that the federal courts lacked jurisdiction to issue divorce and alimony decrees, there was no dissent. See Barber, supra, at 604 (Daniel, J., dissenting) (noting that "upon questions of settlement or of contract connected with marriages, the court of chancery will undertake the enforcement of such contracts, but does not decree alimony as such, and independently of such contracts"). See also Simms v. Simms, , 167 (1899) (stating that "[i]t may therefore be assumed as indubitable that the Circuit Courts of the United States have no jurisdiction, either of suits for divorce, or of claims for alimony, whether made in a suit for divorce, or by an original proceeding in equity, before a decree for such alimony in a state court").

Subsequently, this Court expanded the domestic relations exception to include decrees in child custody cases. In a child custody case brought pursuant to a writ of habeas corpus, for instance, the Court held void a writ issued by a Federal District Court to restore a child to the custody of the father. "As to the right to the control and possession of this child, as it is contested by its father and its grandfather, it is one in regard to which neither the Congress of the United States nor any authority of the United States has any special jurisdiction." In re Burrus, , 594 (1890).

Although In re Burrus technically did not involve a construction of the diversity statute, as we understand Barber to have done, its statement that "[t]he whole subject of the domestic relations of husband and wife, parent and child, belongs to the laws of the States and not to the laws of the United States," id., at 593-594, has been interpreted by the federal courts to apply with equal vigor in suits brought pursuant to diversity jurisdiction. See, e. g., Bennett v. Bennett, 221 U. S. App. D. C. 90, 93, 682 F. 2d 1039, 1042 (1982); Solomon v. Solomon, 516 F. 2d 1018, 1025 (CA3 1975); Hernstadt v. Hernstadt, 373 F. 2d 316, 317 (CA2 1967); see generally 13B C. Wright, A. Miller, & E. Cooper, Federal Practice and Procedure 3609, pp. 477-479, nn. 2832 (1984). This application is consistent with Barber's directive to limit federal courts' exercise of diversity jurisdiction over suits for divorce and alimony decrees. See Barber, supra, at 584. We conclude, therefore, that the domestic relations exception, as articulated by this Court since Barber, divests the federal courts of power to issue divorce, alimony, and child custody decrees. Given the long passage of time without any expression of congressional dissatisfaction, we have no trouble today reaffirming the validity of the exception as it pertains to divorce and alimony decrees and child custody orders.

Not only is our conclusion rooted in respect for this long held understanding, it is also supported by sound policy considerations. Issuance of decrees of this type not infrequently involves retention of jurisdiction by the court and deployment of social workers to monitor compliance. As a matter of judicial economy, state courts are more eminently suited to work of this type than are federal courts, which lack the close association with state and local government organizations dedicated to handling issues that arise out of conflicts over divorce, alimony, and child custody decrees. Moreover, as a matter of judicial expertise, it makes far more sense to retain the rule that federal courts lack power to issue these types of decrees because of the special proficiency developed by state tribunals over the past century and a half in handling issues that arise in the granting of such decrees. See Lloyd v. Loeffler, supra, at 492.

By concluding, as we do, that the domestic relations exception encompasses only cases involving the issuance of a divorce, alimony, or child custody decree, we necessarily find that the Court of Appeals erred by affirming the District Court's invocation of this exception. This lawsuit in no way seeks such a decree; rather, it alleges that respondents Richards and Kesler committed torts against L. R. and S. R., Ankenbrandt's children by Richards. Federal subject matter jurisdiction pursuant to 1332 thus is proper in this case. We now address whether, even though subject matter jurisdiction might be proper, sufficient grounds exist to warrant abstention from the exercise of that jurisdiction.

The Court of Appeals, as did the District Court, stated abstention as an alternative ground for its holding. The District Court quoted another federal court to the effect that " `abstention, that doctrine designed to promote federal state comity, is required when to render a decision would disrupt the establishment of a coherent state policy.' " App. to Pet. for Cert. A 6 (quoting Zaubi v. Hoejme, 530 F. Supp. 831, 836 (WD Pa. 1980)). It is axiomatic, however, that "abstention from the exercise of federal jurisdiction is the exception, not the rule.' " Colorado River Water Conservation Dist. v. United States, 813 (1976). Abstention rarely should be invoked because the federal courts have a "virtually unflagging obligation . . . to exercise the jurisdiction given them." Id., at 817.

The courts below cited Younger v. Harris, (1971) to support their holdings to abstain in this case. In so doing, the courts clearly erred. Younger itself held that, absent unusual circumstances, a federal court could not interfere with a pending state criminal prosecution. Id., at 54. Though we have extended Younger abstention to the civil context, see, e. g., Middlesex County Ethics Comm. v. Garden State Bar Assn.,

(1982); Ohio Civil Rights Comm'n v. Dayton Christian Schools, Inc., (1986); Pennzoil Co. v. Texaco Inc., (1987),we have never applied the notions of comity so critical to Younger's "Our Federalism" when no state proceeding was pending nor any assertion of important state interests made. In this case, there is no allegation by respondents of any pending state proceedings, and Ankenbrandt contends that such proceedings ended prior to her filing this lawsuit. Absent any pending proceeding in state tribunals, therefore, application by the lower courts of Younger abstention was clearly erroneous.

It is not inconceivable, however, that in certain circumstances, the abstention principles developed in Burford v. Sun Oil Co., (1943), might be relevant in a case involving elements of the domestic relationship even when the parties do not seek divorce, alimony, or child custody. This would be so when a case presents "difficult questions of state law bearing on policy problems of substantial public import whose importance transcends the result in the case then at bar." Colorado River Water Conservation Dist., supra, at 814. Such might well be the case if a federal suit were filed prior to effectuation of a divorce, alimony, or child custody decree, and the suit depended on a determination of the status of the parties. Where, as here, the status of the domestic relationship has been determined as a matter of state law, and in any event has no bearing on the underlying torts alleged, we have no difficulty concluding that Burford abstention is inappropriate in this case.

We thus conclude that the Court of Appeals erred by affirming the District Court's rulings to decline jurisdiction based on the domestic relations exception to diversity jurisdiction and to abstain under the doctrine of Younger v. Harris, supra. The exception has no place in a suit such as this one, in which a former spouse sues another on behalf of children alleged to have been abused. Because the allegations in this complaint do not request the District Court to issue a divorce, alimony, or child custody decree, we hold that the suit is appropriate for the exercise of 1332 jurisdiction given the existence of diverse citizenship between petitioner and respondents and the pleading of the relevant amount in controversy. Accordingly, we reverse the decision of the Court of Appeals and remand the case for further proceedings consistent with this opinion.

It is so ordered.

Notes

Ankenbrandt represents that in the month prior to the filing of this federal court action, on August 9, 1989, a juvenile court in Jefferson Parish, Louisiana, entered a judgment under the State's child protection laws, La. Rev. Stat. Ann. 13:1600 et seq. (West 1983), repealed, 1991 La. Acts, No. 235, 17, eff. Jan. 1, 1992, and superseded by Louisiana Children's Code, Title X, Art. 1001 et seq. (1991), permanently terminating all of Richards' parental rights because of the alleged abuse and permanently enjoining him from any contact with the children. Neither the District Court nor the Court of Appeals found it necessary to pass on the accuracy of this representation in resolving the issues presented; nor do we.

The Courts of Appeals have generally diverged in cases involving application of the domestic relations exception to tort suits brought in federal court pursuant to diversity jurisdiction. See, e. g., Bennett v. Bennett, 221 U. S. App. D. C. 90, 682 F. 2d 1039 (1982) (holding that the exception does not bar a claim for damages but that it does bar claims for injunctive relief); Cole v. Cole, 633 F. 2d 1083 (CA4 1980) (holding that the exception does not apply in tort suits stemming from custody and visitation disputes); Drewes v. Ilnicki, 863 F. 2d 469 (CA6 1988) (holding that the exception does not apply to a tort suit for intentional infliction of emotional distress); Lloyd v. Loeffler, 694 F. 2d 489 (CA7 1982) (holding that the exception does not apply to a tort claim for interference with the custody of a child); McIntyre v. McIntyre, 771 F. 2d 1316 (CA9 1985) (holding that the exception does not apply when the case does not involve questions of parental status, interference with pending state domestic relations proceedings, an alteration of a state court judgment, or the impingement of the state court's supervision of a minor); Ingram v. Hayes, 866 F. 2d 368 (CA11 1988) (holding that the exception applies to divest a federal court of jurisdiction over a tort action for intentional infliction of emotional distress).

We read Ohio ex rel. Popovici v. Agler, (1930), as in accord with this conclusion. In that case, the Court referenced the language in In re Burrus, (1890), regarding the domestic relations exception and then held that a state court was not precluded by the Constitution and relevant federal statutes from exercising jurisdiction over a divorce suit brought against the Roumanian vice consul. See id., at 383-384.

See, e. g., Vestal & Foster, Implied Limitations on the Diversity Jurisdiction of Federal Courts, 41 Minn. L. Rev. 1, 28 (1956); Atwood, Domestic Relations Cases in Federal Court: Toward a Principled Exercise of Jurisdiction, 35 Hastings L. J. 571, 584-589 (1984); Rush, Domestic Relations Law: Federal Jurisdiction and State Sovereignty in Perspective, 60 Notre Dame L. Rev. 1, 15 (1984); Note, The Domestic Relations Exception to Diversity Jurisdiction, 83 Colum. L. Rev. 1824, 1834-1839 (1983); Note, The Domestic Relations Exception to Diversity Jurisdiction: A Re Evaluation, 24 Boston College L. Rev. 661, 664-668 (1983).

Justice Blackmun criticizes us for resting upon Congress' apparent acceptance of the Court's earlier construction of the diversity statute in the 1948 codification. See post, at 2-3 (opinion concurring in judgment). We see nothing remarkable in this decision. See, e. g., Flood v. Kuhn, , 283-284 (1972).

The better reasoned views among the Courts of Appeals have similarly stated the domestic relations exception as narrowly confined to suits for divorce, alimony, or child custody decrees. See, e. g., McIntyre v. McIntyre, 771 F. 2d 1316, 1317 (CA9 1985) (opinion of Kennedy, J.) ("[T]he exception to jurisdiction arises in those cases where a federal court is asked to grant a decree of divorce or annulment, or to grant custody or fix payments for support"); Lloyd v. Loeffler, 694 F. 2d, at 492 (same); Bennett v. Bennett, 221 U. S. App. D. C., at 93, 682 F. 2d, at 1042 (same); Cole v. Cole, 633 F. 2d, at 1087 (same).

The courts below offered no explanation, and we are aware of none, why the domestic relations exception applies at all to respondent Kesler, who would appear to stand in the same position with respect to Ankenbrandt as any other opponent in a tort suit brought in federal court pursuant to diversity jurisdiction.

Moreover, should Burford abstention be relevant in other circumstances, it may be appropriate for the court to retain jurisdiction to insure prompt and just disposition of the matter upon the determination by the state court of the relevant issue. Cf. Kaiser Steel Corp. v. W. S. Ranch Co., , 594 (1968).

Though he acknowledges that our earlier cases invoking the domestic relations exceptions speak in jurisdictional terms, Justice Blackmun nevertheless would reinterpret them to support a special abstention doctrine for such cases. See post, at 8-10 (Blackmun, J., concurring in judgment). Yet in briefly sketching his vision of how such a doctrine might operate, Justice Blackmun offers no authoritative support for where such an abstention doctrine might be found, no principled reason why we should retroactively concoct an abstention doctrine out of whole cloth to account for federal court practice in existence for 82 years prior to the announcement of the first abstention doctrine in Railroad Comm'n of Texas v. Pullman Co., (1941), and no persuasive reason why articulation of such an abstention doctrine offers a sounder way of achieving the same result than our construction of the statute.

Appendix C:

President Clinton Letter on the UN Convention on the Rights of the Child

THE WHITE HOUSE

WASHINGTON

April 22 1996
Mr. Stewart Rein
Executive Director
Children's and Human Rights Council
Apartment 6-E
300 East 54th Street
New York, New York 10022

Dear Stewart,

Thank you for your letter regarding the United Nations Convention on the Rights of the Child. I firmly believe that we must protect the world's children against all forms of abuses--from six year olds working long hours in crowded unhealthy factories to youngsters who are forced into prostitution. That is why I decided that the United States would join more than 175 nations in signing the Convention and why I directed Ambassador Albright to sign on behalf of the United States.

Before sending the Convention to the Senate for advice and consent to ratification, we will undertake a final analysis, of how it would be implemented domestically and propose appropriate reservations and understandings. These reservations and understandings will ensure that the Convention does not infringe upon the central role of parents and the family and that it is consistent with our federal system of government. I also want to make clear that this Convention will not serve as a basis for litigation in America's courts.

In conducting this analysis, we want to take into account the considered views of all interested citizens and groups on the Convention. Children are our most important responsibility and they deserve our love and respect. I appreciate knowing your thoughts on this issue, and I'm grateful for your involvement.

Sincerely,

Bill Clinton

Appendix D:

Internet Legal Resources

Please Note that not all links may be accurate or active, but represent those collected at the time of writing.

Law Links

International

Protection from Harassment Act 1997

Bentham Archive of British Law

The English Law Society

U of B English Legal Research

Thunderstone's Webinator

House of Lords - Judicial Business

JURIST: The Law Professors' Network.... The Home Page of Legal Education

JURIST UK: The Law Professors' Network

Smith-Bernal English Casebase

FOREIGN STATES IMMUNITIES ACT 1985

Roman Law

University of Minnesota Human Rights Library

U of M Human Rights Library: International Human Rights Instruments

Multilaterals Project

Human Rights

University of Minnesota Human Rights Library

International Legal Resources

United Nations

Project DIANA

Foreign and International Law Resources on the Internet

The Global Democracy Network WWW Home Page

IANWeb Resources -- International Law

The Public Policy Assessment Society Inc.

RESEARCHING   INDIGENOUS   PEOPLES   RIGHTS   UNDER
INTERNATIONAL LAW

BASIC LAW for the Federal Republic of Germany

EUROLINK : The Pan European Web Index

FindLaw: International Law

United Nations Scholars' Workstation Home Page

The Supreme Court of Canada Home Page

AustLII - Australasian Law on AustLII

Australasian Legal Information Institute

New Zealand Law on the Internet

Ministère de la Justice (Canada)

Hague Case 1 Aust.

Hague Case 2 Aust.

Dr. Francis Boyle, International Law

Journals and Periodicals

European Law Journal

CCTA's UK Government Information Service

The UK Court Service

AdmiNet - The French Connection

Juris -U. of Montreal

France: Le BRAUDO - Dictionnaire de droit privé

French Code Civile

Suiss Federal Supreme Court

Code pénal : Nouveau code pénal, ancien code pénal.

FCIL Newsletter Home Page

Reebok and Human Rights

Causenet & The Reebok Foundation

Multilaterals Project

International and Foreign Legal Materials

Butterworths Legal Information

Academic Council on the United Nations System

CD-ROMs for UN Information

Freedom House

PEN

The Action Coalition

RIGHTS & WRONGS

National

FedWorld/FLITE Supreme Court Decisions Home Page

USSC Plus - U.S. Supreme Court on the Web [HOME]

Selected Historic Decisions of the Supreme Court

FindLaw Legal Dictionary

University Law Review Project

LEGALDOCS - Hold Harmless (Indemnification) Agreement

Legal Documents and Contracts and Law Documents Preparation On the Internet. Legal forms, contracts, leases, will, living trusts.

Tort Links Page

Pennsylvania Legal Resources for Pro se Litigants

The Supreme Court and Other Federal Courts

VersusLaw - Legal Opinions from the US Supreme, Federal, and State Appellate Courts

Legal Information Institute

Colorado Legal Alliance - Research

The American Law Institute Home Page

THE PENNSYLVANIA STATUTES

Journals and Periodicals

FindLaw: Law Journals

V. Library Selection

http://www.hiltonhouse.com/

ALSO!--U.S. Law--Sources

Argentine Expatriate Seeks Justice in 1976 Torture Case

LatinoLink: ARGENTINA SETTLES LAWSUIT BY A VICTIM OF TORTURE

Human Rights Lawsuit Settled Between Jewish Businessman and Argentina

http://www.uscourts.gov/PubAccess.html

Intentional Torts Against Persons

THE LEGAL CITEª - Amicus Curiae - friends of the courts. Law Students, non-profits, professional organizations, commercial law sites.

ARGUENDO...Vol.1 Iss. 1 Page 1

THE LEGAL CITEª - The Courthouse, your pipeline to the court system.

The Law School

THE THURGOOD MARSHALL LAW LIBRARY

New York Laws

Government

FindLaw: Internet Legal Resources

Online Law Library - Internet Edition

GENERAL PROVISIONS

Black's Law Dictionary Definitions Used

Law Dictionaries

Law Dictionary and Legal Encyclopedia - 'Lectric Law Library Reference Room

The Web's Legal Dictionary

Gilbert Law Dictionaries

The Oral Argument Page

The Lawful Path - Title Page for Bouvier's 1856 Law Dictionary

Maxims of Law from Bouvier's 1856 Law Dictionary

The American Standard Law Dictionary

Original Legal Documents

U.S. Immigration and Nationality Act

Nations Law Links

THOMAS: Legislative Information on the Internet

The Law

Legal Material by Topic - Overview

Legal Material by Subject -Topics

Links to Government Servers and Information

DEPARTMENT OF STATE

LawWorld Welcome

P-LAW Legal Resource Locator

Federal Legal Resources

Colorado Legal Alliance

LawWorld Cityscape

Welcome To The White House

THE 'LECTRIC LAW LIBRARY'S REFERENCE ROOM 3.22.96

WWLIA/Legal Dictionary

Hieros Gamos III - Internet Law Library

PRONET Reference Library - Law - Legal

LawWorld Library

The World Wide Web Virtual Library: Law: Law Schools & Libraries

Cornell Law Library Home Page

Washington College of Law

Emory Law Library Electronic Reference Desk

D'Angelo Law Library

Touro Law Center Web Server Home Page

WWlib search -> law

California Law Library

ABA's LawLink (TM) - Law Schools

Edward Bennett Williams Law Library

DOE I v. KARADZIC : TABLE OF CONTENTS

| | | | The Legal List

The World Wide Web Virtual Library: Law

Constitutional Court Access

AMERICAN BAR ASSOCIATION

The Law School

Welcome to Cal Law

The House of Representatives - Internet Law Library - Law school law library catalogues and services

Legal Resources on the Internet

Search Result of U.S. Supreme Court Syllabi

U.S. Courts of Appeals (Web Sites)

CourtTV Home Page

THOMAS: Legislative Information on the Internet

LAW JOURNAL EXTRA! - The Web Site for the Profession

The Freedom Forum First Amendment Center

Chapter Four: The Power of the Sovereign

SECOND CIRCUIT COURT OF APPEALS RULES 1/93

JOINT RULES: SOUTHERN AND EASTERN DISTRICTS OF NEW YORK 3/94

1995 AMENDMENTS TO THE FEDERAL RULES (EFF. 12/01/95)

'LECTRIC LAW LIBRARY'S LAWCOPEDIA™ MEDICINE AND LAW - MEDICAL MALPRACTICE 1.27.96

Dr. Tavel's Self-Help Legal Clinic and Sovereign Library is the homepage of Liberty's Educational Advocacy Forum, Indiana's Fully Informed Jury Association, Inc.

FindLaw: Internet Legal Resources

Legal Research Guide - Contents

State Legal Materials - Pennsylvania

PENNSYLVANIA MINOR JUDICIARY

Opinions and Orders - Pennsylvania State Courts

THE PENNSYLVANIA STATUTES

AOPC Home Page

Constitution of the Commonwealth of Pennsylvania

PENNSYLVANIA RULES OF CIVIL PROCEDURE

DOMESTIC RELATIONS (TITLE 23)

CUSTODY

JUDICIARY AND JUDICIAL PROCEDURE (TITLE 42)

REAL ESTATE SELLER DISCLOSURE ACT

S MISREPRESENTATION AND MISLEADING OR DECEPTIVE CONDUCT

Commonwealth of Pennsylvania - State Government

Pennsylvania State Government

Widener Law School Library, PA Resources

Family Law & Men's Issues

LII: Law about...Children

Center for Children's Justice

Divorce Source: Custody & Visitation Links

Welcome Shared Parenting Forum

Home Page BetterDivorce.com

National Society for the Prevention of Cruelty to Children (NSPCC)

US State Dept: Office of Children's Issues: Parental Child Abduction

U.S. DEPT. OF STATE: CONSULAR AFFAIRS

Hilton Hague Convention Site Important Papers

Children's Rights Council Home Page

Shared Parenting Information Group (SPIG) UK

CRC of New York

Feedback on BetterDivorce.com

Missing Children

National Center for Missing Children: Child Search Start Page

CHILD QUEST INTERNATIONAL - Finding missing children

The UTOPIA Foundation on Rights & Statistics

Population Division Home Page

Men's Issues Page

MEN'S MANIFESTO

The Future of Children: The Packard Foundation

Interstate Family Support Enforcement (UIFSA)

Australian Family Law Act: Australian Legal Info Institute

Dads Place: Custody Updates

Child Abuse: Statistics, Research, and Resources

Family Law Advisor - Massachusetts Divorce Law Dictionary

U.S. Census Bureau Home Page

Family Law Advisor - Volume 1 Issue 6

Men in the Justice System

MenWeb - M.E.N. Magazine

Children, Young Persons, and Their Families Act1989-N.Z.

References

Divorce and Fatherhood

Abarbanel A: Shared parenting after separation and divorce: a study of joint custody. Am. J Orthopsychiatry 49:320-329, 1979

Abelin EL., The role of the father in the separation-individuation process, in Separation-Individuation. Edited by McDevitt JB, Settlage CE New York, International Universities Press, 1971

Abelin EL., Some further observations and comments on the earliest role of the father. Int J Psychoanal 56:293-302, 1975

Benedek EP: Child custody laws: their psychiatric implications. Am. J Psychiatry 129:326-328, 1972

Benedek EP, Benedek RS: New child custody laws: making them do what they say. Am. J Orthopsychiatry 42:825-834, 1972

Benedek EP, Benedek RS: Joint custody: solution or illusion? Am. J Psychiatry 136:1540-1544, 1979

Benedek RS, Benedek EP: Postdivorce visitation: a child's right. J Am Acad Child Psychiatry 16:256-271, 1977

Benedek T: Parenthood as a developmental phase: a contribution to the libido theory. J Am. Psychoanal Assoc 7:389-417, 1959

Bernstein BE: Lawyer and counselor as an interdisciplinary team: preparing the father for custody. Journal of Marriage and Family Counseling 3:29-40, 1977

Bloom BL: Changing Patterns of Psychiatric Care. New York, Human Sciences Press, 1975

Bloom BL, Asher SJ, White SW: Marital disruption as a stressor: a review and analysis. Psychol Bull 85:867-894, 1978

Bloom BL, Hodges WF, Kern MB, et al: A preventive intervention program for the newly separated: final evaluation. Am. J Orthopsychiatry 55.9-2 (1985)

Briscoe CW, Smith TB: Depression and marital turmoil. Arch item Psychiatry 29:811-817 1973

Briscoe CW, Smith TB: Depression in bereavement in Divorce. Arch Gen Psychiatry 32.439-443, 1975

Briscoe CW, Smith TB, Robbins, and E. et al.: Divorce and psychiatric disease. Arch Gen Psychiatry 29.119-125, 1973

Chang PN, Deinard AS: Single-father caretakers: demographic characteristics and adjustment processes. Am. J Orthopsychiatry 52:236-243, 1982

Children of Divorce, Journal of Social Issues 35:1-182, 1979

Coogler OJ: Structured Mediation in Divorce Settlement. Lexington, MA, Lexington Books, 1978

Coogler OJ: Divorce mediation for "low income" families: a proposed model. Conciliation Courts Review 17:21-26, 1979a

Coogler OJ: Reference Guide to the Family Conciliation Unit. Fort Lauderdale, Florida, Circuit Court, 17th judicial Circuit, 1979b

Coogler OJ, Weber RE, McKenry PC: Divorce mediation: a means of facilitating divorce and adjustment. Family Coordinator 28:255-259, 1979

Dell PF, Appelbaum AS: Trigenerational enmeshment: unresolved ties of single-parents to family of origin. Am. J Orthopsychiatry 47:52-59, 1977

Derdeyn AP., Child custody consultation. Am. J Orthopsychiatry 45:791801, 1975

Derdeyn AP., Child custody contests in historical perspective. Am. J Psychiatry 133:1369-1376, 1976

Derdeyn AP, Levy AM, Looney JG, et al: Child Custody Consultation: A Report of the Task Force on Clinical Assessment in Child Custody. Washington DC, American Psychiatric Association, 1982

Despert JL: Children of Divorce. Garden City, NY, Dolphin Books, 1962

Fisher OE., A guide to divorce counseling. Family Coordinator 22:55-61, 1973

Friedman HJ., The father's parenting experience in divorce. Am. J Psychiatry 137:1177-1182, 1980

Gardner RA: Social, legal, and therapeutic changes that should lessen the traumatic effect of divorce on children. J Am Acad Psychoanal 6:231-247, 1978

Gardner RA: The Parents' Book About Divorce, New York, Bantam Books, 1979'

Gasser RD, Taylor CM: Role adjustment of single parent fathers with dependent children. Family Coordinator 25:397-401, 1976

Glick PC., Children of divorced parents in demographic perspective. Journal of Social Issues 35:170-182, 1979

Goldman J, Coane J: Family therapy after the divorce: developing a Strategy, Fam Process 16:357-362, 1977

Goldstein J, Freud A, Solnit AJ: Beyond the Best Interests of the Child New York, Free Press, 1973

Goode WJ: Women in Divorce. New York, Free Press, 1956

Greenberg M, Morris N: Engrossment: the newborn's impact upon the father. Am. J Orthopsychiatry 49:520-531, 1974

Greif JB: Fathers, children and joint custody. Am. J Orthopsychiatry 49:311-319, 1979

Greif, Geoffrey, Single Fathers, Lexington, MA Health

Haynes JM: Divorce mediator: a new role. Social Work 23:5-9, 1978

Herzog E, Sudia CE: Children in fatherless families. Review of Child Development Research 3:141-232, 1973

Hetherington ME, Cox M, Cox R, Divorced fathers. Family Coordinator 25:417-428, 1976

Hozman TL, Froiland DJ: Families in divorce: a proposed model for counseling the children. Family Coordinator 25:271-276, 1976

Ilfeld FW, Ilfeld HZ, Alexander JR, Does Joint Custody Work? A first look at outcome data of relitigation, Am. J Psychiatry 139:62-66, 1982

Jacobs JW: Treatment of divorcing fathers: social and psychotherapeutic considerations. Am. J Psychiatry 140:1294-1299, 1983

Jacobs, John W., Divorce and Fatherhood: The Struggle for Parental Identity, American Psychiatric Press, 1986

Johnston JR, Campbell LEG, Tall MC., Impass to resolution of custody and visitation disputes. Am. J Orthopsychiatry 55:112-129, 1985

Kalter N, Children of divorce in an outpatient psychiatric population. Am. J Orthopsychiatry 47:40-51, 1977

Kalter N, Rembar J: The significance of a child's age at the time of parental divorce. Am. J Orthopsychiatry 51:85-100, 1981

Kaslow FW: Divorce and divorce therapy, in Handbook of Family Therapy. Edited by Gurman AS, Kniskern DP New York, Brunner/Mazel, 1981

Kelly JB, Wallerstein JS: The effects of parental divorce: experience of the child in early latency. Am. J Orthopsychiatry 46:20-32, 1976

Kelly JB, Wallerstein JS: Brief interventions with children in divorcing families. Am. J Orthopsychiatry 47:23-29, 1977

Keshet HF, Rosenthal KM: Fathering after marital separation. Social Work 23:11-18, 1978

Kressel K, Deutch M: Divorce therapy: an in-depth survey of therapists' views. Fam Process 16:413-433, 1977

Kressel K, Jaffee N, Tuchman B, et al: A typology of divorcing couples: implications for mediation and divorce process. Fam Process 19:101116, 1980

Kulka AR, Weingarten H: The long-term effects of parental divorce in childhood on adult adjustment. Journal of Social Issues 35:50-79, 1979

Lamanna, Mary-Anne, Riedmann, Agnes, Marriages & Families, Wadsworth Pub., 4th Ed. 1991

Lamb ME: The role of the father: an overview, in The Role of the Father in Child Development, Edited by Lamb M. New York, Wiley, 1976

Lambert L, Hart S: Who needs a father? New Society 8:80, 1976

Lang, D.M., Papenfuhs R., Walters J., Delinquent females' perceptions of their fathers, Family Coordinator 25:475-481, 1976

Leader, AL., Family therapy for divorced fathers and others out of home, Social Casework 54:13-19, 1973

Lewin, Tamar, Father's Vanishing Act Called Common Drama, NY Times, June 4th, 1990

McDermott JF: Divorce and its psychiatric sequelae in children. Arch L Gen Psychiatry 23:421-427, 1970

McDermott JF: Parental divorce in early childhood. Am J Psychiatry 124:1424-1432, 1968 '

McDermott IF, Tseng W, Char WF, et al: Child custody decision-making: the search for improvement. J Am Acad Child Psychiatry 17:104-116, 1978

Mendes HA: Single fathers. Family Coordinator 25:439-444 1976

Messinger L, Walker KN: From marriage breakdown to remarriage: parental tasks and therapeutic guidelines, Am. J Orthopsychiatry 151:429-438, 1981

Morrison, JR., Parental divorce as a factor in childhood psychiatric illness. Compr Psychiatry 15:95-102, 1974

Nehls N, Morgenbesser M: Joint custody: an exploration of the issues. Fam Process 19:117-125, 1980

New York Times, Sept. 1, 1985

Nieto DS: Aiding the single father. Social Work 27:473-478, 1982

Nye, FI., Child adjustment in broken and unhappy unbroken homes. Marriage and Family Living 19:356 360, 1957

Orthner DK, Brown T, Ferguson D: Single-parent fatherhood: an emerging family life style. Family Coordinator 25:429-437, 1976

Pedersen FA: Does research on children reared in father-absent families yield information on father influences? Family Coordinator 25:4594G4, 1976

Radin N., Father-child interaction and the intellectual functioning of four-year-old boys. Developmental Psychology 6:353-361, 1972

Radin N., Observed paternal behaviors as antecedents of intellectual functioning in young boys. Developmental Psychology 8:369-376, 1973

Roman M, Haddad W: The Disposable Parent: The Case for Joint Custody. New York, Holt, Rinehart & Winston, 1978

Ross JM: The development of paternal identity: a critical review of the literature on nurturance and generativity in boys and men. J Am Psychoanal Assoc 23:783-817, 1975

Santrock JW, Warshak RA: Father custody and social development in boys and girls. Journal of Social Issues 35:112-125, 1979

Sheffner DF, Suarez JM: The postdivorce clinic. Am. J Psychiatry 132:442-444, 1975

Shinn M., Father absence and children's cognitive development. Psychol Bull 85:295-324, 1978

Steinman SS: The experience of children in a joint custody arrangement: a report of a study. Am. J Orthopsychiatry 51:403-414, 1981

Suarez JM, Weston NL, Hartstein NB, Mental health interventions in divorce proceedings. Am. J Orthopsychiatry 48:273-283, 1978

Sugar M, Children of divorce. Pediatrics 46:588-595, 1970

Tepp AV: Divorced fathers: predictors of continued paternal involvement. Am. J Psychiatry 140:1465-1469, 1983

Tooley K: Antisocial behavior and social alienation postdivorce: the "man of the house" and his mother. Am. J Orthopsychiatry 46:33-42, 1976

Wallerstein JS, Kelly JB: The effects of parental divorce: the adolescent experience, in The Child in His Family: Children at Psychiatric Risk Edited by Anthony EJ, Koupemik C. New York, Wiley, 1974

Wallerstein JS, Kelly JB: The Effects of Parental Divorce: experience of the preschool child. J. Am. Acad. Child Psychiatry, 14:600-616, 1975, Wallerstein JS., Kelly JB: The effects of parental divorce: experiences of the child in later latency. Am. J Orthopsychiatry 46:256-269, 1976

Wallerstein JS, Kelly JB: Divorce counseling: a community service for families in the midst of divorce. Am. J Orthopsychiatry 47:4-22, 1977

Wallerstein JS, Kelly JB: Effects of divorce on the visiting father-child relationship. Am. J Psychiatry 137:1534-1539, 1980

Weisfeld D, Laser MS: Divorced parents in family therapy in a residential treatment setting. Fam Process 16:228-236, 1977

Weiss RS: Growing up a little faster: the experience of growing up in a single-parent household. Journal of Social Issues 35:97-118, 1979

Welch GJ, Granvold DK: Seminars for separated/divorced: an educational approach to postdivorce adjustment. J Sex Marital Ther 3:31-39, p 1977

Westman, JC: The psychiatrist and child custody contests. Am. J Psychiatry 127:1687-1688, 1971

Whitaker CA, Miller MH: A reevaluation of "psychiatric help" when divorce impends. Am. J Psychiatry 126:611-618, 1969

Woodruff RA, Guze SB, Clayton PJ: Divorce among psychiatric outpatients. Br J Psychiatry 121:289-292, 1972

Wylder J., Including the divorced father in family therapy. Social Work 27:479-482, 1982

Parental Identity

Derdeyn P: The family in divorce: issues of parental anger. J Am Acad Child Psychiatry 22:385-391, 1983

'Foster H: Child custody and divorce: a lawyer's view. J Am Acad Child Psychiatry 22:392-398,1983

Goldstein J, Freud A, Solnit AJ: Beyond the Best Interest of the Child New York, Free Press, 1973

Hetherington EM, Cox M, Cox R: Beyond father absence: conceptualization of effects of divorce, in Contemporary Readings in Child Psychology, Edited by Hetherington EM, Park R. New York, McGraw 1977

Kelly J, Visiting after divorce, in Research Findings and Clinical Implications in Children of Separation and Divorce. Edited by Abt L, Stuart New York, Van Nostrand Reinhold, 1981

Kestenbaum CJ, Stone MH: The effects of fatherless homes upon daughters: clinical impressions regarding paternal deprivation. J Am Acad Psychoanal 4:171-190, 1976 C c6 New York Times, March 6, 1982

Rutter M: The Quality of Mothering: Maternal Deprivation Reassessed Hammondsworth, England, Penguin Books, 1974

Wallerstein J, Kelly J: Surviving the Breakup: How Children and Parents Cope with Divorce. New York, Basic Books, 1980

Williams FS: Children of divorce: detectives, diplomats or despots? In Marriage and Divorce, edited by Saltzman B., New York, Abraxas Communications Publishing, 1974

Williams FS: Issues in divorce: toward a more creative custody. Presented at the Cedars-Sinai Medical Center Conference on Family Mental Health, Los Angeles, November 1978

Williams FS: What can judges and mediators do to ameliorate the effects of divorce on parents and children? Family Law News 6:5-8, 1982-1983]

Involuntary Child Absence Syndrome

Benedek T: Parenthood as a developmental phase: a contribution to the libido theory. J Am Psychoanal Assoc 7:389-417, 1959

Bloom BL: Changing Patterns of Psychiatric Care. New York, Human Sciences Press, 1975

Bloom BL, Asher SJ, White SW: Marital disruption as a stressor: a review and analysis. Psychol Bull 85:867-894, 1978

Erikson E: Childhood and Society. New York, Norton, 1950

Goldberg B: All dads aren't deadbeats. Newsweek 103 (6):10, 1984

Greif JB: Fathers, children and custody. Am. J Orthopsychiatry

49:311-319, 1979

Hetherington ME, Cox M, Cox R: Divorced Fathers. Family Coordinator 25:417-428, 1976

Jacobs JW: Treatment of divorcing fathers: social and psychotherapeutic considerations, Am. J Psychiatry 14x, 1294-1299, 1983.

Jacobs JW: Divorce and child custody resolution: conflicting legal and psychological paradigms. Am J Psychiatry 143:192-197, 19$6

Keshet HF, Rosenthal KM: Fathering after marital separation. Social Work 23:11-18, 1978

Ross JM: The development of paternal identity; a critical review of the literature on nurturance and generativity in boys and men, J Am.

Psychoanal Assoc 23:783-817, 1975

Wallerstein JS, Kelly JB: Effects of divorce on the visiting father-child relationship. Am. J Psychiatry 137:1534-1539, 19

Wallerstein JS, Kelly JB: Surviving The Breakup: How Children and Parents Cope With Divorce. New York, Basic Books, 1980b

The Forgotten Figures of Divorce

Agopian MW: Parental Child Stealing. Lexington, MA, D.C. Heath, 1981

Killer HB: Father absence, divorce, and personality development, in The Role of The Father in Child Development, edited by Lamb ME. New York, Wiley, 1981

Borys S, Penman D, Goldenberg, S: Sex differences in loneliness. Presented at the Annual Meeting of the Midwestern Psychological Association, Minneapolis, May 1982

Chiriboga DA, Thurnher M: Marital lifestyles and adjustment to separation. Journal of Divorce 3:379-390, 1990

Eisikovits R, Wolins M: Crosscultural uses of research on fathering, in Fatherhood and Family Policy. Edited by Lamb ME, Sagi A. Hillsdale, NJ, Erlbaum, 1983

Eliedman, HJ: The father's parenting experience in divorce, Am J Psychiatry 137:1177-1182, 1980

Furstenberg F, Nord CW, Peterson JL, et al: The life course of children of divorce: marital disruption and parental contact. Am Sociol Rev 48:651-6f 8, 1983

Gardner R: Recent trends in divorce and custody litigation. Academy Forum 29:3, 1985

Geiss G: Foreword, in Parental Child Stealing. Edited by Agopian MW Von, MA, D.C. Heath, 1981

Gelles R.J., Parental child snatching. Prepared for Louis Harris and Associates, December, 1982

George V, Wilding P: Motherless Families. London, Routledge and Kegan Paul, 1972

Gill JE: Stolen Children. New York, Seaview Books, 1981

Gilligan C: In a Different Voice: Psychological Theory and Women's Development, Cambridge, MA, Harvard University Press, 1982a

Gilligan C: New maps of development: new visions of maturity. Am J Orthopsychiatry 52:199-212, 1982b

Gove WR: Sex, marital status, and suicide. J Health Soc Behavior 13:204-213, 1972a

Gove WR: The relationship between sex roles, marital status, and mental illness. Social Forces 51:34-44, 1972b

Greif JB: Fathers, children, and joint custody, Am. J. Orthopsychiatry, 49:311-319, 1979

Hess R, Camara K: Postdivorce family relationships as mediating factors in the consequences of divorce for children. Journal of Social Issues 3-96, 1979

Hetherington EM, Cox G, Cox, R., Divorced fathers. The Family Coordinator 25:417-428, 1976

Hetherington EM, Cox M, Cox R: Effects of divorce on parents and children, in Nontraditional Families: Parenting and Child Development. Edited by Lamb, M.E. Hillsdale, NJ, Erlbaum, 1982

Huntington DS: Theory and method: research on divorce. J Am Acad Child Psychiatry 24:583-589, 1985, C~ c6

Jacobs JW: The effect of divorce on fathers: an overview of the literature. Am j Psychiatry 139:1235-1241, 1982

Jacobs JW: Treatment of divorcing fathers: social and psychotherapeutic Considerations, Am J Psychiatry 140:1294-1299, 1983

Keshet HF: Part-Time Fathers: A Study of Separated and Divorced Men.Doctoral dissertation, University of Michigan, 1977

Lamb ME: Fathers: forgotten contributors to child development. Human Development 18:245-266, 1975

Lamb ME (Ed): The Role of the Father in Child Development, 2nd, 75 Edition, New York, Wiley, 1981 a

Lamb ME: Fatherhood and social policy in international perspective: an introduction, in Fatherhood and Family Policy. Edited by Lamb ME, Sagi ^ ˉ ;dale, NJ, Erlbaum, 1983

The Seasons of a Man's Life. New York, Knopf, 1978

Marriage and Divorce Today Newsletter 9:14, 1983

er for Health Statistics, February 27, 1985

d): The Father-Infant Relationship. New York, Praeger,

Rose KD, Rosow I: Physicians who kill themselves. Arch Gen Psychiatry 29:800-805, 1973

Rosenthal KM, Keshet HF: Fathers without Partners: A Study of Fathers and the Family after Marital Separation. Totowa, NJ, Rowman and Littlefield, 1981

Russell G, Radin N: Increased paternal participation: the fathers' perspective, in Fatherhood and Family Policy. Edited by Lamb ME, Sagi A. Hillsdale, NJ, Erlbaum, 1983

Seagull AA, Seagull EAW: The non-custodial father's relationship to his child: conflicts and solutions. Journal of Clinical Child Psychology Summer, 11-15, 1977

Senior N, Gladstone T, Nurcombe B: Child snatching: a case report. J Am Acad Child Psychiatry 21:579-583, 1982

Taylor SE: Adjustment to threatening events: a theory of cognitive adaptation. American Psychologist 38:1161-1173, 1983

Wallerstein JS, Kelly JB: Surviving the Breakup. New York, Basic Books, 1980

Warshak RA, Santrock JW: The impact of divorce in father-custody and mother-custody homes: the child's perspective, in Children and Divorce: New Directions for Child Development, No. 19, Edited by Kurdek LA. San Francisco, Jossey-Bass, 1983

Waters E, Noyes DM: Psychological parenting vs. attachment theory: the child's best interests and the risks of doing the right things for the wrong reasons. New York University Review of Law and Social Change 12:505-515, 1983-1984

Weiss RS: Loneliness: what we know about it and what we might do about it, in Preventing the Harmful Consequences of Severe and Persistent Loneliness, Edited by Peplau LA, Goldston SE, U.S. Department of Health and Human Services Publication No. (ADM) 84-1312. Washington DC, U.S. Government Printing Office, 1984

Yahm H: Divorce mediation: a psychoanalytic perspective, in Procedures for Guiding the Divorce Mediation Process. Mediation Quarterly 6:59-63, 1984

Zeiss AM, Zeiss RA, Johnson SM: Sex differences in initiation of and adjustment to divorce. Journal of Divorce 4:21-33, 1980

Parental Child Abduction

Dabbagh, Maureen: The Recovery of Internationally Abducted Children, McFarland & Co, Inc., 1997

Davis, Sandra, Rosenblatt, Jeremy, Galbraith, Tanya: International Child Abduction, Sweet & Maxwell, 1993

Index

C